Disability and Art History

This is the first book of its kind to feature interdisciplinary art history and disability studies scholarship. Art historians have traditionally written about images of figures with impairments and artworks by disabled artists, without integrating disability studies scholarship, while many disability studies scholars discuss works of art, but do not necessarily incorporate art historical research and methodology. The chapters in this volume emphasize a shift away from the medical model of disability that is often scrutinized in art history by considering the social model and representations of disabled figures from a range of styles and periods, mostly from the twentieth century. Topics addressed include visible versus invisible impairments; scientific, anthropological, and vernacular images of disability; and the theories and implications of looking/staring versus gazing. They also explore ways in which art responds to, envisions, and at times stereotypes and pathologizes disability. The insights offered in this book contextualize understanding of disability historically, as well as in terms of medicine, literature, and visual culture.

Ann Millett-Gallant is a Senior Lecturer for the Bachelor of Arts in Liberal Studies Program at the University of North Carolina at Greensboro. She holds a PhD in art history at the University of North Carolina at Chapel Hill, and her research focuses on representations of disability in art and visual culture. She is the author of two books, *The Disabled Body in Contemporary Art* and *Re-Membering: Putting Mind and Body Back Together Following Traumatic Brain Injury*, as well as a number of essays for academic journals. Prior to this volume, she has chaired several panels at academic conferences about and co-edited a special issue of the Review of Disability Studies on interdisciplinary art history and disability studies research. She also enjoys painting and drawing. Visit her website at annmg.com.

Elizabeth Howie is Associate Professor of Art History at Coastal Carolina University in Conway, South Carolina. She received her PhD in art history at the University of North Carolina at Chapel Hill. Publications include "Proof of the Forgotten: A Benjaminian Reading of Daguerre's Two Views of the Boulevard du Temple," in *Walter Benjamin and the Aesthetics of Change: An Interdisciplinary Approach*; "Bringing Out the Past: Courtly Cruising and Nineteenth-Century American Men's Passionate Friendship Portraits," in *Love Objects: Emotion, Design, and Material Culture*; and a co-edited (with Ann Millett-Gallant) special issue of the *Review of Disability Studies* on interdisciplinary art history and disability studies research.

Interdisciplinary Disability Studies
Series Editor: Mark Sherry
The University of Toledo, USA

For a full list of titles in this series, please visit www.routledge.com/series/ASHSER1401

Disability studies has made great strides in exploring power and the body. This series extends the interdisciplinary dialogue between disability studies and other fields by asking how disability studies can influence a particular field. It will show how a deep engagement with disability studies changes our understanding of the following fields: sociology, literary studies, gender studies, bioethics, social work, law, education, or history. This groundbreaking series identifies both the practical and theoretical implications of such an interdisciplinary dialogue and challenges people in disability studies as well as other disciplinary fields to critically reflect on their professional praxis in terms of theory, practice, and methods.

Disability and Qualitative Inquiry
Methods for Rethinking an Ableist World
Edited by Ronald J. Berger and Laura S. Lorenz

The Disabled Child's Participation Rights
Anne-Marie Callus and Ruth Farrugia

The Fantasy of Disability
Images of Loss in Popular Culture
Jeffrey Preston

Disability and Art History
Edited by Ann Millett-Gallant and Elizabeth Howie

Forthcoming:

Sport and the Female Disabled Body
Elisabet Apelmo

Disability and Rurality
Identity, Gender and Belonging
Karen Soldatic and Kelley Johnson

Child Pain, Migraine and Invisible Disability
Susan Honeyman

Disability and Art History

Edited by Ann Millett-Gallant
and Elizabeth Howie

LONDON AND NEW YORK

First published 2017
by Routledge

2 Park Square, Milton Park, Abingdon, Oxfordshire OX14 4RN
711 Third Avenue, New York, NY 10017

Routledge is an imprint of the Taylor & Francis Group, an informa business

First issued in paperback 2017

Copyright © 2017 selection and editorial matter, Ann Millett-Gallant and Elizabeth Howie; individual chapters, the contributors

The right of Ann Millett-Gallant and Elizabeth Howie to be identified as the authors of the editorial material, and of the authors for their individual chapters, has been asserted in accordance with sections 77 and 78 of the Copyright, Designs and Patents Act 1988.

All rights reserved. No part of this book may be reprinted or reproduced or utilised in any form or by any electronic, mechanical, or other means, now known or hereafter invented, including photocopying and recording, or in any information storage or retrieval system, without permission in writing from the publishers.

Notice:
Product or corporate names may be trademarks or registered trademarks, and are used only for identification and explanation without intent to infringe.

British Library Cataloguing in Publication Data
A catalogue record for this book is available from the British Library

Library of Congress Cataloging-in-Publication Data
Names: Millett-Gallant, Ann, 1975– editor. | Howie, Elizabeth, editor.
Title: Disability and art history / [edited by] Ann Millett-Gallant & Elizabeth Howie.
Description: New York : Routledge, 2016. | Includes bibliographical references and index.
Identifiers: LCCN 2016020671 | ISBN 9781472453525 (hardback) | ISBN 9781315440002 (ebook)
Subjects: LCSH: People with disabilities in art. | Art and society. | Sociology of disability.
Classification: LCC N8236.P4 D57 2016 | DDC 701/.03—dc23
LC record available at https://lccn.loc.gov/2016020671

ISBN: 978-1-4724-5352-5 (hbk)
ISBN: 978-0-8153-9213-2 (pbk)

Typeset in Times New Roman
by Apex CoVantage, LLC

"*Disability and Art History* makes a definitive claim for the importance of disability in art. Moving seamlessly from the past to the present, and indicating an influential through line between the two, this collection of chapters shows not only how important disability is to art works, but how disability becomes a fascinating focus for artists of all kinds. The book particularly illustrates how transgressive disability art can be and how different bodies and minds redefine what we think about when we think about visual art."

Lennard. J. Davis, University of Illinois, USA

"This original book offers fresh insights as it examines art history's blindness to the burgeoning scholarship in disability studies. Rather than mock the discipline's impairments or seek a cure, the diverse chapters think deeply about their social and cultural significance across an intriguing range of historical periods and places."

Jane Blocker, University of Minnesota, USA

"Millett-Gallant and Howie's *Disability and Art History* provides scholarly examples of how representations of disability reoccur and are recycled in visual culture. From photography to cinema, from Meso-American pottery figures to German Expressionism, from the disabled as artist to the artistic rediscovery of older representations of the disabled, this first-rate collection provides much for the Disability Studies classroom and will add substantially to a rethinking of Art History to introduce the student to the world of visual representations of disability."

Sander L. Gilman, Emory University, USA

This book is dedicated to the many people who played hardworking and vibrant roles in its production: scholars, educators, editors, curators, and foremost, the many artists whose work created the ideas and objects analyzed within its pages.

We must honor and pay tribute specifically to Tobin Siebers (1953–2015), whose teaching, writing, lecturing, and mentoring has contributed to the work in this specific volume, as well as the interdisciplinary projects this book continues.

Contents

List of images ix
Notes on contributors xv
Acknowledgements xviii

Disability and art history introduction 1
ANN MILLETT-GALLANT AND ELIZABETH HOWIE

1 **Artists and muses: "Peter's World" and other photographs by Susan Harbage Page** 12
ANN MILLETT-GALLANT

2 **Exploiting, degrading, and repellent: against a biased interpretation of contemporary art about disability** 29
NINA HEINDL

3 **Nothing is missing: spiritual elevation of a visually impaired Moche shaman** 47
REBECCA R. STONE

4 **Divining disability: criticism as diagnosis in Mesoamerican art history** 60
WILLIAM T. GASSAWAY

5 **Difference and disability in the photography of Margaret Bourke-White** 82
KERI WATSON

6 **Representing disability in post–World War II photography** 99
TIMOTHY W. HILES

7 The disabled veteran of World War I in the mirror of contemporary art: the reception of Otto Dix's painting *The Cripples* (1920) in Yael Bartana's film *Degenerate Art Lives* (2010) 119
ANNE MARNO

8 Disabling Surrealism: reconstituting Surrealist tropes in contemporary art 132
AMANDA CACHIA

9 The dandy Victorian: Yinka Shonibare's allegory of disability and passing 155
ELIZABETH HOWIE

10 Crafting disabled sexuality: the visual language of Nomy Lamm's "Wall of Fire" 178
SHAYDA KAFAI

Index 193

Images

Chapter 1: Ann Millett-Gallant

1.1 Susan Harbage Page, *Peter with Dinosaur Photo*, 20 × 24 inches, silver gelatin print, 1991.   14
1.2 Susan Harbage Page, *Peter with Back to Camera*, 20 × 24 inches, silver gelatin print, 1992.   15
1.3 Susan Harbage Page, *Peter with Comic Book*, 20 × 24 inches, silver gelatin print, 2000.   16
1.4 Susan Harbage Page, *Peter with Cramer*, 20 × 24 inches, silver gelatin print, 2001.   18
1.5 Susan Harbage Page, *Peter with Cape*, 20 × 24 inches, silver gelatin print, 1994.   19
1.6 Susan Harbage Page, *Peter the Teenager*, 20 × 24 inches, silver gelatin print, 1999.   23
1.7 Susan Harbage Page, *Peter's Hands*, 20 × 24 inches, silver gelatin print, 1999.   24

Chapter 2: Nina Heindl

2.1 Jake and Dinos Chapman, *Ubermensch*, 366 × 183 × 183 cm, Fiberglass, resin and paint, 1995, private collection. © VG Bild-Kunst, Bonn, 2015.   32
2.2 Marc Quinn, *Alison Lapper Pregnant*, 355 × 180.5 × 260 cm, Marble, 2005, Trafalgar Square, London. Photo: Marc Quinn Studio.   35
2.3 Jacques-Louis David, *Bonaparte franchissant le Grand Saint Bernard*, 272 × 232 cm, oil on canvas, 1801, Musée national des châteaux de Malmaison et de Bois-Préau, Malmaison. © bpk | RMN—Grand Palais | Daniel Arnaudet.   36
2.4 Christoph Schlingensief, *Freakstars 3000*, six-part television series (2002) and film (2003). Photo: Thomas Aurin.   38

x *Images*

Chapter 3: Rebecca R. Stone

3.1 Moche effigy of a vision-impaired man. 17.8 × 10.5 cm (7 × 4 1/8 in.). Ceramic. c. 300 CE. Michael C. Carlos Museum, accession number 1989.8.71. © Michael C. Carlos Museum. Photo by Bruce M. White, 2011. 48

3.2 Moche effigy of a man wearing espingo seeds. 24.7 × 14 cm (9 3/4 × 5 1/2 in.). Ceramic. c. 300 CE. Michael C. Carlos Museum, accession number 1989.8.68. © Michael C. Carlos Museum. Photo by Michael McKelvey. 49

3.3 Moche portrait head cup. 14.8 × 10.6 cm (5 13/16 × 4 3/16 in.). Ceramic. c. 300 CE. Michael C. Carlos Museum, accession number 1999.3.115. Ex coll. William S. Arnett. © Michael C. Carlos Museum. Photo by Bruce M. White, 2012. 52

3.4 Moche effigy of a survivor of leishmaniasis. 21.4 × 13.8 cm (8 7/16 × 5 7/16 in.) Ceramic. c. 300 CE. Michael C. Carlos Museum, accession number 1989.8.72. © Michael C. Carlos Museum. Photo by Michael McKelvey. 53

3.5 Moche effigy of an older man. 27.3 × 13.3 cm (10 3/4 × 5 1/4 in.) Ceramic. c. 300 CE. Michael C. Carlos Museum, accession number 1989.8.69. Gift of William C. and Carol W. Thibadeau. © Michael C. Carlos Museum. Photo by Michael McKelvey. 56

Chapter 4: William T. Gassaway

4.1 Potrero Nuevo Monument 2 ("Atlantean altar"), Olmec, Early Preclassic (1800–1200 BCE), stone, H. 37 in. (94 cm). Museo de Antropología, Xalapa, Veracruz, 04019 (after Diehl 2004: fig. 14). 62

4.2 Enthroned elite looking into mirror held by dwarf, with another dwarf sipping an unknown liquid from a large vessel, Maya, Late Classic (CE 600–900), ceramic with polychrome, H. 9.5 × Diam. 6.7 × Circum. 19.4 in. (24 × 17 × 49.2 cm). National Museum of Australia, 82.22.92 (photograph K1453 © Justin Kerr, www.mayavase.com). 63

4.3 Dwarf figurine whistle, Maya (Jaina), Late Classic (CE 600–800), ceramic with red and white pigment, H. 4 1/2 in. (11.43 cm). The Los Angeles County Museum of Art, gift of Constance McCormick Fearing, AC1992.134.20 (artwork in the public domain; photograph © Los Angeles County Museum of Art, www.lacma.org). 64

4.4 Dwarf figurine whistle, Maya (Jaina), Late Classic (CE 600–800), ceramic with red and white pigment, H. 3 13/16 in. (9.53 cm). The Los Angeles County Museum of Art, gift of Constance McCormick Fearing, AC1992.134.21 (artwork in the public domain; photograph © Los Angeles County Museum of Art, www.lacma.org). 65

4.5	Dwarf wearing a deer headdress and holding a mirror, Maya (Jaina), Late Classic (CE 600–800), ceramic, H. 6 1/8 × W. 3 3/16 in. (15.6 × 8.1 cm). Ethnologisches Museum, Berlin/SMB, IV Ca 50146 (photograph by the author).	66
4.6	Mask, Olmec, Middle Preclassic (900–500 BCE), jadeite, H. 6 3/4 × W. 6 5/16 in. (17.1 × 16.5 cm). The Metropolitan Museum of Art, bequest of Alice K. Bache, 1977.187.33 (artwork in the public domain; photograph © The Metropolitan Museum of Art, www.metmuseum.org).	70
4.7	Mask, Olmec, Middle Preclassic (800–400 BCE), jadeite, H. 8 1/8 × W. 7 × D. 4 1/4 in. (20.64 × 17.78 × 10.8 cm). The Dumbarton Oaks Research Library and Collection, PC.B.020 (photograph © Dumbarton Oaks, Pre-Columbian Collection, Washington, DC).	71
4.8	Diminutive figurine resembling purported "fetal typology," Olmec, Middle Preclassic (1000–800 BCE), volcanic stone, dimensions unknown. Museo Nacional de Antropología, Mexico City (photograph by the author).	74

Chapter 5: Keri Watson

5.1	Margaret Bourke-White, *Girls Lined Up without Shoes, Letchworth Village*, 1933. Photo © Estate of Margaret Bourke-White/Licensed by VAGA, New York, NY.	84
5.2	Margaret Bourke-White, *Men with Hoes, Letchworth Village*, 1933. Photo © Estate of Margaret Bourke-White/Licensed by VAGA, New York, NY.	85
5.3	Margaret Bourke-White, *Boys Digging in a Trench, Letchworth Village*, 1933. Photo © Estate of Margaret Bourke-White/Licensed by VAGA, New York, NY.	86
5.4	Dorothea Lange, *Spring Plowing. Guadalupe, California. Cauliflower Fields*, March 1937. FSA-OWI Collection, Prints and Photographs Division, Library of Congress.	88
5.5	Margaret Bourke-White, *Happy Hollow, Georgia, You Have Seen Their Faces*, 1937. Photo © Estate of Margaret Bourke-White/Licensed by VAGA, New York, NY.	91
5.6	Margaret Bourke-White, *Belmont, Florida, You Have Seen Their Faces*, 1937. Photo © Estate of Margaret Bourke-White/Licensed by VAGA, New York, NY.	92
5.7	Margaret Bourke-White, *Sweet Fern, Arkansas, You Have Seen Their Faces*, 1937. Photo © Estate of Margaret Bourke-White/Licensed by VAGA, New York, NY.	94

Chapter 6: Timothy W. Hiles

6.1	Ralph Morse, *Nine-Year-Old Neil Koenig, Who Has Cerebral Palsy, Walking Unassisted*, 1950. Published in *Life* magazine, April 30, 1951, p. 85. Getty Images.	101

xii *Images*

6.2 Ralph Morse, *Normal Pupils Watching Their Handicapped Classmates through a One-Way Window*, 1950. Published in *Life* magazine, April 30, 1951, p. 89. Getty Images. 103
6.3 Cornell Capa, *Sunday Visit*, published in *Life* magazine, October 18, 1954, p. 121. Magnum Photos. 106
6.4 Cornell Capa, *Eileen and Her Family*, published in *Life* magazine, October 18, 1954, p. 124. Magnum Photos. 107
6.5 Cornell Capa, "Mentally Retarded Eileen Stares Emptily Out into Space, Lost in Her Own Infantile World," published in *Life* magazine, October 18, 1954, p. 123. Magnum Photos. 108
6.6 Nina Leen, *Jackie Robinson Signs Autographs*, 1949. Getty Images. 109
6.7 Bruce Davidson, *USA, Palisades, New Jersey, The Dwarf* (in restaurant), 1958. Magnum Photos. 111
6.8 Bruce Davidson, *USA, Palisades, New Jersey, The Dwarf*, 1958. Magnum Photos. 112
6.9 Garry Winogrand, *American Legion Convention, Dallas*, 1964. © The Estate of Garry Winogrand, courtesy Fraenkel Gallery, San Francisco. 114

Chapter 7: Anne Marno

7.1 Otto Dix, *The Cripples*, 150 × 200 cm, oil on canvas, 1920, in: Beck, Rainer. *Otto Dix 1891–1969: Zeit, Leben, Werk*. Konstanz: Stadler, 1993, 69, fig. 114. Permission source: Artist Rights Society, New York. © 2015 Artists Rights Society (ARS), New York / VG Bild-Kunst, Bonn. 120
7.2 Section from Yael Bartana, *Degenerate Art Lives* (*Entartete Kunst Lebt*), 2010, video still, courtesy of Annet Gelink Gallery, Amsterdam, and Sommer Contemporary Art, Tel Aviv. 123
7.3 Section from Yael Bartana, *Degenerate Art Lives* (*Entartete Kunst Lebt*), 2010, video still, courtesy of Annet Gelink Gallery, Amsterdam, and Sommer Contemporary Art, Tel Aviv. 124
7.4 Section from Yael Bartana, *Degenerate Art Lives* (*Entartete Kunst Lebt*), 2010, video still, courtesy of Annet Gelink Gallery, Amsterdam, and Sommer Contemporary Art, Tel Aviv. 125

Chapter 8: Amanda Cachia

8.1 André Masson, *Le génie de l'espèce III*, 64.5 × 19.3 cm, India ink, 1939, photo © Centre Pompidou, MNAM-CCI, Dist. RMN-Grand Palais / Philippe Migeat © 2015 Artists Rights Society (ARS), New York / ADAGP, Paris. 135

Images   xiii

8.2	Lisa Bufano, *Home Is Not Home*, video still, 2011, courtesy Jason Tshantrè, photo by Jason Tshantrè.	136
8.3	André Masson, Max Ernst, Max Morise, *Exquisite Corpse*, 20 × 15.5 cm, graphite and colored crayons on ivory wove paper, March 18, 1927, Lindy and Edwin Bergman Collection, 104.1991, The Art Institute of Chicago. Photography © The Art Institute of Chicago. © 2015 Artists Rights Society (ARS), New York / ADAGP, Paris.	137
8.4	Hans Bellmer, Untitled *(Unica Bound)* 16.2 × 16.2 cm (6 3/8 × 6 3/8 in.), gelatin silver print, 1958, Ubu Gallery, New York. Photo by Joelle Jensen.	139
8.5	Chun-Shan (Sandie) Yi, *Can I Be Sexy for Once?* (no printed size), digital photo, 2005, courtesy the artist, photo by Cheng-Chang Kuo.	141
8.6	Jacques-André Boiffard, *Gros orteil*, 31 × 23.9 cm, gelatin silver print, 1929, Photo © Centre Pompidou, MNAM-CCI, Dist. RMN-Grand Palais / Philippe Migeat © Mme Denise Boiffard, © 2015 Artists Rights Society (ARS), New York / ADAGP, Paris.	143
8.7	Chun-Shan (Sandie) Yi, *Footwear Close-Up* (no printed size), digital photo, 2005, courtesy the artist, photo by Cheng-Chang Kuo.	144
8.8	Jacques-André Boiffard, *Sans titre*, 23.8 × 17.8 cm, silver gelatine print, 1929, Photo © Centre Pompidou, MNAM-CCI, Dist. RMN-Grand Palais / Bertrand Prévost, © Mme Denise Boiffard © 2015 Artists Rights Society (ARS), New York / ADAGP, Paris.	145
8.9	Chun-Shan (Sandie) Yi, Untitled (no printed size), digital photo, 2013, courtesy the artist, digital image edit by Shu-Ching Chou.	146
8.10	Brassaï, *Nu, la poitrine* (no known original dimensions), silver gelatin print, 1931–1932 © RMN-Grand Palais / Michèle Bellot, © Estate Brassaï—RMN-Grand Palais, © 2015 Artists Rights Society (ARS), New York / ADAGP, Paris.	147
8.11	Chun-Shan (Sandie) Yi, *Animal Instinct*, 78.7 × 55.8 cm (31 × 22 in.), digital chromogenic print, 2005, courtesy the artist, photo by Cheng-Chang Kuo.	148
8.12	Hans Bellmer, *The Doll*, 24.1 × 23.7 cm (9 1/2 × 9 5/16 in.), gelatin silver print, 1935–1937, Samuel J. Wagstaff, Jr. Fund © 2015 Artists Rights Society (ARS), New York / ADAGP, Paris.	149
8.13	Artur Żmijewski, *An Eye for an Eye (Undressed Ib)*, 100 × 100 cm (39 3/8 × 39 3/8 in.), color photograph, 1998, courtesy the artist and Galerie Peter Kilchmann, Zurich.	151

xiv *Images*

Chapter 9: Elizabeth Howie

9.1 Yinka Shonibare, *Diary of a Victorian Dandy: 11.00 Hours*, 183 × 228.6 cm [72 × 90 in.], C-print, 1998. © Yinka Shonibare MBE. All Rights Reserved, DACS/ ARS, NY 2015. Courtesy James Cohan, New York / Shanghai. 159

9.2 Yinka Shonibare, *Diary of a Victorian Dandy: 14.00 Hours*, 183 × 228.6 cm [72 × 90 in.], C-print, 1998. © Yinka Shonibare MBE. All Rights Reserved, DACS/ ARS, NY 2015. Courtesy James Cohan, New York / Shanghai. 160

9.3 Yinka Shonibare, *Diary of a Victorian Dandy: 17.00 Hours*, 183 × 228.6 cm [72 × 90 in.], C-print, 1998. © Yinka Shonibare MBE. All Rights Reserved, DACS/ ARS, NY 2015. Courtesy James Cohan, New York / Shanghai. 161

9.4 Yinka Shonibare, *Diary of a Victorian Dandy: 19.00 Hours*, 183 × 228.6 cm [72 × 90 in.], C-print, 1998. © Yinka Shonibare MBE. All Rights Reserved, DACS/ ARS, NY 2015. Courtesy James Cohan, New York / Shanghai. 162

9.5 Yinka Shonibare, *Diary of a Victorian Dandy: 03.00 Hours*, 183 × 228.6 cm [72 × 90 in.], C-print, 1998. © Yinka Shonibare MBE. All Rights Reserved, DACS/ ARS, NY 2015. Courtesy James Cohan, New York / Shanghai. 163

Chapter 10: Shayda Kafai

10.1 Nomy Lamm performing "Wall of Fire" in Sins Invalid 2008 show. Photograph by Richard Downing © 2008. Courtesy of Sins Invalid. 182

10.2 Nomy Lamm performing "Wall of Fire" in Sins Invalid 2008 show. Photograph by Richard Downing © 2008. Courtesy of Sins Invalid. 185

10.3 Nomy Lamm performing "Wall of Fire" in Sins Invalid 2008 show. Photograph by Richard Downing © 2008. Courtesy of Sins Invalid. 187

Notes on contributors

Amanda Cachia is an independent curator from Sydney, Australia, and is currently a PhD candidate in Art History, Theory, and Criticism at the University of California, San Diego. Her dissertation will focus on the intersection of disability and contemporary art. Cachia completed her second master's degree in Visual and Critical Studies at the California College of the Arts in San Francisco in 2012, and received her first master's in Creative Curating from Goldsmiths College, University of London, in 2001. Cachia held the position Director/Curator of the Dunlop Art Gallery in Regina, Saskatchewan, Canada, from 2007 to 2010, and has curated approximately thirty exhibitions over the last ten years in the United States, England, Australia, and Canada. Her critical writing has been published in numerous exhibition catalogues and journals such as *Canadian Journal of Disability Studies*, *Disability Studies Quarterly*, *Journal of Literary & Cultural Disability Studies*, *Journal of Visual Art Practice*, *Museums and Social Issues: A Journal of Reflective Discourse*, and *The Review of Disability Studies: An International Journal*. Cachia is a dwarf activist and has been the Chair of the Dwarf Artists Coalition for the Little People of America since 2007.

William T. Gassaway is a doctoral candidate in the Department of Art History and Archaeology at Columbia University. His research focuses on pre-Columbian visual culture, phenomenology and art, Latin American modernism, and critical theory. He is the recipient of several research fellowships in the United States, including awards from the Metropolitan Museum of Art, the National Endowment for the Humanities, and the Dumbarton Oaks Research Library and Collection. Gassaway is currently at work on his dissertation, "Extraordinary Bodies: The Art of Deformation in Postclassic Mexico," which examines the representation and meaning of anomalous, disabled, or otherwise exceptional bodies in indigenous American art.

Nina Heindl, MA (Ruhr-University Bochum and University of Cologne, Germany), studied art history and philosophy. She is PhD student in Art History at the Ruhr-University Bochum, Germany. Her dissertation project is about artistic forms of comics based on Chris Ware's oeuvre. She works as Graduate Assistant at the Department of Art History, University of Cologne, Germany.

xvi *Notes on contributors*

Her research focuses on comics; contemporary art, especially sculpture; and the representation of disability.

Timothy W. Hiles is Associate Professor at the University of Tennessee. He received his PhD from Penn State University where his studies emphasized the early modern movement in Germany and Austria. His recent research encompasses visual perception within twentieth-century American photography and film. Among his publications are *Thomas Theodor Heine: Fin-de-Siècle Munich and the Origins of Simplicissimus* (1996); "Klimt, Nietzsche and the Beethoven Frieze," *Cambridge Studies in Philosophy and the Arts* (1998); "Reality and Utopia in Munich's Premier Magazines," *The Oxford Critical and Cultural History of Modernist Magazines* (2013); and "Shifting Perception: Photographing Disabled People during the Civil Rights Era," *Review of Disability Studies* (2014). His most recent research—culminating in "The Art of Becoming: The Symbiosis of Time, Space and Film in *Pull My Daisy*" in *Gotthold Lessing's Legacy: Space and Time in Artistic Practices and Aesthetics*—is in press and expected to be released in 2016.

Elizabeth Howie is Associate Professor of Art History at Coastal Carolina University in Conway, South Carolina. She received her PhD in art history at the University of North Carolina at Chapel Hill. Publications include "Proof of the Forgotten: A Benjaminian Reading of Daguerre's Two Views of the Boulevard du Temple" in *Walter Benjamin and the Aesthetics of Change: An Interdisciplinary Approach*; "Bringing Out the Past: Courtly Cruising and Nineteenth-Century American Men's Passionate Friendship Portraits" in *Love Objects: Emotion, Design, and Material Culture*; and a co-edited a special issue of the *Review of Disability Studies* on interdisciplinary art history and disability studies research.

Shayda Kafai is a lecturer at California Polytechnic University, Pomona's Ethnic and Women's Studies Department. She earned her PhD in Cultural Studies from Claremont Graduate University. As a queer, disabled woman of color, she is committed to exploring the numerous ways we can reclaim our bodies from intersecting systems of oppression. Her research focuses on disability studies, gender studies, and performance art.

Anne Marno is an art historian, medical historian, and physician. She is an assistant lecturer at the Institute of Art History and cooperator of the Institute of Medical History at the Heinrich-Heine-University in Duesseldorf (Germany). She has finished an interdisciplinary PhD in Art and Medical History with her work on Otto Dix's graphic cycle *The War* (1924). Her academic training includes studies of arts (Academy of Arts in Düsseldorf), art history, German language and literature studies, pedagogics (University of Duesseldorf), and human medicine (universities of Duesseldorf, Würzburg and Cologne). Her areas of research are the works of Otto Dix, arts prior to World War I, and Contemporary Arts.

Ann Millett-Gallant is a Senior Lecturer for the University of North Carolina at Greensboro, where she teaches for the Art Department and the Bachelor of Studies Program. She earned her PhD in Art History at the University of North Carolina at Chapel Hill. Her research focuses on representations of disability in art and visual culture. She is the author of two books, *The Disabled Body in Contemporary Art* and *Re-Membering: Putting Mind and Body Back Together Following Traumatic Brain Injury*, as well as a number of chapters for academic journals. Prior to this volume, she has chaired several panels at academic conferences about and co-edited a special issue of the *Review of Disability Studies* on interdisciplinary art history and disability studies research. She also enjoys painting and drawing.

Rebecca R. Stone (also published under the name Rebecca Stone-Miller) holds a doctorate in the History of Art from Yale University. She has taught at the Johns Hopkins University (1987–1988) and Emory University (1988–present), attaining the rank of Professor. Stone is also the Faculty Curator of the Art of the Americas at Emory's Michael C. Carlos Museum and has curated numerous exhibitions and reinstallations there, plus the 1992 Columbus Quincentennial show at the Museum of Fine Arts, Boston (authoring its catalogue, *To Weave for the Sun: Andean Textiles from the Museum of Fine Arts, Boston*). Subsequent publications include: *Art of the Andes from Chavín to Inca* (1995, 2002, 2012), *Seeing with New Eyes: Highlights of the Michael C. Carlos Museum Collection of Art of the Ancient Americas* (2002), and *The Jaguar Within: Shamanic Trance in Ancient Central and South American Art* (2011). Currently she is working on a coauthored text on the art and culture from Ecuador to Honduras for Yale University Press. Her scholarly interests include disability studies, shamanism, and the textile arts.

Keri Watson is an Assistant Professor of Art History at the University of Central Florida. She specializes in modern and contemporary art and the history of photography. She has published on topics including Patricia Cronin's public sculpture, Eudora Welty's photography, and Judy Chicago's feminist pedagogy, as well as curated exhibitions on disability in sideshow banners and photographs, the photography of the civil rights movement, the history of immigration in Alabama, and the women's art movement. Currently, she is researching the intersections of text, image, race, and disability in Depression-era photo-books.

Acknowledgements

We would like to acknowledge key individuals for their contributions to this book. Special thanks go to Mark Sherry, who edits this series for Routledge; our editorial team at Ashgate/Routledge: Claire Jarvis, Lianne Sherlock, Shannon Kneis, and Katherine Wetzel; Lennard J. Davis, for all his work in disability studies and its dissemination to diverse academic fields, activists, and students; and Megan Conway, as well as others who contributed to our special issue of the *Review of Disability Studies (2015)*. Ann would like to thank Susan Harbage Page, who photographed Peter, herself, and many other subjects and sites all over the world, as well as the cast of characters at Ann's 2008 wedding. She also must acknowledge her co-workers and students at the University of North Carolina at Greensboro. Elizabeth would like to acknowledge the support of Coastal Carolina University, which facilitated the development of these ideas at venues including SECAC and the Society of Disability Studies Conference. We are grateful to our authors for their outstanding contributions to this project.

Disability and art history introduction

Ann Millett-Gallant and Elizabeth Howie

This is the first volume to feature interdisciplinary art history and disability studies scholarship, despite the commonalities these disciplines share in their investigations into culture and representation. Where disability studies and art history overlap most compellingly is in terms of visual experience. The appearance and performance of disability in visual culture has been analyzed by disability studies scholars such as Lennard J. Davis, Rosemarie Garland-Thomson, and Tobin Siebers.[1] These scholars' theories have been revisited and reinvigorated in this volume in art historical terms—chapters in this book address the relationship between "the stare" and "the gaze"; the mainstream public's reaction to and sometimes repulsion from visibly disabled individuals and representations of them; the social construction of disability, specifically in relation to visibility and visual culture; and the consequences of representation of and for individuals with visible versus invisible disabilities.

Chapters in this volume explore ways in which art responds to disability, envisions disability, at times stereotypes and pathologizes disability, and raises questions about the visibility of disability. Along similar lines, these chapters raise questions about conventional diagnostic assumptions, both physical and psychological, made about disability.

This volume makes no claims to be comprehensive, but the gaps are reflective, to some extent, of the newness of this form of inquiry. Admittedly, most of these chapters center on physical and visible disabilities, as visual art is primarily, but of course not exclusively, a visual practice, and certainly an exhaustive compendium of scholarship on this topic would need to address, for example, sculpture designed for a blind audience, sound-based works, and so on.

Disability studies is a multidisciplinary academic field and political movement, beginning in the 1980s, which still aims to combat historical notions of disability as a medical problem or a metaphor for destruction or disintegration.[2] The recognition of disability as a category of identity that must be acknowledged in social terms has been facilitated in the United States by the 1990 passing of the Americans with Disabilities Act (ADA), which prohibits discrimination in public services, telecommunications, employment, and public accommodations.[3] Disability studies challenges the medical model, which operates on the idea that disability is an illness or problem that must be cured or fixed, as well as a misfortune or tragedy that elicits pity.[4] Instead, disability studies asserts the social model, which recognizes disability as a social construct that marginalizes people with impairments.

If the medical model focuses on fixing the non-normative body, the social model addresses changing cultural structures that oppress disabled people.[5] Hence, disability studies differentiates between "impairment" and "disability." Impairment is a term that refers to the specific corporeal (including both physical and psychological) ways in which a body might diverge from the so-called normal or average body in ways that create functional limitations. The term "impairment" also serves as a reminder that more than other marginalized identities, disability is one that anyone may pass in and out of because of the relationship of impairment to accident or illness; moreover, the affected individual may at times choose whether to be identified as disabled. The term "disability" in this context refers to the social consequences of an impairment in relation not only to the body, but also to social constructions that result in limitations as well as a social and personal identity. Disability studies has also coined the term "ableism" to align the oppression of disabled people with that of other marginalized groups; "ableism" strategically raises associations with racism, sexism, classism, homophobism, and so on, to draw attention to the way that dominant culture's marginalization of otherness relates to disability.

Like other forms of identity politics, disability culture, in art as in other areas, seeks to allow its members to identify and define themselves, rather than be defined by others. Wherever possible we have sought to distinguish conventional, pathologizing terms for disability from terms that are embraced by disability culture. There is not necessarily a consensus about preferable terms; some seemingly derogatory terms have been recuperated and reframed. Examples of such terms that require definition in relation to disability culture and disability studies are "freak" and "crip." "Freak" is a term that originates with the exploitative display of disabled individuals with highly visible impairments, and evokes the idea of disability as spectacle, but at the same time can articulate voluntary performance, display, and celebration of non-normative appearance. "Crip" is a term that has been recuperated to represent the disability community at large in relation to disability rights, and also allies the disability community with queerness.[6]

Disability studies as a discipline may have emerged in the 1980s, but Lennard J. Davis has thoroughly investigated how categories of "normal" versus "abnormal" individuals were constructed in the nineteenth century.[7] The chapters in this volume confirm this concept that disability is a social construct related specifically to sociohistorical contexts. Disability as a social category is at least in part a product of changing attitudes toward the body that arose during the Industrial Revolution. This same historical period, the era of Modernism, also witnessed new expressions of and understandings of identity and identification. During that time, photography's ability to seemingly document truth fed the public's growing fascination with visible otherness, and with disability in particular. Disability studies and women's studies scholar Rosemarie Garland-Thomson has most thoroughly analyzed the "stare," which disabled people receive in everyday public encounters, and how photography in particular articulates and reproduces it.[8]

Disability studies in the second half of the twentieth century has followed the political movements of civil rights and feminism; disability art has, influenced by the work of second-wave feminist artists, provided new avenues for artists to complicate notions of the performance of identity, as discussed in chapters by Shayda Kafai and Elizabeth Howie in this volume. Addressing disability through art history opens ways to think about art historical tropes that tie together appearance, character, and identity, in diverse geographical and historical contexts. Disability studies–based analysis also extends beyond modern and contemporary Western art, as exemplified by chapters in this volume by William Gassaway and Rebecca Stone.

Art history, also interdisciplinary, conceives that an artwork is an object that visually represents an idea or experience, which in turn creates related but distinct experiences in the viewer. Art history addresses artworks as forms of individual expression, historical documents, and acts of social communication. Through analysis of aesthetics, production, and historical context, art history examines visual and material culture, whether historical or contemporary, in terms of its meaning both originally and over the history of its existence. In addition, art history not only points out what the art shows, but how it shows—not just what objects or ideas the artwork displays, but how, through form (media, composition, etc.) it represents its subject. And in some cases, art history interprets works of art in terms of what they fail to show, or even hide. Many art historians analyze artworks, especially figurative examples, through the lens of identity, both that of the artist and of the subject of representation. "Identity" here means that art history often incorporates discourses on race, gender, class, nationality, and sexuality, although disability as a social and historical construct and as a vital element of human diversity has been, until very recently, largely overlooked by art historical analysis.

Art history seems at times to excel at ignoring the obvious. There are many works that represent disabled individuals—for example, Raphael's *Resurrection of Christ* (1502), the Master of Alkmaar's *The Seven Works of Mercy* (1504), Pieter Bruegel the Elder's *The Beggars* (1568), Rembrandt's *Hundred Guilder Print* (1650), and Velázquez's *Las Meninas* (1656). Art history as a discipline emerged in the nineteenth century, when the medical model of disability became entrenched, and thus perhaps unsurprisingly, art history's interest in disability has traditionally followed the medical model, with the result that analyses of such works have largely overlooked the social and political status of the disabled subjects depicted in them. Despite the frequency of representations of disability in art history and visual culture (with widely varying degrees of accuracy and/or appropriateness), art history has only recently begun to focus on and reconsider such examples.

Tellingly, historical works of art that represent disability, and the scholarship that addresses them, are hard to track down using academic databases. They are frequently not indexed by the term "disability," nor are essays that discuss them. Instead, the researcher must use pejorative terms such as "cripple" and "lame," or even more troubling, perhaps, "fool," as well as other descriptive terms such as "blind," in order to find art historical analysis of such works. And even if such images can be found, most art historical articles written before the 2000s discuss the presence of individuals with disability in terms of their symbolic function, that is, in a moralizing sense as Christian figures deserving of charity and pity, as in images of Christ among beggars, cripples, and lepers, or as motifs (the monstrous or marvelous).[9] Even when they are identified as historical individuals, they nonetheless often remain pictorial motifs rather than actual social subjects. While these contexts and investigations remain important, they tend to reiterate the stereotype of the disabled person as being in need of medical attention, assistance, and/or pity.

James Holderbaum's essay "A Bronze by Giovanni Bologna and a Painting by Bronzino," published in the *Burlington Magazine* in 1956, provides an example of how art history has traditionally addressed disability.[10] While it may seem a cheap shot to target such a dated article, it does serve as a painful instance of art history's failures, in an essay which is otherwise brilliant in its investigations; certainly the approach exemplified in Holderbaum's article is not unique in art history or humanities scholarship in general. Holderbaum analyzes sculptural representations of Braccio di Bartolo, a dwarf[11] known as Morgante, who was a member of the court of Cosimo de'Medici.[12] Describing a small bronze sculpture, *The Dwarf Morgante* (1561) by Bologna, the paper fails to even indicate that the image is based on a historical individual. Several pages in the author notes that this same subject had interested another artist, Bronzino, but the "subject" could as easily be literary or mythological as factual. Holderbaum writes, "The bronze is a remarkably objective presentation of a fat and lively little body, and the artist has not underscored a joke of nature with caricature."[13] The issue here is that the description is based on his visual interpretation and thus points out disciplinary and cultural biases. Holderbaum not only has the audacity to state that the representation is "objective," which seems inappropriate considering his lack of knowledge of the true appearance of Morgante, but calling Morgante a "joke of nature" dehumanizes and enfreaks Morgante. Holderbaum compares this sculpture of Morgante to one by Valerio Cioli of Morgante as Bacchus (1560) that does caricature: "Unlike the nimble little bronze figure, here the body is sluggish and cumbersome, with every detail lingeringly ridiculed . . ."[14] Holderbaum's chapter is certainly useful in its comparison of two different approaches to representations of disability, but its failure to engage with the social reality of the represented individual is, while reflective of the scholarship of its day, excruciating. In contrast, an article from 2013 by Touba Ghadessi identifies Morgante as Braccio di Bartolo, who was from Poggio Fornione in the province of Bologna.[15] Ghadessi contextualizes the representation of Morgante in relation to Renaissance ideas about physical difference. Clearly there is much art historical work left to do to both identify and investigate such works from a disability studies perspective.

Art history has also examined artwork by disabled artists in terms of its influence on mainstream art, but often not in terms of its own merit. For example, art by institutionalized people with mental illness was appreciated for the way it was perceived to have circumvented cultural norms, but only as influence on or inspiration for so-called normal artists. An example is the work of Adolf Wölfli, who was institutionalized in Bern, Switzerland, from 1895 until his death in

1930, and who produced thousands of drawings. Such work, termed "art brut" by Jean Dubuffet, inspired abstract artists who sought new forms of abstracted and/or expressionistic painting.[16]

Furthermore, art historians have assessed impairing conditions experienced by canonical artists, for example, Goya's deafness; van Gogh's seeming mental instability; the rheumatoid arthritis experienced by Renoir late in his life; Toulouse-Lautrec's possible pycnodysostosis, a hereditary genetic disease of the bones that resulted in his small stature (and now known as Toulouse-Lautrec syndrome); the impairment experienced by the elderly Matisse following surgery for intestinal cancer; and Chuck Close's partial paralysis. In some cases, such artists are categorized as inspiring survivors whose careers continued, or even flourished, "in spite of" disability. In other cases, the artist's disability often colors interpretation of the work to a degree that it may occlude other relevant readings. For example, Frida Kahlo's luscious, colorful, and sometimes heartbreaking paintings have been conventionally seen as self-indulgent and as compensating for her emotional and physical trauma, without consideration for Kahlo's powerful influence on art, society, and politics; scholarship has also largely ignored Kahlo's subordinate status and lack of adaptive tools, state-of-the-art prosthetics, and mobility equipment, as a disabled woman in early twentieth-century Mexico.

Disability imagery also relates to the long-running academic debates between idealization and naturalism. In this sense, non-normative bodies may serve to offset the normative, or disabled individuals may be presented as "monsters" whose difference contrasts with the ideal forms of other pictured figures, for example, in portraits of royal figures accompanied by dwarfs, such as Alonso Sánchez Coello's *Infante Isabel Clara Eugenia and Magdalena Ruiz* (1585–1588).[17] Additionally, portraiture of the aristocracy tends to occlude visible signs of disability, as in the case of King Charles I, who had rickets as a child, as a result of which his legs were considered unsightly and were covered by tall boots in portraits.[18]

Modernism, with its interest in the representation of everyday life, made way for individuals to be represented more prosaically. At the same time, a figure such as Manet's *Olympia* (1863), whose naturalism was shocking in Manet's day, was perceived as physically deformed and even disabled: one critic wrote, "She does not have a human form; Monsieur Manet has so pulled her out of joint that she could not possibly move her arms of legs."[19] The perception of her appearance as revolting, expressed here in terms that could refer to human impairments, resulted from her ordinariness and failure to live up to the curvaceous female form first depicted nude in works by Titian, as well as because of Manet's deliberately unpolished painting technique, which failed to depict the model with light and shadow in the way to which viewers were accustomed, among other innovations.[20]

Modernism also facilitated a departure from the naturalism/idealism binary by introducing abstraction. The late disability studies scholar Tobin Siebers focused much of his research on a "disability aesthetic" across examples of art and visual culture, specifically in relation to the abstraction typical of Modernism. Siebers explored the way in which distortion of the human form relates to visible disability.[21] Siebers also stated that Ann Millett-Gallant's *The Disabled Body in*

Contemporary Art was unique in its merging of art history and disability studies.[22] Millett-Gallant forged a path for the scholarship that is framed in this volume.

The subjects of analysis in this book vary in terms of time periods and cultures, ranging from ancient Mesoamerican figurines and South American ceramic effigy vessels to 1920s German painting, documentary and fine art photographs from the early twentieth century to the present, and many contemporary artworks in a variety of media, as well as film. Scholars contributing to this volume integrate art historical and theoretical research by, among others, Hal Foster, RoseLee Goldberg, Rosalind Krauss, W.J.T. Mitchell, and Alan Trachtenberg, with disability studies work by Robert Bogdan, Allison C. Carey, Rosemarie Garland-Thomson, David Hevey, Alison Kafer, Petra Kuppers, Simi Linton, Paul K. Longmore, Ann Millett-Gallant, David T. Mitchell, Martha Craven Nussbaum, Carrie Sandahl, Tom Shakespeare, Tobin Siebers, Sharon L. Snyder, and Abby Wilkerson.

Some consistent themes emerged as we put this volume together, and we have arranged the chapters to draw connections between them. Both Ann Millett-Gallant and Nina Heindl examine responses to images that reveal negative biases towards disability, whether in popular culture or academic contexts. Also addressing negative biases, Rebecca Stone and William Gassaway reevaluate artworks of the ancient Americas that have been addressed problematically in terms of disability, based on the medical model. Their new readings seek to interpret their subjects within a social model of disability. Keri Watson and Timothy Hiles also re-examine work in which issues relating to disability have been overlooked or misinterpreted, in this case, documentary and journalistic photography. Anne Marno and Amanda Cachia examine ways that contemporary artists dialogue with artists of the past, in this case Dada and Surrealist artists, respectively, demonstrating ways that earlier artistic approaches to representations of disability reflected the biases of their times, as well as ways that contemporary artists may productively recuperate such content. Elizabeth Howie and Shayda Kafai address contemporary artists whose work involves performance of the problematic visibility, or lack thereof, of disability in relation to other typically oppressed identities.

Ann Millett-Gallant analyzes contemporary artist Susan Harbage Page's photographs of her developmentally disabled nephew, Peter, from age five to twenty-five. Millett-Gallant compares and contrasts Page's portraits of Peter with other visual representations of children and of developmentally disabled subjects, including Western paintings and professional portraits of children; family photographs; Diane Arbus's *Untitled* series (1970–1971), photographic portraits of developmentally disabled residents of group homes; pseudo-anthropological exhibitions of "freaks" and human/animal hybrids, and the photographs of these freak subjects; as well as Page's own self-representations. Millett-Gallant argues that Page's photographs produce multidimensional and humanistic representations of Peter and conceives of Page's and Peter's relationship as one of artist and muse, to emphasize the intersubjectivity of their collaborative artwork.

Exploring negative biases in a different context, Nina Heindl examines the sculpture *Ubermensch* (1995), a portrait of scientist Stephen Hawking, by British artists Jack and Dinos Chapman, and the television series and later film *Freakstars*

3000 (2002) by German artist and stage director Christoph Schlingensief. Heindl places these representations in larger contexts of fine art, the freak show, and reality and competition television shows, and shows the way that these contexts represent physically and intellectually disabled subjects. Both the works Heindl primarily discusses were surrounded with controversy, and the artists were accused of exploiting disabled persons just for public attention, yet Heindl emphasizes that this criticism was both informed by and contributed to negative associations with or assumptions about disability in contemporary society. Heindl contends that *Ubermensch* and *Freakstars 3000* represent two concepts of transgressive art that challenge the viewers' biased attitudes regarding disability.

Rebecca Stone discusses ancient South American ceramic effigies as images of the 'dis'abled, a term meant to differentiate between the term "disabled," according to the problematic medical model, and the still pervasive cultural stereotype of being outside of, and specifically below, the norm. Stone identifies the effigies as high-status spiritual specialists and visionaries, or shamans, who exhibit visual impairment, a characteristic correlated with elevated status and key socio-religious roles in their societies and spiritual traditions. She argues that celebration of physical anomaly was a widespread phenomenon in the indigenous Americas and particularly important in relation to the religious role of shaman, drawing attention to the social construction of the various meanings of disability, according to cultural context.

William Gassaway focuses on the appearance, interpretation, and spiritual significance of corporeal forms with atypical physical characteristics in Mesoamerican art, more specifically the role of the dwarf figure in ancient art. He contends that scientifically based analyses of the figures have tended to identify these figures' physical deviations from the norm, and to diagnose the presence of historical individuals in these communities with anomalous disorders. Instead, Gassaway recognizes that such dwarf figures were associated in indigenous thought with the benevolent forces of sun and rain, as well as with the divine retribution for mankind's earthly sins. He goes on to argue that these figures functioned as symbols of authority, nobility, and prestige, which underscores their high value among New World elites generally. Furthermore, he contends that the conventional medical analysis of such individuals dismisses their art historical and divine status.

Addressing images of disabled people that have been overlooked by art historical analyses, Keri Watson focuses on the work of Margaret Bourke-White, who was known globally for her documentary photographs of political and social movements of the twentieth century. Bourke-White contributed photographs to influential books, such as the 1937 bestselling *You Have Seen Their Faces*, which documented the effects of contemporary U.S. history on the poor and marginalized. Watson compares Bourke-White's photographs of physically disabled people in this book with her little-known 1932 photographs of residents of Letchworth Village, a New York State institution for people with developmental disabilities. These latter photographs contributed to publications that were meant to resolve controversy regarding Letchworth Village's effectiveness and alleged abuse of it residents. Watson argues that both these series of photographs challenged the popular use of disabled body as signifier of the Great Depression, which contributed to making the disabled body the scapegoat of social anxiety, as well as questioned the social construction of raced, gendered, and abled identities.

Also addressing the ways in which twentieth-century American photography shaped ideas about disability, Timothy Hiles investigates how the cultural awareness of disability following the two world wars was documented by photography of the time period and how the photographs convey different notions of roles for disabled people in society. Hiles argues that in the post–World War II era, American photographic representation of disabled individuals shifted markedly from portrayals that reinforced hierarchical preconceptions and stereotypes to those that questioned the dominance of the representative "normal." He identifies three distinct visual constructs in the photographic representation of disabled individuals: separation of the disabled from the normal, a more inclusive view of disabled individuals within a normative structure, and a redefinition of normal that shows physical difference as a legitimate aspect of society. Analyzing the photographs of Ralph Morse, Cornell Capa, Bruce Davidson, Garry Winogrand, and Paul McDonough, Hiles points to how these photographs exhibit such visual constructs and relates them to changing social attitudes toward and the development of services and programs for the disabled in America in the decades following World War II, which led to more integration of disability into mainstream, "normal" society.

Contemporary artists investigating disability at current times open dialogues with works of art from an earlier time period. Anne Marno analyzes the influence of German artist Otto Dix's Dadaist painting *The Cripples* (1920) on contemporary Israeli artist Yael Bartana's film *Degenerate Art Lives* (2010). Pointing to multimedia details and techniques, Marno argues that Bartana brings Dix's representation of veterans, disabled by war, into a present context, to critique not only the twentieth- and twenty-first-century conflicts in Israel, which have surrounded Bartana's cultural landscape, but also global war in general, as well as the political and economic causes used to justify them. Further, Marno maintains that both Dix's and Bartana's works call for the respect and rights of disabled war veterans, as well as perhaps disability rights in general.

Also investigating relationships between earlier twentieth-century art and contemporary artworks that address disability, Amanda Cachia juxtaposes the work of Surrealist artists Hans Bellmer, Jacques-André Boiffard, Brassaï, and André Masson with disability-themed performances, sculptures, and photographs by contemporary disabled and nondisabled artists Lisa Bufano, Chun-Shan (Sandie) Yi, and Artur Żmijewski. She compares and contrasts these artists' representations of the disabled body, as well its implications and contexts. Cachia argues that these contemporary artists engage with Surrealist corporeal forms, but rather than symbolizing the imagination and psychoanalysis, their imagery of bodies and body parts depict flesh and bone, in the forms of their personal experiences and body images in the world. Destabilizing Surrealist iconography, they take control of, arm, and adorn their own bodies with Surrealist imagery and iconography. Cachia maintains that Bufano, Yi, and Żmijewski transform Surrealism's often objectifying and even abusive themes of body representation to produce empowering and eroticized images of their own and other disabled subjects' bodies.

The visibility of disability in relation to the performance of identity is explored by Elizabeth Howie and Shayda Kafai. Howie dismembers the lavish, performative, and beguiling photographs of contemporary, physically impaired artist Yinka Shonibare. In *Diary of a Victorian Dandy*, Shonibare stages himself as a nineteenth-century dandy, exploring the visibility of identity in terms of race and disability. He poses self-assuredly in ornate settings of conventional Victorian, upper-class gatherings of white ladies and gentlemen, all of whom gather around and admire their ironic guest of honor. Howie demonstrates how Shonibare's photographic mise-en-scènes showcase intersections of race and disability in themes of performing, passing, and manipulating the gaze/stare of viewers. Finally, she argues that the photographic series enact scenarios of mistaken identity that question the role visibility plays in the construction of social hierarchies.

Kafai analyzes the work of San Francisco–based artist Nomy Lamm, who performs before an audience, playing music, singing erotic lyrics, moving suggestively wearing in a sexy dress, and removing her prosthetic leg. As a self-proclaimed fat, Jewish, physically disabled woman, Lamm reclaims her sexuality and that of other marginalized peoples. Kafai places Lamm's work in the framework of disability performance art that seeks to rewrite the political, sociocultural, and medical mandates of ableism, specifically the notion that disabled people are not sexual subjects. Kafai argues that by performing her sexual reclamation in such a vocal and visible way, Lamm undoes oppression, confronts the silencing effects of shame, and emphasizes that disabled bodies are desiring and desirable.

These chapters present a broad, but certainly not comprehensive, approach to interdisciplinary art history and disability studies work. They prove that analyzing representations of disabled bodies and themes of disability through art historical methodologies, and interrogating images drawn from art history through the lens of disability studies, leads to innovative and exciting new perspectives on art, on bodies, on looking, and on both academic fields of study. However, there are vast contexts and subjects of both disciplines that are not addressed here; this volume hopes to inspire and enable further thinking, research, and writing/speaking on these rich subjects.

Notes

1 Lennard J. Davis, *Enforcing Normalcy: Disability, Deafness, and the Body* (Brooklyn, NY: Verso, 1995). Davis has also edited and contributed to all four editions of *The Disability Studies Reader* (New York: Routledge, 1997; 2006; 2010; 2013). Rosemarie Garland-Thomson, *Extraordinary Bodies: Figuring Disability in American Literature and Culture* (New York: Columbia University Press, 1996); ed., *Freakery: Cultural Spectacles of the Extraordinary Body* (New York: Columbia University Press, 1996); "Seeing the Disabled: Visual Rhetorics of Disability in Popular Photography," in *The New Disability History: American Perspectives*, ed. Paul K. Longmore and Laurie Umansky (New York: New York University Press, 2001), 335–374; ed., with Sharon Snyder and Brenda Jo Bruggeman, *Disability Studies: Enabling the Humanities* (New York: MLA Press, 2002); and *Staring: How We Look* (Oxford University Press,

2009). Tobin Siebers, *The Mirror of Medusa* (Oakland: University of California Press, 1983); *The Subject and Other Subjects: On Ethical, Aesthetic, and Political Identity* (Ann Arbor: Michigan University Press, 1998); *The Body Aesthetic: From Fine Art to Body Modification* (Ann Arbor: Michigan University Press, 2000); *Disability Theory* (Ann Arbor: Michigan University Press, 2008); and *Disability Aesthetics* (Ann Arbor: Michigan University Press, 2010).
2   An exact origin of disability studies as a discipline is impossible to determine, but its first investigations emerged in the 1970s; the Society for Disability Studies, the oldest formal organization dedicated to this topic, was founded in 1982. See Philip M. Ferguson and Emily Nusbaum, "Disability Studies: What Is It and What Difference Does It Make?" *Research and Practice for Persons with Severe Disabilities* 37, no. 2 (2012): 70–80.
3   For more information on the ADA, see http://www.eeoc.gov/eeoc/history/35th/1990s/ada.html.
4   See Simi Linton, *Claiming Disability: Knowledge and Identity*, forward by Michael Bérubé (New York and London: New York University Press, 1998).
5   See Ann Millett-Gallant, *The Disabled Body in Contemporary Art* (New York: Palgrave MacMillan, 2010), 7.
6   See, for example, Robert McRuer's *Crip Theory: Cultural Signs of Queerness and Disability* (New York: NYU Press, 2006).
7   Davis, *Enforcing Normalcy*.
8   Rosemarie Garland-Thomson, *Extraordinary Bodies*; "Seeing the Disabled;" and *Staring: How We Look*.
9   These are academically important articles in prominent journals, and the editors imply no disrespect for these scholars, but instead seek to provide examples of art historical scholarship that addresses works of art with content related to disability. The research done by these scholars will certainly be of significance for future investigations into representations of disability. See, for example, Larry Silver and Henry Luttikhuizen, "The Quality of Mercy: Representations of Charity in Early Netherlandish Art," *Studies in Iconography* 29 (2008): 216–248; Kahren Jones Hellerstedt, "The Blind Man and His Guide in Netherlandish Painting," *Simiolus: Netherlands Quarterly for the History of Art* 13, no. 3/4 (1983): 161–181; Robert Baldwin, "'On Earth We Are Beggars, as Christ Himself Was': The Protestant Background of Rembrandt's Imagery of Poverty, Disability, and Begging," *Konsthistorik Tidskrift* LIV, no. 3 (1985): 122–153; Erwin Pokorny, "Bosch's Cripples and Drawings by His Imitators," *Master Drawings* 41, no. 3 (Autumn 2003): 293–304; Sandra Cheng, "The Cult of the Monstrous: Caricature, Physiognomy, and Monsters in Early Modern Italy," *Preternature: Critical and Historical Studies on the Preternatural* 1, no. 2 (2012): 197–231.
10 James Holderbaum, "A Bronze by Giovanni Bologna and a Painting by Bronzino," *The Burlington Magazine* 98, no. 645 (Dec. 1956): 439–445.
11 The acceptability of the term "dwarf" varies across the community of individuals with shorter than average stature. The resourceful and community-building organization the Little People of America was founded in 1957 and has encouraged many "people of short stature" to identify themselves by its empowering terminology. See http://www.lpaonline.org/, accessed April 3, 2016. Some people have reclaimed the term "dwarf"; others prefer to be described as people with dwarfism; still others prefer the descriptive term "short-statured." All of these terms are considered highly preferable to "midget." As editors, we are committed to whenever possible using the language preferred by the disability community, and are grateful to Amanda Cachia for sharing her insight into this issue.
12 Touba Ghadessi, "Lords and Monsters: Visible Emblems of Rule," *I Tatti Studies in the Italian Renaissance* 16, no. 1/2 (2013): 496.
13 Holderbaum, "Bronze," 439.

14 Holderbaum, "Bronze," 439.
15 Ghadessi, "Lords," 496.
16 See Hal Foster, "Blinded Insights: On the Modernist Reception of the Art of the Mentally Ill," *October* 97 (Summer 2001): 3–30.
17 See Janet Ravenscroft, "Invisible Friends: Questioning the Representation of the Court Dwarf in Hapsburg Spain," in *Histories of the Normal and the Abnormal: Social and Cultural Histories of Norms and Normativity*, ed. Waltraud Ernst (London and New York: Routledge: 2012), 26–52.
18 Iris Brooke, *A History of English Footwear* (London: Saint Giles Publishing Co., 1948), 55.
19 T.J. Clark, *The Painting of Modern Life* (Princeton, NJ: Princeton University Press, 1984), 98.
20 Clark, *Painting*, 134.
21 See Siebers, *Disability Aesthetics*.
22 Tobin Siebers, "Review of The Disabled Body in Contemporary Art," *Journal of Literary and Cultural Disability Studies* 6, no. 2 (2012): 234–237, 240.

1 Artists and muses
"Peter's World" and other photographs by Susan Harbage Page

Ann Millett-Gallant

My nephew Peter was born with disabilities. He has always had trouble with balance and sports. He finally learned to read at 14 and has always been interested in animals, imaginary action figures, musicals and now professional sports. He lives in a group home in Pittsburgh, Pennsylvania, near his mother. Most of these images were made during family gatherings; summer vacations, Thanksgiving, Christmas, Easter. I began photographing Peter when he was five years old. The early images are just me responding to him and I believe trying to come to terms with who he was. The next phase in the image making was totally controlled by Peter. He would plan backdrops and costumes for these images. Currently the images are more collaborative.[1]

Susan Harbage Page

The camera has been employed as an instrument of empirical judgment, surveillance, social documentation, and artistic creation. Photographic portraiture in particular crosses these diverse contexts, as photographic conventions for displaying the body serve as visual codes for measuring, stereotyping, and memorializing human beings. Photography, through repeated visual conventions, has established cultural codes for notions of "normal" versus "pathological" human appearance, behavior, and character. Yet, the camera has also been an instrument of memory and nostalgia, as well as a medium for the representation of a loved one, or muse. This chapter contemplates and compares all these contexts while gazing at photographs of bodies, specifically Susan Harbage Page's photographs of her developmentally disabled nephew, Peter. The photographs produce multidimensional and humanistic representations of him, which I will demonstrate by comparing and contrasting them with other visual representations of children and of developmentally disabled subjects. Page's photographs of Peter incorporate elements from the other images I analyze; yet, they strongly distinguish themselves from these counter-examples by being intimate and yet defiant of cultural stereotypes of developmentally disabled subjects. I will also conceive of Page's and Peter's relationship as one of artist and muse, to emphasize the intersubjectivity of their collaborative artwork and to undermine the conventional power dynamics between a non-disabled photographer and a disabled, objectified subject.

The opening passage is taken from photographer Susan Harbage Page's unpublished book of photographs, "Peter's World 1985–2005," which features

Peter from age five to twenty-five. Arranged chronologically, the photographs document Peter's childhood and early maturation in his mother's home, group home, neighborhood, and immediate surroundings. The photographs display Peter at work, play, leisure, and deep in thought; showcase his fascinations for animals, sports, and toy action figures; or include Peter as a silhouette against a landscape or genre scene. Shot with strong blacks and whites, a grainy quality to the tones, and sometimes blurred backgrounds, the photographs resemble both family snapshots and also documentary photographs, which have historically called for social reform. Yet, rather than sentimentalizing or typecasting Peter, the images offer a fluid, unclassifiable, and even rich depiction of developmental disability and of Peter as an individual. I chose the term "developmental disability" strategically, for it characterizes certain impairments and their manifestations, yet it is also specifically collective and abstract. While this term might problematically lump a number of intellectual and physical disabilities, I chose it for its descriptive, rather than prescriptive, function. This chapter, like Page's portraits of Peter, refuses to diagnose or brand Peter according to his specific impairments. I will argue for these interpretations of "Peter's World" by contextualizing them in relation to art historical representations of children; Diane Arbus's *Untitled* series (1970–1971), portraits of developmentally disabled residents of group homes; pseudo-anthropological exhibitions of "freaks" and human/animal hybrids; and Page's own self-representations. Page's images of Peter, as a photographic series, reflect on, yet contradict problematic histories of representing developmentally disabled subjects. Peter's body and activities both saturate and overflow the frames of "Peter's World," while both artist and muse emerge inter-subjectively.

While it is difficult to classify the portraits of "Peter's World" by genre, they share common motifs. Peter's fascination with objects is the subject of *Peter with Dinosaur Photo* (1991, fig. 1.1), in which a shirtless Peter looks serious, even impassioned. The viewer sees Peter's childlike body with rounded belly emerging from the edge of white cotton briefs, which he sticks out farther in his slouched pose as he points to a dinosaur image, a photograph he took. Thus this is also an image of a photographer showing his work. In *Peter with a Doll in His Pocket* (1993), Peter looks strained, serious, and perhaps in pain. Shadows cross his body and face, as the photographer plays with light and shadow as elements of drama. *Peter with Catwoman Doll* (1992), evidences Peter's interest in superheroes. Wearing the same clothes as in *Peter with Catwoman Doll*, Peter, in *Peter with Back to Camera* (1992, fig. 1.2), turns away from a bright studio light, which is visible inside the left-hand frame of image. This marked presence of a spectator in the photograph makes Peter's pose one of resistance or self-removal. In contrast, *Peter at Work* (2005), reveals a decidedly more mature face, again leaning over in concentration on an undistinguishable activity with cards.

Visual representations of children and childhood, particularly since early modern times, are lush and often contradictory. Art historian Anne Higonnet analyzes such representations in fine art and in various media of visual culture, including

Figure 1.1 Susan Harbage Page, *Peter with Dinosaur Photo*, 20 × 24 inches, silver gelatin print, 1991.

commercial images, formal family portraits, and everyday snapshots. According to Higonnet, images of children are often constructed to imply innocence, idealism, and optimism.[2] Yet, they also suggest implicit danger or corruption. Ideal childhood innocence is a modern, Romantic concept, Higonnet argues, as children are often represented as little adults in dress and pose, who portray proper masculine and feminine ideals.[3] A famous example is Thomas Gainsborough's *The Blue Boy* (c. 1770), in which a dapper young man stands with one foot forward, holds a riding helmet, and wears a period suit of sumptuous, sapphire fabric with silky white details, which overwhelms his boyish frame. He is staged as the archetype of proper masculinity, for boys and for men.

Higonnet refers to such examples of painted portraiture, yet focuses on photography because it implies fact, yet is also known for deception. Photographs portray the "real," but are subject to infinite forms of alteration. Photography also crosses

Artists and muses 15

Figure 1.2 Susan Harbage Page, *Peter with Back to Camera*, 20 × 24 inches, silver gelatin print, 1992.

and often confuses genres. Photographs are the pastimes of amateurs and the works of professionals; they are found abundantly in everyday culture, fine art, and a range of popular and commercial contexts. Higonnet further explains, in relation to images of children's bodies, how photography bears unique associations with pornography.[4] Photographs have indexical and visceral relationships with the subject portrayed, and many photographers have been accused of exploiting children, sometimes their own children, in the guise of depicting naked innocence.[5] Further, questions of consent and agency become convoluted when the subject matter is children's bodies.

Children have been conventionally represented with mothers, across historical, cultural, and visual contexts, and are considered appropriate or predictable subjects for women artists. The Romantic child, according to Higonnet, was conventionally represented as protected by a mother's love.[6] No one protects Peter.

16 *Ann Millett-Gallant*

Yet, Page remembers the family always being present at the settings, and indeed, she has numerous photographs of Peter participating in and even directing his cousins' play. She chose to include in her book the photographs that feature and allow Peter to dominate the frame. In Page's eyes and through her camera, Peter is all-powerful.

Page approaches her subject through her familial relationship with Peter, and her images hint at these dynamics. In *Peter with Comic Book* (2000, fig. 1.3), Peter is not ashamed of his nakedness as he lies on the bed reading before his aunt's gaze and the camera. Peter's reclining torso is shot diagonally, with soft focus and blurry details. His nude, reclining upper body is central to the image, and his lower half is more abstracted, as bended legs emerge inconspicuously beneath his book. The book shields his face and takes center stage in the image; his penis, concealed by his leg, plays a minor role. Page may have angled the

Figure 1.3 Susan Harbage Page, *Peter with Comic Book*, 20 × 24 inches, silver gelatin print, 2000.

shot specifically to avoid objectifying Peter, as she focuses on his activities and accomplishments. The image documents Peter's ability to read, a skill he obtained in adolescence. In this semi-nude portrait, Peter is specifically personalized, rather than objectified.

All of the photographs focus solely on Peter as their star, yet this characteristic staging places Peter in isolation. Particularly in the images shot at family gatherings, such as holiday celebrations, Peter is featured alone. *Peter at Christmas* (2000), features Peter in solitude, asleep on the floor of a vacant family living room in front of a lit Christmas tree. More formal, staged portraits in visual history depict children as the bearers of noble lineage, and often, children are posed within their royal families. They represent their families' legacy. Higonnet argues that like these formal painted portraits, family snapshots display the desires, successes, and lifestyles of parents.[7] In contrast, Peter's family is noticeably absent in "Peter's World."

Page's portraits of Peter allude to but conceal Peter's relationships. In *Peter with Cramer* (2001, fig. 1.4), the foreground is dominated by the back of a frisky, jumping black dog that licks Peter's smiling face. Pairings of children with cute, cuddly, specifically domesticated animals abound in visual culture. Yet here, both the dog and Peter appear enraptured and wild. Peter does not control or dominate Cramer, but rather interacts with him at the mouth. *Peter Talks with His Girlfriend* (2002) features Peter standing with his back to the family garage as he talks on a cell phone. In all the other photographs of Peter's face, he looks serious and sometimes stern; these two photographs show glimpses of Peter's smile. These images of friendship suggest that Peter is part of a loving community, yet they show Peter visibly alone.

Peter assumes his role as solitary leading man with gusto. As represented in several of Page's photographs, Peter loves Halloween. *Peter with Clown Mask* (1994), shows Peter in a mask with a strong, menacing grin. In this photograph, he is an evil clown. In *Halloween: Peter with Walker the Rat* (2005), Peter poses with a toy rat, and in *Peter with Cape* (1994, fig. 1.5), Peter stands before an outdoor wall, glaring at the camera with a slightly downward gaze. Peter, in these photographs, tries on different identities and fantasizes. Further, he performs before the camera. The Halloween images, like many others of Peter and his activities, emphasize the narrowing of his eyes; the white, round mass of his forehead; and his characteristically vacant stare. His facial features and expression reflect his developmental disabilities in these images, as well as in many others, and he could problematically be deemed unusual by the viewer. Or maybe Peter is just a typical, agitated teenager. Peter's body, in the flesh and in silhouette, shows a child blossoming and stumbling into adulthood.

Like photographer Diane Arbus's *Untitled* series (1970–1971), shot at the end of her life at various facilities for people with developmental disabilities, Page's photographs of Peter refuse to diagnose. Many of Arbus's images feature the subjects costumed for Halloween and directly influenced Page's portraits of Peter on Halloween. "Peter's World" also shares with Arbus's series a repeated image of a developmentally disabled, awkward manchild, yet adolescence is inevitably

Figure 1.4 Susan Harbage Page, *Peter with Cramer*, 20 × 24 inches, silver gelatin print, 2001.

gawky for everyone. Arbus made repeated visits to the facilities where she photographed developmentally disabled subjects, many in rural New England. The photographs spotlight their subjects as performative, in their costumes and dynamic actions, like Page's portraits of Peter.

Unlike Arbus's numerous singular portraits and photographic slices of life, *Untitled*, as a series, and like the series "Peter's World," suggests a narrative. The

Artists and muses 19

Figure 1.5 Susan Harbage Page, *Peter with Cape*, 20 × 24 inches, silver gelatin print, 1994.

heavily printed edges make the *Untitled* series appear like images on a reel of film. In choreographies of dance and sometimes gymnastic-like movements, the subjects command their spaces and overwhelm their frames, as does Peter. The characters roll on the grounds, hold hands, frolic at outdoor picnics, and parade their Halloween costumes. Despite their age, many of the adults proudly display their almost childish, food-covered faces and tacky finery. Many of the *Untitled* subjects pause in their play to pose, while smiling and sometimes drooling. Like Peter in some of Page's photographs, some return a vacant gaze, like deer caught in headlights, while others flirt with the camera. Yet few turn away from Arbus's attention, raising questions regarding whether they knew they would be shown publicly as spectacles, by nature of their already conspicuous bodies and bodily displays.

Arbus's work has been said to "enfreak"[8] her disabled subjects, in form and composition, and thus construct them as freaks. Her photographs of developmentally disabled subjects do indeed share discursive and visual similarities with freak show displays, specifically in their staging as "wild" subjects closer to nature. In the nineteenth century, anxieties about evolution and human development were projected onto freak show bodies.[9] Specifically, contextual social values and scientific theories of human development and evolution were projected onto developmentally disabled bodies, marking them with metaphorical associations specific to nature. The "mentally retarded," as they are often called in freak show literature, were commonly exhibited as wild people; feral children, sometimes raised by wolves; pinheads (individuals with microcephaly); human/animal hybrids; lost races of non-Western, uncivilized peoples (such as Bartola and Maximo, the "Lost Aztec Children"); and geeks (performers who killed live chickens or snakes with their teeth and ate them, often dressed in "wild" costumes to exaggerate connections between the primitive and the cannibal).[10] In these roles, many individuals with developmental disabilities wore skins and fur costumes, were marketed as being some form of alien, or primitive tribe, and were largely infantilized. Freak show historian Rachel Adams points out how such pseudo-anthropological freak show displays exaggerated racial and ethnic stereotypes.[11] The *Untitled* series enacts a similar anthropological gaze/stare and represents the "Other" through exaggerating qualities that mark their difference or deviance from the norm.

Comparisons between so-called monstrous, wild people and developmentally disabled subjects in freak shows and in Arbus's images reveal a deep history of representation. In one example, an 1887 study by J. Langdon Down (for whom Down syndrome is named) characterizes Down syndrome as an "Aztec-type."[12] Here, he references specifically the exhibition, beginning in 1849, of microcephalic children whose background was unclear (possibly abandoned children from Mexico or San Salvador), as the "Lost Aztec Children." Maximo and Bartola, these so-called Lost Aztecs or Aztec Lilliputians, were framed by the freak show as culturally primitive, as well as physically and mentally delayed. They were specifically staged as remnants of a lost race, perhaps even the survivors of European colonial genocide (historically, the Aztecs were a fierce Mexican Indian society defeated by the conquest of Hernán Cortés in the seventeenth century). The "Lost Aztecs" were said to be cretins, a term that described little people whose intelligence is mostly average, but who experience limited sexual development.[13] Maximo and Bartola were first presented as twins who toured Europe and the United States for freak performances, but were later married 1867 as a publicity stunt.[14] This suggestively incestuous act increased their associations with the animalistic and primitive, yet was marketed as sweet and innocent due to their childlike asexuality. They were ambivalently sentimentalized and eroticized.[15] In contrast, images from "Peter's World" feature Peter frolicking in the outdoor areas surrounding his home, showing his playful, specifically humanized activities.

Different from "Peter's World" in visual qualities and intention, collectible, souvenir photographs, or *cartes de visite*, framed and circulated freak show narratives.[16] Nineteenth-century *cartes de visite* of the so-called Aztec children with their owner, many of which were shot by period photographer Charles Eisenmann, portray Maximo's body, displayed as abnormal by his unusually rigid, turned-down hand gesture, turned-in feet, and slightly hunched stance; likely, he was posed this way strategically. According to literature, the "marriage" was never consummated due to Maximo's sexual immaturity rather than Bartola's, who appears in the photographs as "normal" in pose and dress, according to the standards of American and European audiences.[17] She does diverge from conventional, or Caucasian, appearance in her dark skin, emphasized by the photograph in strong frontal lighting and by her white dress and pearl necklace, a formal quality shared with many of Arbus's *Untitled* portraits. Costume also functions rhetorically: a white Victorian crocheted dress in another *carte* further accentuates the color of Bartola's skin. Correspondingly, Maximo dons a proper and fashionable nineteenth-century man's suit, again on an awkwardly posed, abnormally marked body. The Eisenmann photographs stage them as ironically dignified in a conventional nineteenth-century family portrait format, which emphatically offsets their non-Western, non-human "wildness"—highlighted particularly in the animal-like qualities of their black, bushy, tangled hair. The children were costumed and staged as microcosmic metaphors—personifications of contemporary, pseudo-scientific theories. Photographs both enacted and document these affronts to civil and human rights.

Such historical offenses circulate in and around Arbus's *Untitled* photographs. Arbus's own descriptions of her subjects as "retarded people, idiots, imbeciles and morons" begin to point to the inadequacy of conventional language for and representation of individuals with developmental disabilities.[18] Terms such as Arbus's socially construct the developmentally disabled accordingly. For example, the most popular term, "retarded," stems from the verb "retard," which in everyday use means to slow up, to prevent or hinder advancement or accomplishment, and to impede.[19] "Retarded," as a label for individuals, further encompasses various forms of developmental disabilities, such as Down syndrome, autism, brain damage, or a somewhat miscellaneous grouping of "multi-handicapped," all of which may include diverse sensorial and anatomical impairments. Conflating individuals under the umbrella term "retarded" may de-particularize individual lived experiences, personalities, educational needs, and abilities and options for work, self-sufficiency, and autonomy. Referring to Arbus's subjects as "retardees" exercises what disability studies theorist Paul K. Longmore has postulated about the conventional language of disability as working to reduce individuals to the singular characteristics of their impairments, rather than considering them as multidimensional in identity and personality. Longmore argues that conventional language for disability largely medicalizes, constructing disabilities as tragic and pathological.[20]

However, even the word "retarded" exceeds frames. "Retarded" was invented in the twentieth century to replace other offensive terms such as "feebleminded," "idiot," and "moron."[21] "Retarded" goes in and out of favor socially, and oscillates between colloquial, derogatory slander (as a slang synonym for stupidity), perhaps progressive reclamation of language, and often a clinical and professional term.[22] Alternative terms such as intellectual disability and neurodiversity have been raised by academics and other professionals to offset more disparaging, slang usage of the term "retarded." Organizations of and for individuals with developmental disabilities, such as the Special Olympics and Best Buddies, have actively protested the term "retarded"; for example, the R-Word website discusses contemporary connotations of the term and advocates a movement to focus more on the unique abilities of people.[23] Considering all these voices, the connotation of "retarded" may only be determined by context and reception.

Arbus's images, as well as Page's photographs of Peter, are likewise indeterminate. In one particularly moving image, *Untitled #55* (1970–1971), viewers get a vivid sense of their own exclusion from a world existing off the page and extending beyond their empirical reach. Here, a solitary young woman with Down's syndrome (as revealed by her characteristic facial features) poses on an outdoor picnic bench in a bonnet made of paper. Her highly vivid body, in crisp detail, is offset by a blurry background, which obscures the buildings of her institution. She stares off in the distance, at something beyond the frame which the viewer cannot see or perhaps, metaphorically, will never access, in an intense, somewhat alarmed gaze and in complete oblivion to the world around her. The paper and pencil in her hand might demonstrate a daily activity of schoolwork or doodling, or they could identify her as a writer, recording her thoughts. She is perhaps caught in a moment of reverie, imagination, and creativity. The indistinct background heightens the sense of no place, or any place, as if she is transported telepathically, or shape-shifts to a privileged time traveler due to her socially unrestrained imagination. In other words, perhaps her developmental disabilities and her status as a so-called "special case" liberate her from responsibilities and allow her to freely fantasize and create. The viewer is excluded from her imaginative narrative, as the photograph frames the interior world of the subject. And although her broad facial features may hint at her disability, her illusive gaze serves as another performative mask. The conventions of physiognomy for reading character and particularly pathology from facial features and expressions fail to signify in this portrait. Page's *Peter the Teenager*, (1999, fig. 1.6) reveals Peter maturing, with similar facial features as Arbus's subject. He displays a shy smile and is visibly aware that he is being photographed. His idiosyncratic facial features produce a look of reflection, rather than abnormality, as his wide eyes show an intense and thoughtful gaze and his lips are parted, as if he intends to speak. Comparing Arbus's photograph to Page's makes the viewer look twice and question what he or she assumes about the young person each image frames.

I raise these examples to discuss a history of visual representations of developmentally disabled subjects. These comparisons suggest what a viewer might assume about Page's photographs of a "developmentally disabled subject," yet such assumptions would only scratch the surface. Page's photographs, in sharp contrast to those from the freak show tradition, humanize and even cause the viewer to marvel affectionately and admiringly at Peter. They are intimate, familial, and showcase Peter as multidimensional. The photographs of "Peter's World" do bear similarities to some of Arbus's *Untitled* images, as they stage the

Figure 1.6 Susan Harbage Page, *Peter the Teenager*, 20 × 24 inches, silver gelatin print, 1999.

developmentally disabled subject as the subject of artistic display, a muse, and significantly, as a unique individual. *Peter's Hands* (1999, fig. 1.7, and 2002), is the title of two of Peter's portraits. Rosemarie Garland-Thomson-argues that conventional photographs of disabled subjects fetishize the sites of impairment, making disability, derogatorily, all encompassing of one's identity.[24] Photographs of Peter's hands, however, expand Peter's multidimensional identity.

Rather than fetishizing Peter, the photographs of his hands mask his impairments and highlight his tools of creative work. The 1999 photograph is a close-up of Peter's hands against the legs of his jeans. They are worker's hands, stained and scarred, like the soiled hands of the domestic worker in Tina Modotti's *Hands Washing* (1927). Modotti worked for the cause of revolution in Mexico, with contemporary Edward Weston, photographing impoverished laborers, and often, their hands at work. In *Hands Washing*, a bright white cleaning cloth highlights the

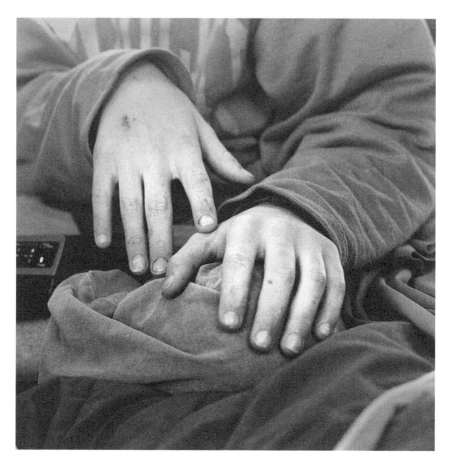

Figure 1.7 Susan Harbage Page, *Peter's Hands*, 20 × 24 inches, silver gelatin print, 1999.

dark-skinned hands of the worker. In *Hands of a Puppeteer* (1929), Modotti again employs strong lighting, as shadows of the hands, wrapped in the strings and control bar and of a marionette, create drama. Like Peter, the puppeteer exhibits worker's hands, but his work is art. In *Peter's Hands* (2002), Peter stretches his arms with fingers spread over high vines and weeds. A strong, overhead light emphasizes that his hands are objects of awe and display, like a still life object, additionally alluded to by the long foliage behind them. Bathed in light from above, Peter's hands are inspiring and inspired—the hands of an artist.

The hands, as well as the eyes, are the sites of Page's work, as Peter serves as her muse. Muses derive from Greek myths about nine female figures who incarnate poetry, history, and the performing arts.[25] They signify the object of unrequited desire and fear. Muses lead to inspiration and risk, self-abandonment, surrender of power or control, and, poignantly, artistic creation; they bring out the artist's greatest vulnerabilities, play upon weaknesses, and incite mischief, social transgression, and often creative genius. The relationship between an artist and his or her muse is one of drama and tension, as having a muse leads to discoveries that always include the discomfort of becoming lost and the process of painful disillusionment. Sometimes, muses cause the viewer of their images, not just the artist, to become moved, altered, and transformed.

Traditionally the artist/muse relationship is gendered male/female and maintains gender power dynamics, yet "Peter's World" makes this relationship symbiotic. The relation between artist and muse, again, is key, as artistic creation becomes a communal activity, and the artist and muse become co-dependent and collaborative. As artist and muse, Page and Peter share a dynamic on both sides of the camera that contrasts sharply with that of the other photographers and subjects discussed in this chapter. Peter serves as Page's muse; while Peter matures and Aunt Susan matures, Page, as a photographer, develops her craft.[26] Page's other photographic series document her own experiences with breast cancer and trials with her body. Page continued working on "Peter's World" as she created her other series, such as documentations and photographic performances of women around the world (nuns in Italy and Arab women in purdah, for example), in veils, with mastectomies, or with impermanent tattoos of self-authored writing and the names of loved ones. All of these images share themes of veiling, concealing, and revealing the self/body. They also involve intense relationships between the subjects behind and in front of the camera.

Page's self-portrait, *A Question of Beauty* (2000), reveals her nude torso with one breast and a post-mastectomy scar. Beneath her bald head (a result of chemotherapy), her face bears little expression, neither inviting nor deterring the viewer's gaze at her body, marked by cancer and consequential emotional battles. The question asked by the photograph is what defines femininity and beauty, particularly for women, or even appearance acceptability. Conversely, the image asks what characterizes a de-feminized or "damaged" body. Hair, particularly long hair, signifies feminine beauty and youth for women, and Page was mistaken for a man socially after losing her hair.[27] The breast signifies an even greater range of characteristics associated with femininity. The naked breast, most frequently fetishized on the female body to eroticize and objectify it for the heterosexual male gaze, may be a source of shame for the woman, when revealed for social or medical scrutiny or when a woman has been made to feel physically inadequate due to the shape, size, or absence of breasts, and therefore considered undesirable. The breastless woman, such as Page and other cancer survivors, likewise faces shame about and stigmatization towards her "diseased" and "disfigured" body. Further, women's breasts bear multiple personal significances; Page has remarked on how in youth, breasts represent a girl's development of womanhood and sexual desirability, while later they provide sustenance and nurturing to children, and then, when faced with breast cancer, the breasts transform from life-givers to life-takers.[28] Removal of the breast, therefore, is a simultaneous loss and relief. Both the present breast and the absent one in Page's photographs of herself and other women represent the process of the body's aging and its inevitable vulnerability, states of the body for which women especially feel ashamed in contemporary culture's obsession with youth and impossible standards for bodily "perfection." The role of motherhood emerges in these works, as it surrounds "Peter's World."

Novelist Francine Prose's *The Lives of the Muses: Nine Women and the Artists They Inspired* turns the tables on conventional, gendered tales of muses and contains many stories of reversal, such that the muse becomes so enveloped in creative passion that the he or she begins to create and becomes an artist.[29] As a result of working with his aunt, Peter created a series of drawings. He also advised Page on the settings of his portraits. The photographs are therefore collaborations, as Page describes in her introduction; they are the works of artist and muse.[30] Peter plays a dual role as director and performer, as he helps craft this presentation of himself. Susan's and Peter's images have been displayed in a number of galleries and museums and are part of the permanent collection of the Museum of Fine Arts, Houston. Page notes the excitement and pride this created for Peter.[31]

My examples throughout this paper point to disturbing histories of representation, far darker than the shadows that fall around Peter within Page's frames. As a series, the photographs of "Peter's World" highlight the passage of time and appear like a family photo album, albeit in the more formal format of a photography exhibition catalogue. Page states that this body of work is influenced by the photographs of Emmet Gowin and Harry Callahan, who made aesthetically beautiful and moving collaborative portraits of their wives over an extended period of time.[32] For Page and these photographers, familial relationships developed along with the photographic images. Page recognizes the changes that occurred in the photographs when she became pregnant and began to assume her own role as a mother. She wanted to photograph Peter, yet protect him. After shooting *Peter with Book* (2000, fig. 1.3), Page began to question her own intentions with the series. She also made a concerted effort to encourage Peter's role in self-representation. Page's relationship with Peter exceeds the frames of the photographs. Peter visits his aunt Susan every year in Durham, North Carolina, where they attend Durham Bulls Baseball games. Sometimes these visits include photo shoots, but only if Peter is in the mood. In this way, and in striking contrast to many of the other examples I analyze in this chapter, "Peter's World" is always a collaborative work in progress.

Notes

1 Susan Harbage Page, "Peter's World 1985–2005" (unpublished manuscript, 2005), 1.
2 Anne Higonnet, *Pictures of Innocence: The History and Crisis of Ideal Childhood* (London: Thames and Hudson, Ltd., 1998).
3 Higonnet, *Pictures of Innocence*, 15–30.
4 Higonnet, *Pictures of Innocence*, 159.
5 For examples, the works of photographers Sally Mann, Lewis Carroll, and Jock Sturges have raised much controversy and received criticism for their photographs of children.
6 Higonnet, *Pictures of Innocence*, 31–49.
7 Higonnet, *Pictures of Innocence*, 193–226.

8 David Hevey, in his argument that Arbus's images oppress the disabled through representation and "enfreak" them, accuses Arbus of "psychoventriloquism," by using "abnormal" bodies as metaphors for her own destructive, chaotic self-image. Ironically, although Hevey characterizes Arbus's framing of disabled bodies as enacting the social isolation of all disabled people, he sees the *Untitled* images as diverging from this scenario, despite the fact that the subjects are photographed in the everyday reality of their social, institutional isolation, because they are self-absorbed and refuse her patronizing attempts to identify with them through rebuffing the gaze. See David Hevey, "The Enfreakment of Photography," *The Disability Studies Reader*, 3rd edition, ed. Lennard J. Davis (New York: Routledge, 2010), 507–521.
9 Daniel P. Mannix, *Freaks: We Who Are Not as Others* (New York: RE/Search Publications, 1999; 1969); Michael Mitchell, *Monsters: Human Freaks in America's Gilded Age: The Photographs of Chas. Eisenmann* (Toronto, Canada: ECW Press, 2002); Leslie Fiedler, *Freaks: Myths and Images of the Secret Self* (New York: Simon & Schuster, Inc., 1978). Specific examples include the Hottentot Venus, Wild Men, and other so-called deformed human/animal hybrids, including Jo Jo (the dog-faced boy), Piebald blacks (or leopard boys), the Frog Boy, the Turtle Boy, the Monkey Woman, the Lion-Faced Boy, the Mule-Faced Woman (Grace McDaniels), the Alligator-Skinned Man and Sister (who exhibited and sold Bibles), Sealo the Seal Boy (whom medical terminology diagnosed as having phocomelia), the Lobster Boy (Grady Styles, as well as his family, known as the Lobster People), and Koo-Koo the Bird Girl (who performed in the Todd Browning cult classic, *Freaks*, and who was not medically deformed but whose title emphasized her intense, so-called ugliness).
10 Mannix, *Freaks: We Who Are Not as Others*, 90.
11 Rachel Adams, *Sideshow USA: Freaks and the American Cultural Imagination* (Chicago: University of Chicago Press, 2001), 25–59.
12 John L. H. Down, "On Some of the Mental Afflictions of Childhood and Youth," *The Lettsomian Lectures Delivered Before the Medical Society of London* (London: J. A. Churchill, 1887).
13 This is according to an extensive study of forms of short stature conducted by Buddie Thompson and quoted by Mannix, *Freaks: We Who Are Not as Others*, 29.
14 Robert Bogdan, *Freakshow: Representing Human Oddities for Amusement and Profit* (Chicago: University of Chicago Press, 1988), 131.
15 Information about Maximo and Bartolo is drawn from Bogdan, *Freakshow*, 127–134.
16 Many examples of *cartes de visite* of freak show performers can be found in Bodgan, *Freakshow*.
17 This image is included in Bogdan, *Freakshow*, 128.
18 This statement is drawn from a letter Arbus wrote to London-based editor Peter Crookston, circa December 1968, and reprinted in *Diane Arbus: Revelations* (New York: Random House, 2003), 196.
19 This was drawn from the entry for "retard" in Merriam-Webster's *Collegiate Dictionary*, 10th edition (Springfield, MS: Merriam-Webster, Inc., 1994).
20 Robert Longmore, "A Note on Language and the Social Identity of Disabled People," *American Behavioral Scientist* 28 (Jan/Feb 1985): 419–423.
21 Tammy Reynolds, C. E. Zupanick, and Mark Dombeck, "History of Stigmatizing Names for Intellectual Disabilities," published on the website of Community Counseling Services, Inc, accessed April 7, 2015, http://communitycounselingservices.org/poc/view_doc.php?type=doc&id=10355&cn=208.
22 Robert Longmore, "A Note on Language," 419–423.
23 The websites of these organizations are as follows: http://www.specialolympics.org/; http://www.bestbuddies.org/; and www.rwor.org. R-word.org is also sponsored by over two hundred organizations from around the world, which are listed at http://r-word.org/r-word-supporting-organizations.aspx.

28 *Ann Millett-Gallant*

24 Rosemarie Garland-Thomson, "Seeing the Disabled: Visual Rhetorics of Disability in Popular Photography," in *The New Disability History: American Perspectives*, ed. P. K. Longmore and L. Umansky (New York: New York University Press, 2001), 335–374.
25 Francine Prose, *The Lives of the Muses: Nine Women and the Artists They Inspired* (New York: HarperCollins Publishing, 2002), 1–23.
26 For information about Page's other bodies of work, see http://susanharbagepage.blogspot.com/
27 Susan Harbage Page in discussion with author, January 2008.
28 Susan Harbage Page in discussion with author, January 2008.
29 Francine Prose, *The Lives of Muses* (New York: Harper Perennial, 2003).
30 Susan Harbage Page, "Peter's World 1985–2005" (unpublished manuscript, 2005), 1.
31 Susan Harbage Page in discussion with author, January 2008.
32 Susan Harbage Page in discussion with author, January 2008.

2 Exploiting, degrading, and repellent

Against a biased interpretation of contemporary art about disability

Nina Heindl

Introduction

> What is the most detestable, the most repellent, and the most pointless work of art you have ever seen? This week I remembered the most hateful work of modern British art, and maybe a candidate for the most repugnant of modern times.[1]
>
> Jonathan Jones, *The Guardian*

> When people who obviously can't assess the situation are exposed in front of the whole "nation," it's pretty perverse and can no longer be justified by its artistic character.[2]
>
> user SnooP, online community *xpbulletin.de*

These statements were made in respect to two contemporary works, a sculpture and an art project: the sculpture *Ubermensch* (1995) by British artists Jack and Dinos Chapman, and the television series and later film *Freakstars 3000*[3] (2002) by German artist and stage director Christoph Schlingensief, respectively. Both works were surrounded with controversy, and the artists (both nondisabled) were accused of exploiting disabled persons just for public attention, as the opening quotes indicate. However, it is not sufficient to analyze these works of art solely with regard to their shock factor—although provocation is unquestionably intended. My aim is to show that negative interpretations of these artistic forms as exploitative, degrading, and repellent are largely based on the viewers' individual perceptions and their sociocultural imprints. I argue that works like *Ubermensch* and *Freakstars 3000* lay bare the viewers' own biased attitudes towards disability, and by doing so, open up a space for reflection on socially given stereotypes of disability and deviations from the so-called norm.

First, I give a short introduction on transgressiveness and ambiguity in contemporary art, with special focus on art concerned with disability. The two following parts are dedicated to the already mentioned *Ubermensch* and *Freakstars 3000*. There I will show how the selected works by nondisabled artists deal with physical and intellectual disability, and what role the viewers play in the possibly biased interpretation of these works.

Transgressiveness and ambiguity of contemporary art about disability

The sentiments of the epigraphs at the introduction's beginning are quite common within current debates about so-called transgressive art. This kind of art can be described as offensive, shocking, and disturbing in its overstepping of moral borders.[4] In his *Aftershock* (2009), art philosopher Kieran Cashell examines the ethical dimensions of this contemporary art form. Cashell argues that transgressive art goes beyond the general assumption that it infringes on conservative views and moral issues only for the value of shock. For Cashell, the viewer's reaction is indispensable for understanding this kind of art.[5] The irritation and shock moment that transgressive art produces in order to offend sensibilities and provoke a moral response in the viewers, Cashell calls "aftershock."[6]

Contemporary art about disability can be separated into two branches: art made by artists with disabilities ("disability art"), and art about disability made by nondisabled artists. Often these nondisabled artists are suspected of exploiting disabled people for a morally and ethically untenable purpose or simply their own profits.[7] By applying Cashell's critical concept of aftershock to the subfield of transgressive art dealing with aspects of disability made by nondisabled artists, new ways of analyzing and examination become possible.

As I will show, reproaching these artists for exploiting disabled persons for public attention takes too narrow a view. It is based on the perception and interpretation of disability as problem. Hence, social scientist Martha Craven Nussbaum and disability studies scholar Tobin Siebers point out that disabled persons in social and public contexts are still struggling with negative connotations, such as tragedy or loss.[8] As a result of "the social illegibility of the disabled body," this negative connotation may extend to discomfort when being confronted with disabled persons, as disability studies scholar Rosemarie Garland-Thomson argues.[9] But where do these negative implications come from? One important explanation lies in contexts of the body. According to Siebers and Garland-Thomson, the perception of the body is to a large extent socially constructed and culturally imprinted.[10] Human beings understand their activities and interactions in relation to their own bodies, their physical condition, and the socially constructed ideal of the body. People who deviate from that norm inevitably have to struggle with negative connotations.

Social scientists Tanya Titchkosky and Rod Michalko call this situation the "disability-as-problem frame."[11] This means that deviations from the norm, that is, physical or psychological otherness, may lead to prejudice and a biased attitude from persons who appear to adjust to or fit the so-called norm. This disregard is a symptom of the social and cultural conditions that provide a reference system for human interaction. Disability studies scholars set their focus on this connection of socially constructed norms and our sociocultural imprint, as Garland-Thomson concludes: "Disability studies points out that ability and disability are not so much a matter of the capacities and limitations of bodies but more about what we expect from a body at a particular moment and place."[12] In this sense disability studies focuses on the thought-provoking "how" of perceiving and representing disability, rather than disability as a secluded and individual problem.

As I will show in the next sections, works of art may provide a frame for these expectations, and thereby evoke self-reflection, by pinpointing the mechanisms of bias at work.[13] Including thoughts about the aforementioned concept of the transgressiveness of art, I question the attitude regarding disability in art by nondisabled artists and challenge the viewers' socioculturally imprinted biases.[14] First, I will examine Jake and Dinos Chapman's *Ubermensch* (1995). The fiberglass and mixed media sculpture depicts the physically disabled physicist Stephen Hawking in his wheelchair on the edge of a cliff. The second work that I will analyze is the project *Freakstars 3000* (2002) by Christoph Schlingensief. *Freakstars 3000* was a television series and later film that included intellectually disabled persons.

An important reason why these two works are able to address possible biases is their ambiguity. Art historian Verena Krieger states that it is commonplace to call works of art and artistic projects ambiguous. But as Krieger argues, it is not sufficient to only state ambiguity. Furthermore, ambiguous aspects have to be analyzed in context of their structure and function within works of art.[15] Although critics reproach the works for one-dimensionality, their interpretation is not fixated on one single meaning.[16] These works of art provide the opportunity to contrast different forms and contexts of ambiguity. In her chapter "At War with the Obvious—Kulturen der Ambiguität," Krieger provides an extensive list of different forms and levels of ambiguity in works of art, for example, in relation to their visual contents and structural design, or the history of their reception (the processes of reinterpretation through the time).[17] In the following I will focus on equivocal aspects of the visual contents and structural design of works of art Krieger calls visual ambiguity.[18] Besides iconographic unclarity (the symbolic content of specific motifs can have several meanings), Krieger defines two other forms of visual ambiguity which are important for the analysis of *Ubermensch* and *Freakstars 3000*: the contradiction between the objects or figures depicted and the way they are depicted as well as the mediation of conflicting information through disparate perspectives.[19]

The visual ambiguity of *Ubermensch* can be described with the first type, dissent in terms of content (the figure depicted) and the type of depiction. It relates to its art historical context, in terms of its title, material, structure, and composition, as well as to the history of representation in general. The art project with the television series and later film, *Freakstars 3000*, focuses on a broader contemporary media and particularly entertainment context. By examining its title, introductory voice-over, and examples from the film, *Freakstars 3000* can be categorized as visual ambiguity that communicates contradictory information. This especially applies to the way the intellectually disabled contestants are staged and the way we usually see disabled persons in television and media context. Both *Ubermensch* and *Freakstars 3000* open up a space for reflection on ambivalent mechanisms. With their historical and contemporary relations to fields of sociocultural imprint in our visual culture these works contribute to an understanding of biased interpretations of contemporary art about disability.

Ubermensch: **mentally superior and physically disabled**

In Jake and Dinos Chapman's *Ubermensch*, a figure in a wheelchair representing Stephen Hawking is situated on the edge of a steep slope (fig. 2.1). It is a quite dangerous position for the figure; in fact, one wheel juts out over the cliff. With a total height of 366 cm, the sculpture also towers above the viewers' heads and

Figure 2.1 Jake and Dinos Chapman, *Ubermensch*, 366 × 183 × 183 cm, Fiberglass, resin and paint, 1995, private collection. © VG Bild-Kunst, Bonn 2015.

conveys the feeling that it is quite risky to linger below the Hawking figure's feet. His head is turned to the right; the right side of his face is wrinkled, and his mouth stands open and lays bare his teeth. His right leg is bent, and the foot protrudes out over the footrest. This kind of jutting out is similar to the way the whole wheelchair projects slightly over the slope, and thereby supports the impression of the figure being in a very unsafe and dangerous position. This effect is strengthened by the viewers' likely knowledge of Hawking's illness.

Stephen Hawking was born in 1942. At the age of 21 he was diagnosed with a slow-progressing form of amyotrophic lateral sclerosis, a disorder in which muscle-controlling neurons die. As a result, the person affected has more and more difficulty moving, speaking, and swallowing. Currently, Hawking uses a wheelchair and communicates via computer by using a single cheek muscle. As a theoretical physicist and cosmologist, Hawking is not only a well-known public figure, but also one of the most important and influential scientists of our time.

Art critic Jonathan Jones contextualizes Hawking's importance in his scathing criticism of the sculpture *Ubermensch*: "Hawking's story really is an epic triumph of the human mind. His defiance of illness is profoundly moving, his ability to mentally explore the universe in spite of it an inspiration for our time and times to come."[20] Jones describes Hawking as a hero who overcomes all adverse circumstances. Consequently, to him, the Chapman brothers' depiction of Hawking seems not in the least adequate for such an important man. In his critique, Jones calls the work a "caricature" as well as a "sneering sculpture," and he sees it as "plainly intended sarcastically."[21] Moreover, he adds that *Ubermensch* "seems to suggest that Hawking, the modern superman, is a prisoner of his sick body. It stresses his carnal weakness and mocks the idea that his mind has somehow conquered matter."[22] Jones provides an explanation of the sculpture, which he expects to be the universal and only valid one: the Chapman brothers make fun of a tragic genius who suffers from his physical disability.

Art critic Robbert Roos, on the other hand, offers a completely different interpretation: "Hawking's brilliant mind trapped in a tormented body towers proudly above us, a superior position based on his analytical brainpower and visionary theories about the cosmos."[23] While Jones rejects the sculpture and describes it with disgust, Roos praises the work to high heaven—he writes of a proud towering that, in my opinion, is not part of sculptural appearance, but of the interpreter's own interpretation of it. Neither in the Hawking figure's facial expression, nor in his physical appearance, can conventional signs of pride be seen, for example, a raised head or a straightened up body in combination with an encapsulation of the figure.[24] Only his exposed and singled-out position on the edge of a steep slope corresponds to this kind of a proud depiction. But that position is also, as we have seen in Jones's critique, the offending object of *Ubermensch*.

Both Jones's reproach and Roos's praises are legitimate interpretations of the sculpture. I argue that there is no definite and unequivocal interpretation for the sculpture; it rather provokes emotional reactions, prompts questions, and thus opens up a space for reflection on personal and social bias.[25] This space for reflection is a result of the ambiguity of the work in question that lies in the sculpture's title, material, its handling and composition.

In *Also sprach Zarathustra* (1883–1885), philosopher Friedrich Nietzsche drafts the concept of "Übermensch" as the striving of humans for surpassing themselves.[26] Becoming an "Übermensch" means that humans have to develop a consciousness of their own needs that follow higher aims, not only human desires, and result in abandoning norms made by society. In Nietzsche's considerations, this is only possible when body and soul are reconciled. In later times, the concept of "Übermensch" has been simplified and thereby seriously distorted. According to the current understanding of the term, it means something like "superman" and is focused on outstanding intellectual as well as biological capabilities. In respect to these general connotations, calling Hawking's disabled body "superhuman" seems not to lack a certain amount of cynicism. But maybe the sculpture, on account of its title and its original meaning in Nietzsche's theory, can also give rise to discussions about the social fixation on physical standards. Is it perhaps possible that outstanding human qualities are no longer tethered to bodily conditions, as long as the person is at ease with him- or herself and his or her bodily condition?

But not only the title *Ubermensch* evokes negative associations at first glance. This also applies to the material qualities that can be analyzed when comparing it to Marc Quinn's *Alison Lapper Pregnant* (fig. 2.2). The marble sculpture with its height of 355 cm was temporarily erected in 2005 on the *Fourth Plinth* at London's Trafalgar Square and shows eight-months-pregnant artist Alison Lapper, who was born with short legs and without arms. Both are works by nondisabled artists who represent a living, physically disabled person as sculpture. But there are definite differences in materiality and depiction that have an important influence on the reception and interpretation of the works.

Quinn uses marble for his sculpture, a natural material with a long tradition in art history and one that is often used in idealized representations.[27] In addition, the surface structure of the sculpture is very smooth and regular, which corresponds to the aesthetic norms of neo-classicism.[28] Quinn refers to a particularly European artistic style of the eighteenth and early nineteenth centuries that revives classical Roman and Greek antiquity. The ideals of neo-classicism in the era of enlightenment that also can be seen in *Alison Lapper Pregnant* are informed by clarity and a certain plainness of the surface structure. Both material and handling lead to the perception of Quinn's sculpture being expensive and valuable. In contrast, the Chapmans use fiberglass, a quite new and inexpensive synthetic material that has its origins in industrial production. As art historian Monika Wagner points out, this kind of material seems ahistorical and ageless because of its malleability—plastic can imitate every surface, but it reveals nothing about its origins.[29] The uneven structure of *Ubermensch* resembles the texture of modeling clay, and the coloring, with its shimmering and glossy parts, supports the less valuable effect in contradistinction to Quinn's marble figure.[30] In combination with the industrial and cheap material, these aspects produce an impression of kitsch, as art critic David Barrett notes.[31]

Furthermore, the way Quinn depicts a disabled body differs to a high degree from the Chapman brothers' approach. Lapper is shown sitting upright and relaxed, her eyes turned skywards. Composition, in addition to medium, make Lapper appear

Exploiting, degrading, and repellent 35

Figure 2.2 Marc Quinn, *Alison Lapper Pregnant*, 355 × 180.5 × 260 cm, Marble, 2005, Trafalgar Square, London. Photo: Marc Quinn Studio.

heroic, graceful, and illustrious in *Alison Lapper Pregnant*. In contrast, Hawking is shown in an uncomfortable and dangerous position right in front of the abyss, tied to his wheelchair with tensed facial expression. It is important to notice that this kind of expression is not unusual for Hawking, at least since the mid-1990s. As can be seen in photographic portraits and press photos, for example, of Hawking's wedding with Elaine Mason in 1995, this expression is part of his appearance.[32] Hawking's appearance in the sculpture is not altered to seem more normalized or idealized, as it often is in non-photographic representations of Hawking.[33]

The Hawking figure's tense position adds an additional aspect to the repellent and shocking nature of the depiction. In art history it is not unusual to show figures in dangerous or tense situations, such as in Jacques-Louis David's *Bonaparte franchissant le Grand Saint Bernard* (fig. 2.3, 1801). Bonaparte sits enthroned

Figure 2.3 Jacques-Louis David, *Bonaparte franchissant le Grand Saint Bernard*, 272 × 232 cm, oil on canvas, 1801, Musée national des châteaux de Malmaison et de Bois-Préau, Malmaison. © bpk | RMN—Grand Palais | Daniel Arnaudet.

on a horse's back, the reins in his left hand, with his right arm outstretched and pointing up the mountain. The horse is on its hind legs, the body convulsing and mouth wide open. This position seems quite dangerous because the horse's hoofs are just a few centimeters away from a sloping rock, and the horse appears to be quite anxious and strained. Bonaparte, on the other hand, has a confident facial expression, seems self-contained, and masters the situation very calmly.

Bonaparte's precarious position on horseback has similarities to the Hawking figure's perilous position in his wheelchair. But whereas the dangerous-looking placement of Bonaparte is interpreted as heroic, path-breaking, and enlightened, the Hawking sculpture is commonly seen as an insult to the portrayed person. The crucial difference between these representations seems to be their physical appearance—or more precisely the implications of their appearance in terms of function and ability. While Bonaparte can manage the dangerous situation with his bodily presence—he has power over the frightened horse and shows him what to do—Hawking seems to be a victim of fate and cannot help himself out of this situation.

Closely associated with physical presence is the attribution of intelligence: because of his strength and physical superiority, Bonaparte is also interpreted as a person of outstanding intellect and a leader for the nation. As art historian Martin Warnke points out, the physicality of the sovereign's representation is an indicator of his character and mental state.[34] This tradition of representation can be traced back to ancient times and remains valid to this day. More generally formulated, an outstanding normalized or—as can be seen in David's portraiture of Bonaparte— even idealized physical presence allows positive conclusions about the depicted person's intellectual qualities.[35] In Hawking's case this culturally imprinted correlation of superior body with superior intellect does not fit, and therefore causes negative judgments about the sculpture *Ubermensch*.

Looking back in art history the tradition of representation shows us to what extent perception is influenced by our sociocultural background. Jake and Dinos Chapman's *Ubermensch* has the potential to make us aware of this circumstance. Instead of portraying a well-known public figure in an idealized fashion, the sculpture with its title and its inexpensive as well as kitschy medium contests conventional attributions of value. The interaction of these challenges to conventional expectations of sculpture blurs the clarity of meaning, and opens up different interpretations of each element and the sculpture as a whole. In this way, the sculpture gets the viewers to think about socioculturally imprinted norms and their own attitudes. *Ubermensch* challenges the viewers' expectations of the representation of a physically disabled person and evokes moral responses that possibly lay bare viewers' own biased attitudes.

Freakstars 3000: **intellectually disabled actors freaking out**

Freakstars 3000[36] (2002) (fig. 2.4) directed by Christoph Schlingensief,[37] mainly deals with intellectual disabilities instead of physical ones. The television series and later film are comprised of a combination of different television show formats,

Figure 2.4 Christoph Schlingensief, *Freakstars 3000*, six-part television series (2002) and film (2003). Photo: Thomas Aurin.

including a singing competition, the talk shows *Freakmann* and *Presseclub 3000*, a home shopping series, the folk music program *Das Hitparade*, and a weather program, as well as a short live-action report in a hostage drama. All contestants of the competition are disabled and are involved in each of the other television formats. Furthermore, one of them, Achim von Paczensky, is the director of the television series alongside Schlingensief. So the contestants are shown not only in front of the camera, but also behind the scenes, involved in the production processes.

Both series and film focus on the singing competition format, including all of its conventional components: mass casting and audition processes, vocal and dance coaching, producing of an album, and finally, the first live performance of the newly formed band *Mutter sucht Schrauben* (*Mother Looks for Screws*). The whole process is interspersed with interviews and behind-the-scenes sequences (e.g. a love story among two contestants) just like in the corresponding singing-competition role model *Deutschland sucht den Superstar* (the German version of *American Idol*).

The disabled contestants in *Freakstars 3000* all live in the Tiele Winckler House in Berlin-Lichtenrade, a home for intellectually disabled people. There are only a few notes and questions about the contestants' disabilities in interview sequences in the whole film.[38] Additional information about the contestants is also available through the *Freakstars 3000* website, where portraits of the contestants and later band members can be found. The site provides their dates and places of birth, career preferences, and hobbies. In none of these online portrayals is the disability of the contestants mentioned at all. It seems as if their disabilities play no role in this contest.

In contrast to how the television series, film, and website handle the issue of disability discreetly, the guestbook entries on the *Freakstars 3000* website (which are no longer accessible) and statements on online discussion boards (as quoted in the beginning) judge the show harshly, and some users express their outrage about the shamelessness of Schlingensief to show disabled persons in a reality television format, to parade and exploit them.[39] Germanist Nina Ort, who analyzed some of the guestbook entries, explains that these guestbook writers aim to protect the disabled contestants from humiliation, but furthermore, as Ort concludes, such statements are in fact discriminatory and contribute to their exclusion from public life.[40]

But in addition to the contemptuous comments, there are a lot of thoughtful as well as reflective posts, in which viewers communicate their discomfort while watching the show and reflect thereby on their own biased attitudes, as well as positive reactions to *Freakstars 3000*.[41] Scholars also interpret the television series/film positively: Ort, for example, describes the *Freakstars* contestants as refreshingly authentic and credible, in contrast to the contestants of common reality television formats.[42]

The biased attitude inherent in these arguments is comparable with the results of history and disability studies scholar Paul K. Longmore's analysis of the representation of disability on television. According to Longmore, the negative connotation of disability in public and cultural contexts can even extend to discomfort for viewers and stigmatization of disabled persons.[43] As disability scholars Colin Barnes and Geof Mercer summarize different research results regarding the media representation of disability, the stereotypes extend from pitiable, pathetic, and heroic to a burden for society.[44] Between the poles of the so-called pity-hero-trap—the biased interpretation of the disabled person as either a tragic figure who has to be protected from his or her surroundings, or a heroic one who overcomes his or her tragic deviation from the norm and endeavors to live a "normal" life—all facets are included in stereotyping disability on television. The comments on *Freakstars 3000* reflect the poles of the pity-hero-trap described by Barnes and Mercer.[45] Moreover, the comments mirror the intense and emotional public debate Schlingensief saw himself confronted with because of doing a show with intellectually disabled persons. This fact I consider particularly important, as ascriptions of helplessness, mental incapacity, or even inviability are typically attributed to humans with intellectual disabilities.[46] Schlingensief encourages these stereotypes at first glance, but the discussion of the title as well as the opening credits of the film show that the interpretation of *Freakstars 3000* is highly influenced by our perception of mass media, especially reality shows, and the stereotypes of the representation of disability in television and media context.

The title *Freakstars 3000* refers to the term "freak show." Freak shows were popular in the nineteenth and twentieth centuries and exhibited humans with extraordinary bodies for profit and the amusement of audiences looking at them. As Germanist Morgan Koerner shows, there are tremendous similarities between the narratives of freak shows categorized by Garland-Thompson and Schlingensief's *Freakstars 3000*.[47] Besides the amusement of staring at something so marvelous, strange, and scary at the same time, according to Garland-Thomson, the viewers felt normalized in comparison to the displayed humans who are visually more deviating from existing body norms.[48]

Garland-Thomson describes this kind of comparison as one possible and natural concept of staring: "We stare when ordinary seeing fails, when we want to know more. (. . .) The eyes hang on, working to recognize what seems illegible, order what seems unruly, know what seems strange."[49] In the direct confrontation of starer and staree, we are faced with the social convention that one should not stare at anyone else, because it is impolite.[50] In *Freakstars 3000*, this uneasy feeling of staring remains, but our staring is anonymous, so the starees cannot return the gaze. The viewers therefore have a special position: they can stare privately and without reaction from those at whom they stare. Nevertheless, some guestbook entries indicate that such staring still results in feelings of discomfort and uneasiness.[51]

Freakstars 3000's opening credits underscore the references to the freak show suggested by the title. A voice-over reads a text displayed on screen:

> Dear film fans! Step right up and see cool young people who, with talent and 100 percent commitment, fulfill their dream of a big music career. Step right up and hear German eccentrics who, while they sing, nonchalantly point to the big problem of nondisabled. During the shooting, actors were consistently abused and forced to portray disability. Every attack and every crackup is therefore guaranteed to be authentic and not repeatable.[52]

The spoken text suggests the characteristic style used by sideshow barkers in circuses, fairs, and freak shows. But whereas sideshow barkers praise the advertised show, we are confronted with a highly ironic introduction: the contestants are not addressed as disabled, but as eccentric Germans. The term "eccentric" describes someone who behaves or appears in a way that is unusual and different from most people. With that the deviations of the actors from the so-called norm are not clearly defined, but remain vague. Also in the following sentences disability is only implied within its opposite as nondisabled, or mentioned in context of acting as disabled ("portray disability"). As the voice-over explains the disabled contestants will take care of the problems of the nondisabled—the "big problem" cannot be found in the contestants but in the nondisabled who do not feel comfortable with watching disabled actors—the before mentioned quotes from the *Freakstars 3000* guestbook or online discussion boards can illustrate the "big problem" someone can have with the series/film. In the last two sentences we learn that the disabled actors are abused and exploited. Even worse, they are also shown in situations no bigger crowd should be watching—during real and unique attacks and mental breakdowns that may be related to the disabilities of the actors. These are the reproaches Schlingensief was confronted with right from the start of the television series. By mentioning these accusations at the beginning of the film, viewers have to question their own attitudes: Am I one of the nondisabled who has problems with disability? Do I operate with stereotypes when confronted with disability?

The authenticity and uniqueness mentioned in the opening credits allude to the singing competition format. This kind of production is part of the so-called reality television principle.[53] As sociologists Irmhild Saake and Veronica Maier point out, singing competitions and reality television in general are to a great extent staged. At the same time, real persons function as contestants to reach a certain goal—becoming a famous singer, dancer, or a combination of both.[54] In the staged competition framework, the participating characters add and suggest authenticity. Furthermore, as musicologist Ralf von Appen points out, competition shows represent principles and ideals of hierarchy, discipline, and conformity in the judging and elimination processes and in working hard on one's own characteristics, talents, and attitude.[55] Communication theorist Jo Reichertz suggests that the mostly youthful contestants are aware of being judged in these shows regarding their abilities, and they want to find out who they are themselves and what they are capable of.[56]

Being confronted with the title *Freakstars 3000* and its close connection to freak shows, their entertaining character and our lust to stare, we are challenged in our sociocultural imprint and usual behavior. In other words, Schlingensief makes us feel ashamed for looking/staring and being "cultural tourists," as Cashell states in regard to other works of transgressive art which play with forbidden stares.[57] A cultural tourist is someone who lives for a temporary time outside of daily life responsibilities and moral commitments while gazing at monuments, cityscapes, and cultural artifacts, without considering moral issues associated with them. *Freakstars 3000* shows a singing competition format that is familiar from conventional television. But with disabled contestants, Schlingensief adds an ethically challenging question: Is it appropriate to watch a singing competition when its contestants are intellectually disabled?

By combining the title's reference to freak shows with conventional singing competitions for a show with intellectual disabled contestants, Schlingensief is deliberately trying to shock the viewers. As film critic Georg Seeßlen points out, in his performances and productions, Schlingensief makes visible what remains otherwise incomprehensible.[58] In this case, that means Schlingensief is laying bare the stereotypes and norms of mainstream television productions, but also the attitude of the viewers regarding disability and deviation from the "norm." The first aspect, making stereotypes and hierarchies obvious, can be found in the dramaturgy of the singing competition. While there are some disabled persons in the competition process, and later in the band, who have already worked with Schlingensief in other productions,[59] viewers are not made aware of this connection. Schlingensief treats his previously known contestants in the same fashion as the new participants. This fact questions the authenticity of format and contestants, and results in uncertainty: Is the singing competition a set-up? Was it clear from the beginning that the other disabled persons would not have a chance to be part of the band? With these questions in mind we not only query the seemingly unfair production process, but also the reference to mass media reality television shows, where allegations like these arise over and over again.[60]

For such uncertainties in Schlingensief's works, Germanist Susanne Hochreiter uses the term "VerUneindeutigung": making something seemingly unequivocal more open to interpretation. Through Schlingensief's concept of "VerUneindeutigung," mechanisms of hierarchy and power, as well as thought patterns of normalization, can be evaded.[61] This creates a space for viewers' reflections and raises the question of whether Schlingensief's contestants are real participants who want to be part of a band. In my point of view, there is enough evidence to assume that the disabled are only playing the role of competition contestants in a competition and don't really want to be part of the band at all.

In the other segments integrated in *Freakstars 3000*, actor Mario Garzaner imitates a weatherman or journalist, and at the premiere of the television series, actor Kerstin Graßmann portrays German politician Angela Merkel, a leading politician of the conservative party CDU, and German chancellor since 2005. All these represented figures are well known in diverse television formats, and it is obvious that the disabled participants are in these parts actors who are playing roles. But in general, scholars and critics who are engaged with Schlingensief's work question neither the authenticity of the reality television format nor that of the disabled persons. It is especially the socioculturally imprinted connotations of disability that are responsible for causing this connection to be overlooked. In the end, and as Koerner points out, we cannot decide how much acting and how much authenticity are part of the production.[62] But in this very concept of "VerUneindeutigung" lies the possibility to become aware of biased attitudes towards (intellectual) disability and challenge them.

Conclusion

Ubermensch and *Freakstars 3000* represent two concepts of transgressive art that challenge viewers' biased attitudes regarding disability. As I have shown, there are very negative and also highly positive interpretations of both works that can be assigned to one of the poles of the so-called pity-hero-trap. On one hand, the disabled may be seen as persons who have to be protected against exploitation by nondisabled artists. On the other hand, disabled persons, due to their disability, may be seen as heroic and admirable. Both interpretations are possible and are to the same extent inherent in *Ubermensch* and *Freakstars 3000*, because of their ambiguous structures. The artists use titles, motifs, and strategies of representation that can have different meanings and give space for interpretations in contrary directions. But the root of the matter is that these interpretations are strongly related to the viewers' own sociocultural imprints, and result in potentially biased attitudes we have to reflect in order to find out what role we are playing ourselves in imputing to these works of art only one valid meaning.

Notes

1 Jonathan Jones, "Thin Line Between Art and Hate: Is this the Most Repellent Work of Modern Art?" *The Guardian*, accessed April 29, 2015, http://www.theguardian.com/artanddesign/jonathanjonesblog/2012/jan/12/art-hate-repellent-work-modern.

2 "wenn Leute, die das offensichtlich nicht selbst einschätzen können, dazu gebracht werden und vor der 'Nation' bloßgestellt werden, dann ist das schon ziemlich pervers und kann auch imho nicht mehr mit dem Kunstcharakter gerechtfertigt werden." SnooP, June 30, 2002 (10:47 p.m.), posting #14 in thread "Freakstars3000," accessed April 29, 2015, http://www.xpbulletin.de/gesellschaft-f10/freakstars3000-t1383.html.
3 Besides, a website is part of the art project consisting of television series and later film: http://www.Freakstars3000.de. The viewers could write comments in the guestbook or leave their tip on who will win the singing competition. The television series was not shown in the United States/Canada, but the film can be purchased. The DVD (multi-region PAL/NTSC DVD player is required) has English subtitles.
4 For general assumptions regarding shocking art, see Dave Beech, "Shock: A Report on Contemporary Art," in *Jake and Dinos Chapman. Bad Art for Bad People*, ed Christoph Grunenberg and Tanya Barson (Liverpool: Tate Liverpool, 2006), 99–110, especially 104–106.
5 Kieran Cashell, *Aftershock: The Ethics of Contemporary Transgressive Art* (London and New York: I. B. Tauris, 2009), 12.
6 Cashell, *Aftershock*, 12.
7 This circumstance is, for example, pointed out by art historian Ann Millett-Gallant; see Millett-Gallant, *The Disabled Body in Contemporary Art* (New York: Palgrave Macmillan, 2010), 16. Especially for the works of art I analyze in this chapter, see the reproaches of Jonathan Jones in regard to *Ubermensch*, Jones, "Thin line," and Germanist Nina Ort's examination of the discussion about *Freakstars 3000*, Nina Ort, "'Ihr seid krank!'—'Ihr seid schon jetzt alle Gewinner!'" *Medienobservationen*, August 16, 2004, accessed April 29, 2015, http://www.medienobservationen.de/artikel/gesellschaft/ort_freakstars.html.
8 Martha Craven Nussbaum, *Hiding from Humanity: Disgust, Shame, and the Law* (Princeton: Princeton University Press, 2004), 305 and 127, and Tobin Siebers, *Disability Theory* (Ann Arbor: The University of Michigan Press, 2008), 10.
9 Rosemarie Garland-Thomson, *Staring: How We Look* (Oxford: Oxford University Press, 2009), 38.
10 See, for example, Tobin Siebers, "Disability in Theory: From Social Constructionism to the New Realism of the Body," *American Literary History* 13, no. 4 (2001): 737–754, especially 737, 740, and Rosemarie Garland-Thomson, "Staring back: Self-Representations of Disabled Performance Artists," *American Quarterly* 52, no. 2 (2000): 334.
11 Tanya Titchkosky and Rod Michalko, "The Body as the Problem of Individuality: A Phenomenological Disability Studies Approach," in *Disability and Social Theory: New Developments and Directions*, ed. Dan Goodley, Bill Hughes and Lennard Davis (New York: Palgrave Macmillan, 2012), 127–129.
12 Rosemarie Garland-Thomson, "Disability and Representation," *PMLA* 120, no. 2 (2005): 524.
13 Previous considerations about the role of art in reflecting socio-cultural imprint can be found in Nina Heindl, "Becoming Aware of One's Own Biased Attitude: The Observer's Encounter With Disability in Chris Ware's Acme Novelty Library No. 18," *Review of Disability Studies: An International Journal* 10, no. 3/4 (2014): 40–51.
14 In this I share an underlying aim with Ann Millett-Gallant, which she explicates in her book; see Millett-Gallant, *Disabled Body*, 6, 17, 19.
15 See Verena Krieger, "At war with the obvious—Kulturen der Ambiguität: Historische, psychologische und ästhetische Dimensionen des Mehrdeutigen," in *Ambiguität in der Kunst: Typen und Funktionen eines ästhtetischen Paradigmas*, ed. Verena Krieger and Rachel Mader (Cologne, Weimar, and Vienna: Böhlau, 2010), 13, 45.
16 For reproaches of one-dimensionality see, for example, Jones, "Thin line," and the statements Morgan Koerner collected in endnote 13 in her chapter, Morgan Koerner, "Subversions of the Medical Gaze: Disability and Media Parody in Christoph Schlingensief's

Freakstars 3000," in *Cinema and Social Change in Germany and Austria*, ed. Gabriele Müller and James M. Skidmore (Waterloo: Wilfried Laurier University Press, 2012), 74.
17 For the whole, but as Krieger mentions, not exclusive list, see Krieger, "Kulturen der Ambiguität," 22–24.
18 Krieger, "Kulturen der Ambiguität," 23–24.
19 Krieger, "Kulturen der Ambiguität," 24.
20 Jones, "Thin line."
21 Jones, "Thin line."
22 Jones, "Thin line."
23 Robbert Roos, "Dinos & Jake Chapman," in *Difference on Display: Diversity in Art, Science & Society*, ed. Ine Gevers (Rotterdam: NAi Publishers, 2010), 111.
24 See, for example, painted and sculpted whole-body representations of sovereigns through the epochs, for example, Marcus Aurelius (121–180), Heinrich VIII (1491–1547), Louis XIV (1638–1715) or Queen Elizabeth (Queen Mum, 1900–2002).
25 In this I argue against Kieran Cashell, who attests to the literalness and seemingly obvious meaning of works by Jake and Dinos Chapman, Cashell, *Aftershock*, 113.
26 Friedrich Nietzsche, "Also sprach Zarathustra," in *Friedrich Nietzsche: Sämtliche Werke*, vol. 4, ed. Giorgio Colli and Mazzino Montinari (Munich, Berlin and New York: dtv, 1980), especially 14–19.
27 Nina Heindl, "Temporär bespielt. Die plastischen Werke auf der Fourth Plinth zwischen Intervention und Denkmalsetzung" *Kunsttexte.de Sektion Gegenwart* 4 (2014): 21, accessed April 29, 2015, http://edoc.hu-berlin.de/kunsttexte/2014–4/heindl-nina-4/PDF/heindl.pdf. See also Monika Wagner, "Reinheit und Gefährdung: Weißer Marmor als ästhetische und ethnische Norm," in *Material of Sculpture: Between Technique and Semantics*, ed. Aleksandra Lipińska (Wrocław: Wydawn. Uniwersytet Wrocławskiego, 2009), 243.
28 Millett-Gallant, *Disabled Body*, 56–57.
29 Monika Wagner, *Das Material der Kunst. Eine andere Geschichte der Moderne* (Munich: Beck, 2001), 190.
30 As Monika Wagner points out for art theory and production since the eighteenth century, the colored sculpture is seen as not as valuable as a white marble one; see Wagner, "Reinheit und Gefährdung," 242–243.
31 David Barrett, *Jake & Dinos Chapman* (London: Royal Jelly Factory, 2007), 44.
32 See for example Hans Hoyng, "Ehe vor Schwarzen Löchern," *Spiegel* 34 (1999): 119. The image in the article shows Stephen Hawking at his and Elaine Mason's wedding in 1995 in the same wheelchair depicted in *Übermensch*. See also the way Hawking is represented as a wax sculpture at London's *Madame Tussauds*, first shown in 1994.
33 Often he is shown in graphical depictions in his current condition but with relaxed facial features, eyebrows lifted meaningfully, and head slightly tilted. See, for example, a digital painting by the artist Tamiart, accessed April 29, 2015, http://tamiart.deviantart.com/art/Stephen-Hawking-194025707 or a figure of Kevinbolk (K-Bo) in manga style, accessed April 29, 2015, http://kevinbolk.deviantart.com/art/Stephen-Hawking-Art-Card-by-K-Bo-445137690.
34 Martin Warnke, "Herrscherbildnis," in *Handbuch der politischen Ikonographie*, vol. 1, ed. Uwe Fleckner, Martin Warnke, and Hendrik Ziegler (Munich: C.H. Beck, 2011), 481–490.
35 Gerrit Walczak, "David, der General, Carteux und sein König: Über Bonaparte am Großen St. Bernhard," *Wallraf-Richartz-Jahrbuch* 73 (2012): 211–212.
36 *Freakstars 3000* was first broadcast as a television series with six episodes, each 30 minutes, on German music channel VIVA Plus in 2002. In 2003 the film version *Freakstars 3000* followed, which includes a collection of clips of the whole series (75 minutes). My following explanations refer to the film.
37 Christoph Schlingensief (1960–2010) was a well-known German performance artist and director of theatre as well as film productions. Many of his performances are

closely linked to the current politics, culture, and mass media. In 1998 he formed the party *Chance 2000* with the election slogan "Failure as an opportunity" ("Scheitern als Chance"). With his party he laid bare the mechanisms of the conventional parties and made nonsense of election campaigns. In 2000 Schlingensief installed a container as part of the Wiener Festwochen for the performance *Please love Austria* (*Bitte liebt Österreich*). Twelve contestants who were introduced as asylum seekers lived in this container and were filmed all the time. By voting the public was able to decide which contestant had to leave the container and the land as well. Schlingensief addressed with this performance the political and moral responsibility of society. For more information see, for example, Solveig Gade, "Putting the Public Sphere to the Test: On Publics and Counter-Publics in Chance 2000," in *Christoph Schlingensief: Art without Borders*, ed. Tara Forrest and Anna Teresa Scheer (Bristol and Chicago: Intellect, 2010), 89–103 and Susanne Hochreiter, "Den Skandal erzeugen immer die anderen: Überlegungen zu künstlerischen und politischen Strategien Christoph Schlingensiefs," in *Der Gesamtkünstler Christoph Schlingensief*, ed. Pia Janke and Teresa Kovacs (Vienna: Praesens Verlag, 2011), 444–448.

38 In an interview Schlingensief talks to contestant Kerstin Graßmann: "'Kerstin was schizophrenic, but you're not anymore.' Kerstin replies: 'I still am.'" *Freakstars 3000* (2003), 11:00–11:08 min. Another interview part shows Achim von Paczensky and Schlingensief asks: "'Achim, are you handicapped? Really?' and 'Where are you handicapped?' Achims answers ironically 'Yes, on my ass.'" *Freakstars 3000* (2003), 14:25–14:28 min. As Morgan Koerner argues, through "its treatment of the participants as individuals and refusal to pinpoint their specific disabilities, the film resists and ridicules the medical notion of disability." Koerner, "Medical Gaze," 72.

39 See, for example, Tara Forrest, "Productive Discord: Schlingensief, Adorno, and Freakstars 3000," in *Christoph Schlingensief: Art Without Borders*, ed. Tara Forrest and Anna Teresa Scheer (Bristol and Chicago: Intellect, 2010), 131 and Koerner, "Medical Gaze," 69, 74, endnote 13.

40 Ort, "Ihr seid krank."

41 See, for example, entry 27 (10 August 2004) in the guestbook: "I want to know whether I can die laughing without thinking about my morals or whether what has concocted there is serious? [. . .] Am, however, really SERIOUSLY confused. Have unfortunately absolutely NO idea what it is." Quoted after Forrest, "Productive Discord," 131. See also some postings in the thread "Freakstars3000," for example: "This television series is absolutely necessary! It hurts, it is uncomfortable, and it is loud and hysterical and anything but feel-good television! Freakstars 3000 shows the very people who most other people want to ignore" ("Diese Sendung ist absolut nötig! Sie tut weh, sie ist unbequem, sie ist laut und hysterisch und alles andere als Wohlfühlfernsehn! [. . .] *Freakstars 3000* setzt genau die Leute in Szene, bei denen achsoviele lieber zur Seite schauen, wenn sie die Strassenbahn betreten."). Yog-Sothoth, July 18, 2002 (04:44 p.m.), posting #24 in thread "Freakstars3000," accessed April 29, 2015, http://www.xpbulletin.de/gesellschaft-f10/freakstars3000-t1383.html.

42 Ort, "Ihr seid krank."

43 Paul K. Longmore, "Screening Stereotypes: Images of Disabled People in Television and Motion Pictures," in *Why I Burned My Book: And Other Chapters on Disability*, ed. Paul K. Longmore (Philadelphia: Temple University Press, 2003), especially 132.

44 Colin Barnes and Geof Mercer, *Exploring Disability: A Sociological Introduction*, 2nd edition (Cambridge and Malden: Polity Press, 2010), 193.

45 The contrasting interpretations of *Ubermensch* show similar tendencies in stereotyping disability. This leads to the clue that the findings of Longmore as well as Barnes and Mercer regarding television and media can be extended to a broader field of the representation of disability in cultural contexts.

46 Koerner, "Medical Gaze," 71.

47 Koerner, "Medical Gaze," 69.

48 Rosemarie Garland-Thomson, "Introduction: From Wonder to Error—A Genealogy of Freak Discourse in Modernity," in *Freakery: Cultural Spectacles of the Extraordinary Body*, ed. Garland-Thomson (New York and London: New York University Press, 1996), 5.
49 Garland-Thomson, *Staring*, 3.
50 Garland-Thomson, *Staring*, 5, 13–14.
51 See for example Ort, "Ihr seid krank."
52 *Freakstars 3000* (2003), 00:00–00:28 min., translation by Morgan Koerner, Koerner, "Medical Gaze," 59.
53 Morgan Koerner analyzes the camera perspectives and usage in *Freakstars 3000* and comes to the conclusion that also on a filmic level, Schlingensief is adapting reality TV formats, Koerner, "Medical Gaze," 65.
54 Irmhild Saake and Veronica Maier, "Gefühlte Kritik: Casting Shows als Visualisierung des moralischen Diskurses," *Soziale Systeme* 16, no. 1 (2010): 177.
55 Ralf von Appen, "Die Wertungskriterien der Deutschland sucht den Superstar-Jury vor dem Hintergrund sozialer Milieus und kulturindustrieller Strategien," in *Keiner wird Gewinnen: Populäre Musik im Wettbewerb*, ed. Dietrich Helms (Bielefeld: Transcript, 2005), 206.
56 Jo Reichertz, *Die Macht der Worte und der Medien* (Wiesbaden: VS Verlag, 2007), 96.
57 Cashell, *Aftershock*, 26.
58 Georg Seeßlen, "Radikale Kunst: Über Schlingensiefs Ästhetik der Öffnung," in *Der Gesamtkünstler Christoph Schlingensief*, ed. Pia Janke and Teresa Kovacs (Vienna: Praesens Verlag, 2011), 76.
59 Harald Mühlbeyer, "*Freakstars 3000*—Christoph-Schlingensief-Edition #11," *Screenshot. Texte zum Film*, accessed April 29, 2015, http://screenshot-online.blogspot.de/2008/04/christoph-schlingensief-edition-11.html.
60 Mühlbeyer, "*Freakstars 3000*."
61 Hochreiter, "Den Skandal erzeugen immer die anderen," 447.
62 Koerner, "Medical Gaze," 64.

3 Nothing is missing

Spiritual elevation of a visually impaired Moche shaman

Rebecca R. Stone

Native American or First Nations peoples[1] seem to have maintained an unusually high regard for human physical difference from the statistical norm. The indigenous American cultural and artistic traditions serve as important exceptions to the widespread "rule" that those with unusual bodies are somehow "less than" others in some fundamental way. This chapter will explore an example of art as evidence of a positive, elevated view of anomalous-bodied individuals, using terms such as "different," "unusual," and "anomalous" interchangeably. I will discuss one ancient South American ceramic effigy as an image of the 'dis'abled, a category found throughout the Americas.

Here placing single quotes around 'dis' underscores that our term "disabled" may not be relevant within the Amerindian value system, in which difference tends to be more accepted.[2] Our current term emphasizes the idea of something as lacking, at least in the popular sense. If the visual evidence asserts ability rather than its opposite, "disabled" becomes misleading. "Special"—defined as positively different—remains the applicable concept in relation to Amerindian effigies.

I will identify the vision-impaired individual (fig. 3.1) as a high-status spiritual specialist, or shaman in contemporary parlance. This Moche effigy, from northern coastal Peru (c. 300 CE), shows a man with completely white eyes. This probably indicates the effect of advanced cataracts, as I will discuss later. In addition, according to the figure's dress and pose, he enjoyed elevated status and played a key socio-religious role.

Precious objects such as this, beautifully sculpted, fired, and preserved in a grave, seem to function as companions on the afterlife journey of the deceased's spirit. It suggests that artistry was lavished upon the subject matter of an individual with physical differences from the norm. Further, it embodies empowerment of the visually impaired, along with hundreds, possibly thousands, of other images of the 'dis'abled across the indigenous Americas.[3]

Shamans[4] were and remain the spiritual intermediaries and visionaries central in the shared indigenous Native American religious system.[5] Shamanism is a trance-based practice in which the visionary out-of-body experience is considered to cure human ills, whether physical, social, and/or political; predict the future and fathom things distant in space; and affect all terrestrial fertility, from game to

48　*Rebecca R. Stone*

Figure 3.1 Moche effigy of a vision-impaired man. 17.8 × 10.5 cm (7 × 4 1/8 in.). Ceramic. c. 300 CE. Michael C. Carlos Museum, accession number 1989.8.71. © Michael C. Carlos Museum. Photo by Bruce M. White, 2011.

birthing to abundant rains. Shamans are midwives, herbalists, and diviners; their roles crosscut our doctors, psychologists, mediums, and dreamers. I have argued that anomalousness was a prerequisite for becoming a shaman, a person necessarily outside of society and its norms.[6]

Figure 3.2 Moche effigy of a man wearing espingo seeds. 24.7 × 14 cm (9 3/4 × 5 1/2 in.). Ceramic. c. 300 CE. Michael C. Carlos Museum, accession number 1989.8.68. © Michael C. Carlos Museum. Photo by Michael McKelvey.

The de-emphasis on the usual bodily experience underlies shamanic visions and sets the stage for this correlation with anomalousness. People who feel themselves transforming into another being, and their culture that promotes the validity of that experience, do not privilege a "normal" human appearance. Transformation into animal-selves is common in Amerindian visionary reports. To become a jaguar, an eagle, a caiman, a snake, or a deer, and access their powers, perceptions, wisdom, and characteristics, is a major component of shamanic trance. It is the indication that shamans have succeeded. Artists of most styles depict shamans in their animal-selves by blending characteristics of humans and (other) animals in myriad ways.[7] This leads to the important but rather touchy subject of resembling an animal. In the West, calling people animals has been highly derogatory. The Western negative connotation of looking like an animal is based on the Judeo-Christian divide between human and animal: the Bible exhorts humans to dominate the animals, making animals inherently lesser. However, it is the opposite in a shamanic society; in the ancient tropics, animals are dominant. In shamanic terms, to look like an animal is a strong and inherently positive indication of your animal-self.[8] Since in the ancient tropics animals are often dominant, animal-like human bodies become acceptable, especially among shamans.

Furthermore, more than simple empathy, an isomorphism (similarity in form) exists between helpers and clients, all of whom are "wounded." The logic of the "wounded healer," a phrase adapted from T.S. Eliot,[9] presupposes that surviving trauma, disease, or a genetic condition makes one more able to help others in similar situations.[10] Certainly the idea has a general, common-sense, universal appeal; however, for Native Americans there is more to the connection: disease and anomaly are believed to have spiritual origins, so that someone who has prevailed over challenges is ascribed spiritual power, as Halifax argues.[11] Likewise attributed a propensity to garner the help of other shamans and spirits, such a survivor multiplies his or her powers.

Even with this empowering framework of belief, the term "wounded" must be questioned. It implies harm, but also suggests the person carries around a permanent condition of woundedness. Thus it implies again a negative condition, by focusing on the damage, missing something, or lacking wholeness. Perhaps "survivor-healer" might better convey the Native perspective. In this worldview, the specialness that is evidenced by having a different body is seen as a spiritual blessing.[12] The artistic choices made in the following Moche example will serve as a test case for this hypothesis.

The Moche

Moche ceramic effigies are among the most recognizable, accessible Andean works. Their degree of realism is unusual, especially within Andean representational tradition, which tends towards abstraction. Moche vessels depict spotted dogs, subjects holding up their tribute, men seemingly asleep, and metallurgists smelting ore; however, naturalism does not necessarily indicate an interest in terrestrial appearances alone. Despite Moche art's seemingly everyday aspect, it does not comprise an encyclopedia of culture, but rather emphasizes certain themes, often with deep spiritual content. For instance, no known images show women cooking, children playing, or farmers digging the fields. Sacrifices on mountaintops, ceremonial dances, skeletons, men wearing necklaces of visionary plants (fig. 3.2), and rituals involving human blood offerings are typical of its ceremonial imagery. There is also a large group of generic images of Moche people, which only occur in full-body versions and are lower in status (according to their repetitive faces, undifferentiated bodies, and the lack of any items associated with the leaders in the royal tombs). They are purposefully and nearly interchangeable.[13]

In contrast to the "everyman" effigies, about seven hundred Moche mimetic portraits clearly convey important men's distinctive physiognomies; each person differs noticeably from the next.[14] While this number may seem like a lot, there are at least 150,000 extant Moche ceramics, probably more. From facial contours to wrinkles and inset eyeballs, the full range of realistic elements is present. Some of the physiognomic portraits are full-body, but most focus on the head alone. Some faces are elegant, others handsome, crooked, plump, thin, young, middle-aged, or elderly. The subject of figure 3.3 is a mature man, with nascent jowls, mouth lines, outwardly slanting eyes, and a strong nose. Some series of portraits trace the same individual throughout his life, notably a boy with a scarred lip who lived to old age or another with puffy eyelids and high eyebrows.[15] Some portraits include frankly fantastical headwear—with mushroom-shaped emanations—that strongly suggest they were important shamans.[16] Many sit in the hands-on-knees meditation pose that signifies they were spiritual intermediaries in trance states.

Of interest here, some of those immortalized in portraits are missing one or both eyes, or both eyes are sunken or open but are completely white. There are faces missing lips, eyelids, and the tip of the nose (evidence of leishmaniasis, a disease in which the face is eaten away by a parasite borne by sandflies [fig. 3.4]), as well as some evincing facial clefting and scarring.[17] There are bodies that have a single foot, arm, leg, or some combination thereof, and those that appear to depict achondroplasia (a form of dwarfism in which the individual displays a large head plus a truncated torso and limbs). These unusual bodies are elevated by being depicted very precisely, their portraits as detailed and physiognomic as the others. While the "diagnoses" of these long-dead immortalized shamans are not necessarily germane, and a medical model of disability is potentially objectionable,[18] the fact that the Moche took pains to distinguish various unusual conditions is significant. Hypothetical diagnoses in this case help determine what might have contributed to making a person with x condition a successful shaman and allow us to explore how Moche artists chose to communicate this concept.

Since shamanism is heavily dependent on trance visions, it is significant that some of the head and body portrait vessels depict people who are vision-impaired in the terrestrial realm. In general, alterations to the eyes often signal the trance state, as I have argued.[19] Among the various "trance eyes" are round eyes substituted for human ones to directly convey the animal-self, and exaggeratedly opening almond-shaped human ones to show the experience of fear, excitement, and the sensation of bulging eyes that visionaries report.[20] Wide-open eyes are like those of this figure. Another type of "trance eye" depiction is purposefully tightly

Figure 3.3 Moche portrait head cup. 14.8 × 10.6 cm (5 13/16 × 4 3/16 in.). Ceramic. c. 300 CE. Michael C. Carlos Museum, accession number 1999.3.115. Ex coll. William S. Arnett. © Michael C. Carlos Museum. Photo by Bruce M. White, 2012.

squeezed shut, which relates to the vision-impaired who have lost an eye(s) or whose eyes have never functioned and the person keeps them closed.

This "eyes-closed seeing" communicates trance because visionaries also report that their visions are clearer if they do not have any perceptions simultaneously entering through their physical eyes.[21] This leads to a very important point: visions

Figure 3.4 Moche effigy of a survivor of leishmaniasis. 21.4 × 13.8 cm (8 7/16 × 5 7/16 in.) Ceramic. c. 300 CE. Michael C. Carlos Museum, accession number 1989.8.72. © Michael C. Carlos Museum. Photo by Michael McKelvey.

take place in the head (we would say the brain), not in the eyes. Therefore, one need not have eyes at all to have visions; indeed, if vision is distracting to visions, then someone who is blind has the advantage in this arena. We can make a distinction between "Seeing" (as in visions) and "seeing" (as in physically functioning eyes). Shamanic societies value Seeing far more; in shamanic terms, nothing is considered to be "missing" from the blind.

To argue that the subject in figure 3.1 represents a shaman Seeing, first we must establish that it is a portrait of a particular person, then a shaman, and finally consider his all-white eyes as regards visions and a possible animal-self. He does not display the same rounded, even-featured, bilaterally symmetrical face as the generic men (compare figs. 3.1 and 3.2). Seen from the side, his lower face juts out and nose turns up, versus the everyman's flat profile and straight nose. The front view communicates how his eyes droop and mouth turns down toward the outside. Again, such naturalistically irregular features indicate the face is a portrait.

Around his neck, this figure wears decorative square elements or beads on a string clearly painted as a line that links them. The squares could represent either carved *Spondylus* (spiny oyster shell)[22] or gold plaques. Both are high-status materials. The best clue is in the back view, where the last two squares are not joined, suggesting it is sewn on the robe's neckline, not encircling the neck like a choker. Sumptuous Moche burials found at the site of Sipán and elsewhere include hundreds of metal pieces originally sewn to cloth, making this the more likely referent.[23] The crisscrossed woven bands draped over his shoulders are another seemingly ceremonial dress item. The back view specifically shows how the bands' tapered ends dangle down his shoulder blades. This is a highly individualized combination of neck appliqués and bands, differing from other portrait head and full-body images,[24] as a cursory look through Donnan's *Moche Portraits from Ancient Peru* will demonstrate.

Also individualized are the marks incised asymmetrically on his face. If indicative of something in the terrestrial realm, this could represent tattooing, which has been found recently on the Moche queen known today as La Señora de Cao.[25] However, it is more likely to represent scarification because of its purposeful three-dimensionality, cut into the clay, like scars would be into the flesh. Less likely is body paint, since that is routinely indicated by painted-on darker slip (fig. 3.3). Incisions are uncommon in the Moche portraits and the ceramic corpus overall, though they are found on several other effigies of vision-impaired shamans.[26]

However, it is worth considering that the incised patterns may not realistically depict actual facial markings. Rather, they could be symbolic of the geometry the blind visionaries see in visions. Geometric patterns are universally reported as the first images experienced during trance consciousness, and often continue throughout the vision.[27] The grid on this figure's nose, upper lip, and chin is a typical geometric introductory image, in fact.[28] In addition, in Andean art and culture there is a premium placed on internal qualities manifested outwardly; the Inka word *ukhu* means "the hidden revealed."[29] In other words, these apparently real and external facial patterns could simply disclose what the shaman is seeing in the trance worlds. Like an X-ray, often the kind of perspective gained in trance as well,[30] the patterns show his visionary experience, manifesting it outwardly so the viewer can understand his special consciousness. The realities that exist for shamans and in images of shamans are complex and non-linear, yet shamanic art must communicate them in the terms of the terrestrial world, a fascinating and creative paradox with many solutions.

The idea that the man represented in figure 3.1 is Seeing visions is also underscored by his legs being tucked under and his hands being placed on his knees. Generic figures do not assume this position, while figures sitting on benches, in healing ceremonies, and showing the various types of trance eyes do. This has long been identified as the pose of shamanic meditation.[31] The man with the face eaten away by leishmaniasis also takes this pose (fig. 3.4). Arguably, another related shamanic feature is that the vision-impaired man has enlarged ears, perhaps an indication of enhanced hearing, as visions are full of dramatic aural and other sense experiences.

This blind shaman's particular visual impairment is also individualistic; all-white eyes are not common in the corpus. The generic figures' eyes tend to remain the overall red-brown of the piece (fig. 3.2), while portraits of the non-blind have painted irises realistically floating in the whites (figs. 3.3, 3.5). The most likely explanation for the unusual all-white eyes is that the man had advanced cataracts, the clouding of the lenses.[32] Protein consolidates into a film, which prevents images from focusing on the retina. Eyes cloud over, become yellowish, and sight blurs. Cataracts are strongly associated with aging, especially common after age sixty, but also can be the result of prolonged exposure to light, trauma to the eye, or diabetes. In some cases, they are congenital.

In relation to this figure, the Moche lived in a very sunny environment on the north coast of Peru; sun exposure could well be the culprit. The yellowish cast of the eyes is rendered in the cream slip paint, the usual light-color slip in a two-color palette, but congruent with cataracts in this case. This particular figure is mature rather than elderly: other mimetic Moche figures have wrinkles (fig. 3.5). He still might have had age-related onset, or he may have had cataracts due to the other reasons mentioned. In a shamanic society, being born with apparently sightless eyes could be a dramatic indication of future potential to have special sight, that is, visions. Sightless eyes are by definition different, anomalous, and draw attention to seeing the terrestrial world as considered less important than seeing the Other Side during trance experiences. To have survived an accident or attack that affected one's eyesight would also indicate special powers, as per the wounded healer discussion earlier.

No overt animal-self is definitely indicated here; this is not unusual, since in general shamanic imagery follows a continuum from human to animal and everything in between.[33] However, there is a relevant shamanic and visionary animal whose eyes periodically become white: snakes at the onset of molting.[34] The eye membranes detach and become milky white, leaving the snake with blurry vision until the head skin begins to peel off and molting proceeds. This might be simply an interesting fact, except that snakes—continuously growing and being reborn via molting—are strongly symbolic of life, regeneration, and fertility, as well as

Figure 3.5 Moche effigy of an older man. 27.3 × 13.3 cm (10 3/4 × 5 1/4 in.) Ceramic. c. 300 CE. Michael C. Carlos Museum, accession number 1989.8.69. Gift of William C. and Carol W. Thibadeau. © Michael C. Carlos Museum. Photo by Michael McKelvey.

the most common animal to see in trances, according to all accounts.[35] This makes the snake a charged animal in shamanic experience, and may link a white-eyed person to regeneration, a power necessary to the healing endeavor. Other effigies of Moche blind Seeing shamans do have depicted animal spirits: one wears an iguana headdress.[36] Covered by a thin skin but still visible, iguanas have a literal third or parietal eye in their foreheads.[37] The presence of a hidden eye would be most apt in suggesting a blind shaman who experiences visions. Such molting or extra-eyed animals, plus ones that regrow body parts (e.g., lizards can reproduce new tails) or heal easily (e.g., whale sharks) strongly embody self-healing, and so logically participate in the "wounded healer" logic. There is a key curing figure in Moche iconography known as Lizard,[38] and a slightly later Chancay style whale shark-woman shaman effigy serves as a good example.[39]

In sum, the shaman effigy under discussion is one of quite a few, at least forty or more, vision-impaired portraits in the Moche corpus. The others share most of his traits, including the large ears, meditation pose, facial incision, and higher-status clothes and jewelry. The sculptors were paying close attention to their subjects, valuing them as individuals as well as Seers, likely ascribed powers to help others see what was most important.

Conclusion

Many physical anomalies that would today be considered problematic medical conditions are commemorated in ancient American art and occur in myriad styles.[40] In Costa Rican art, for example, intersexed, khyphotic, and scioliotic individuals are known, as are those surviving osteomalacia.[41] Celebrating physical anomaly is a widespread phenomenon in the indigenous Americas and particularly important in relation to the religious role of shaman.

This example suggests that the modern connotation of "disabled" may be a misnomer when applied to Amerindian art and culture, particularly that of ancient times. Since such an individual seems to have been considered sacred, and performed shamanic roles in these effigy representations, the usefulness of the term "disabled" for explicating across all cultures and time periods is unsupported. Therefore, I propose the notation 'dis'abled to help create distance from the modern category, while retaining the recognition of differentness from the norm. These ancient South American effigies depict people who were not considered to be missing anything, except in the terrestrial realm; rather, they are shown as having more powers in the spiritual one. In the world history of art and culture, in disability studies, and in religious studies, these diverse and remarkable ceramic effigies add a positive Native American voice to the dialogue.

Notes

1 Terminology is fraught because of the original mistake by Columbus in identifying the indigenous peoples of the continent as "Indian." "Native American" is commonly used, although to many that signifies the peoples of the northern continent only. "First Nations" is the phrase employed in Canada and is perceived as specifically referring

58 *Rebecca R. Stone*

to those groups who now coincide with that country's borders. However, any of these terms can be extended to all Amerindian peoples. Since they did not have a term for themselves in antiquity, and the European terms artificially unify groups, none of these broad categories is satisfying. Yet to make generalizations some kind of encompassing terminology must be utilized.

2 For instance, in the Arctic and the American Southwest (Navajo), transgender is accepted. See Bernard Saladin D'Anglure, "Rethinking Inuit Shamanism through the Concept of 'Third Gender'," in *Shamanism: A Reader*, ed. Graham Harvey (New York: Routledge, 2003), 235–241; and Marjorie Mandelstam Balzer, "Sacred Genders in Siberia: Shamans, Bear Festivals, and Androgyny," also in *Shamanism: A Reader*, 252. For the Navajo see Joseph Campbell, *Where the Two came to their Father: A Navajo War Ceremonial Given by Jeff King* (Princeton: Princeton University Press, Mythos Series, 1991), 78. Peruvian novelist Mario Vargas Llosa, winner of the Nobel Prize in Literature in 2010, includes a character in his virtuoso ethnographic novel, *The Storyteller*, who has the eaten-away face left by leishmaniasis (see fig. 3.4 here) but is accepted by the community; see Vargas Llosa, *The Storyteller*, trans. Helen Lane (New York: Farrar, Strauss, and Giroux, 1989). These are among many examples of this broadly Amerindian inclusive worldview.

3 See Gassaway, chapter 4, this volume; Rebecca R. Stone, *The Jaguar Within: Shamanic Trance in Ancient Central and South American Art* (Austin: University of Texas Press, 2011). Further afield culturally, but nevertheless relevant, is a Navajo example of positive difference found in Joseph Campbell, *Where the Two came to their Father*, 78. Older sources include Juan B. Lastres, Abraham Guillen, Jorge C. Muelle, and J. M. B. Tarfán, *Representaciones Patológicos En La Cerámica Peruana: Texto Medico* (Lima, Peru: Museo Nacional, 1943). The main untapped source consists of around three hundred Moche examples in the Museo Arqueológico Rafael Larco Herrera in Lima, Peru. Their catalogue is on line: http://www.museolarco.org/coleccion/catalogo-en-linea/ and the search term is, predictably, "pathologies."

4 The term "shaman" originates with the Tungus language of the Altai region of Siberia, one of the world heartlands of this early, pervasive, and long-lasting approach to the supernatural. The Americas were peopled from this very region of Asia, according to genetic studies (see James Shreeve, "The Greatest Journey," *National Geographic* 209, no. 3 (2006): 60–69). This makes the Tungus name relevant, although many different terms are used in Native American languages. See Stone, *The Jaguar Within*, 2, 211, note 1.

5 Jeremy and Francis Huxley Narby, *Shamans through Time: 500 Years on the Path to Knowledge* (New York: Thames and Hudson, 2001).

6 Stone, *The Jaguar Within*, 54–55.

7 Stone, *The Jaguar Within*, 54–55.

8 In the Bible, Genesis 1:27: "So God created humankind in his image, in the image of God he created them; male and female he created them. 1:28 God blessed them, and God said to them, "Be fruitful and multiply, and fill the earth and subdue it; and have dominion over the fish of the sea and over the birds of the air and over every living thing that moves upon the earth."

9 Eliot's actual term was the "wounded surgeon," though surgeon now refers more specifically to one who operates, not one who heals. T. S. Eliot, *Four Quartets* (London: Faber and Faber, 1944), 20.

10 Joan Halifax, *Shaman: The Wounded Healer* (New York: Thames and Hudson, 1982), 10.

11 Halifax, *Shaman*.

12 Halifax, *Shaman*.

13 Walter Alva and Christopher Donnan, *Royal Tombs of Sipán* (Los Angeles, CA: Fowler Museum of Cultural History, University of California, 1993).

14 Christopher B. Donnan, *Moche Portraits from Ancient Peru* (Austin, TX: University of Texas Press, 2004).

15 Donnan, *Moche Portraits*, 144–156.
16 Donnan, *Moche Portraits*, 57.
17 Stone, *The Jaguar Within*, 96–97, 171–176.
18 For instance, see Simon Brisenden, "Independent Living and the Medical Model of Disability," in *The Disability Reader: Social Science Perspectives*, ed. Tom Shakespeare (London: Continuum, 1998), 20–27.
19 Stone, *The Jaguar Within*, 78ff.
20 Stone, *The Jaguar Within*, 87–90.
21 Stone, *The Jaguar Within*, 15–18, 89–91.
22 The *Spondylus sp.* bivalve inhabits warm waters of the Caribbean and the Pacific, its red, orange, maroon, and purple inner lining a prized art material throughout the ancient Americas. See http://scholarblogs.emory.edu/blackjaguar, 2013; Rebecca Stone-Miller, *Seeing with New Eyes: Highlights of the Michael C. Carlos Museum Collection of Art of the Ancient Americas* (Atlanta: Michael C. Carlos Museum, 2002), 40–41 and 194–197.
23 Alva, *Royal Tombs of Sipán*, 76.
24 See Donnan, *Moche Portraits*.
25 Rebecca R. Stone, *Art of the Andes from Chavín to Inca*, Thames & Hudson World of Art (New York, NY: Thames & Hudson, 2012), 109.
26 Stone, *The Jaguar Within*, 155–160.
27 Stone, *The Jaguar Within*, 34–39.
28 Stone, *The Jaguar Within*, 36.
29 Stone, *Art of the Andes from Chavín to Inca*, 19.
30 Stone, *The Jaguar Within*, 27, 192.
31 Armand Labbé, *Shamans, Gods, and Mythic Beasts: Colombian Gold and Ceramics in Antiquity* (New York: American Federation of Arts, 1998), 50–57.
32 National Eye Institute, "https://www.Nei.Nih.Gov/Health/Cataract/Cataract_Facts," (2015).
33 Stone, *The Jaguar Within*, 93ff.
34 Stone, *The Jaguar Within*, 81.
35 Stone, *The Jaguar Within*, 39–44ff.
36 Stone, *The Jaguar Within*, 174, 175.
37 Melissa Kaplan, Herp Care Collection, http://www.Anapsid.Org/Parietal.Html.
38 Christopher B. and Donna McClelland Donnan, "The Burial Theme in Moche Iconography," in *Studies in pre-Columbian art and archaeology* (1979), 1–46.
39 Stone, *The Jaguar Within*, 157–164.
40 See Gassaway, chapter 4, this volume.
41 Sarah V. Parks, "Dis'abilities as Divine: Bodily Anomalies and Shamanic Power in Ancient Costa Rican Ceramic Effigies" (Honors Thesis, Emory University, 2013). Rebecca Stone and Sarah V. Parks, "Transcending Gender, Transforming Bones," *Journal of Disabilities, Art, and Culture*, forthcoming.

4 Divining disability
Criticism as diagnosis in Mesoamerican art history

William T. Gassaway

Introduction[1]

Based on the large number of hunched backs, paralytic limbs, contorted spines, and other corporeal distinctions that appear in the arts of the ancient Americas, a number of scholars of pre-Hispanic history contend that disability and so-called "bodily deformation" were once endemic among New World populations.[2] These archaeologists and art historians have relied primarily on visual analysis of artworks carried out in relation to contemporary Western medical pathology, resulting in interpretations including diagnoses of spina bifida, facial paralysis, syphilis, and widespread achondroplasia (the most common form of dwarfism).[3] However, in electing to articulate disability as a "pathology" or "sickness" (*enfermedad*) rather than as an imposed social, cultural, or political identity, such analyses assume that many of the most extraordinary examples of non-Western art were modeled on literal, even prosaic, examples of bodily anomaly. Consequently, these sculptural figurines have come to be viewed not as objects of artistic creativity, but rather as historical records of identifiable illness. Such is the case in scholarly discussions of one Mesoamerican artistic motif in particular: a short-statured figure known in Mesoamerican scholarship as "the dwarf."[4]

Over the past several decades, researchers have made tremendous progress in reconstructing the social and religious contexts in which atypical sculptural types were created, deployed, and viewed in the Mesoamerican world. Principally, these findings make clear that indigenous people regarded corporeal distinction as essential to the continuation of the earth's fecundity, the daily rise of the sun, and the regular progression of seasons.[5] At the same time, though, historical accounts by Europeans affirm that uncharacteristic bodies were a form of punishment, or divine retribution, for man's worldly sins.[6] As multivalent indices of virtue and iniquity, these atypical bodies thus pose a number of conceptual paradoxes that significantly challenge our modern investigations into the pre-Hispanic past.

While examinations of the supernatural and affective role of distinctive bodies within pre-contact cosmologies have provided grounds for what disability studies scholar Simi Linton calls a productive, "epistemological basis for inquiries" into the cultural construction of disability as such,[7] there is nevertheless a lingering tendency within Mesoamerican scholarship to regard disability as a medical issue. As this chapter will demonstrate, the naturalistic appearance of many of the most extraordinary morphological features in art of the past has encouraged the belief that people long ago duplicated observable traits that we associate today with physical impairment, spinal cord disability, injuries to the head and limbs, and other types of disability.[8] As such, it has been problematically suggested that distinctive body types can be explained in etiological terms and, by extension, bear clear evidence of pathological conditions. As one of several disability theorists who seek to correct such generalizations, feminist disability scholar Alison Kafer notes, "The medical model of disability frames atypical bodies and minds as deviant, pathological, and defective, best understood and addressed in medical terms."[9] Indeed, I argue that these are precisely the terms in which we have come to conceptualize—or rather, reimagine—people of the distant past. But by incorporating recent advances in the field of disability studies, I believe that this reductive view of nonconforming bodies can be reinvigorated and made receptive to new explanations of, and possibilities for, disability representation.

Art has an expressivity beyond mere scientific fact, and it is important to consider that artists of the past did not always illustrate in some slavish way the diversity of human anatomies. Therefore, in an effort to present a more equitable assessment of the role of disability in the pre-contact Americas, I propose that we must first recognize our tendency to "diagnose" art rather than interpret it. To this end, the following chapter will focus specifically on the appearance and meanings of dwarfism in ancient art, as I believe the contemporary focus on this issue reveals more about scholars' own preoccupations than it does those of indigenous sculptors. It is my hope that with the groundwork laid here, future studies might take up the crucial work of historicizing disability as one of several oppressed identity categories vis-à-vis ancient and contemporary Mesoamerican religious and social practices, in ways akin perhaps to discussions of race, gender, and sexuality addressed elsewhere.[10]

Problems of scale or perspective?

In the arts of pre-Columbian Mexico and Central America, there exists a distinct category of figures whose diminutive statures and short, fleshy limbs are believed to resemble those of individuals termed "dwarfs" in modern parlance.[11] Bare-chested and wearing simple loincloths, their habitual associations with elite contexts and supernatural phenomena are as conspicuous as their flamboyant headdresses. As they appear in nearly every artistic medium, their presence in the Mesoamerican artistic corpus spans at least three thousand years and a vast array of cultures.

One of the earliest and most celebrated works in all of pre-Hispanic art is Potrero Nuevo Monument 2 (1800–1200 BCE), a stone dais featuring a pair of small-scale figures hoisting a slab of rock high above their heads (fig. 4.1). With their stout, muscular frames, large heads, shortened extremities, and flattened facial features, these two crouching individuals embody many of the most salient characteristics of the dwarf type in Mesoamerican art. But what can be said of their role in this work of art? One interpretation is that they represent Atlas-like "sky-bearers."

62   *William T. Gassaway*

Figure 4.1 Potrero Nuevo Monument 2 ("Atlantean altar"), Olmec, Early Preclassic (1800–1200 BCE), stone, H. 37 in. (94 cm). Museo de Antropología, Xalapa, Veracruz, 04019 (after Diehl 2004: fig. 14).

As anthropologists Susan Milbrath and Karl Taube note, the monolith they support represents the schematic rendering of a celestial serpent's maw on its upper ledge.[12] Furthermore, evidence suggests that this monument likely served long ago as the throne of an Olmec chief. Thus, as pillars of both cosmic and political order, these individuals were apparently regarded at one time as figures of tremendous significance.[13]

Depicted alongside kings in Maya art as well, dwarfs are continually represented as symbols of authority, nobility, and prestige, which underscores their high value among New World elites generally (fig. 4.2).[14] In fact, it was because of their wisdom and exceptional self-assurance that the Aztec ruler Moctezuma held dwarfs in such high esteem. The colonial chronicles confirm that when the former grew tired of his other entertainers, only the palace dwarf was asked to stay behind and advise the supreme lord in matters of state and religion.[15] Significantly, it is in this same role (or guise) that they are most frequently portrayed in Maya art as well (figs. 4.3–4.5).[16] Festooned with amulets of precious stone, ankle-length skirts, and ceremonial deer- or bird-shaped headdresses, dwarfs have a privileged access to luxurious wares that distinguishes them as official counselors, modish courtiers, and courtly mystics.

Figure 4.2 Enthroned elite looking into mirror held by dwarf, with another dwarf sipping an unknown liquid from a large vessel, Maya, Late Classic (CE 600–900), ceramic with polychrome, H. 9.5 x Diam. 6.7 x Circum. 19.4 in. (24 x 17 x 49.2 cm). National Museum of Australia, 82.22.92 (photograph K1453 © Justin Kerr, www.mayavase.com).

Despite the noble implications of these costumes, there is still a great deal of uncertainty as to what roles dwarfs and their images actually performed. Were they, for example, portraits of historical figures? If so, were these portraits intended to be honorific or satirical? Did they possess the power to ward off evil, or perhaps encourage rainfall, as has often been suggested?[17] Or, as art historian Carolyn Tate has recently argued, could they perhaps represent history's oldest surviving example of medical illustration?[18] Each of these possible functions has been put forth and defended, and at one time or another, most have been dismissed.

So what is to be done with this enormous archive of atypical bodies: a corpus of images at once so abundant yet so capricious? Scholars of art history, and more recently medical history, have sought to clarify the historical significance of dwarfs by first taxonomically identifying and classifying their physical characteristics. As art historian Virginia Miller argues, among the Maya, dwarfism is represented more often than any other form of physical diversity. Most of these depictions, she continues, share a common set of features, such as "small stature, abnormally short and fleshy limbs, a protruding abdomen, and a disproportionately large head with prominent forehead, sunken face, and drooping lower lip"— the combination of which she regards as "diagnostic of the most common type of dwarfism, usually called achondroplasia . . . [or] short-limb dwarfism" (e.g., figs. 4.3–4.5).[19] Beyond this subset, Miller identifies additional representations of figures with compressed torsos, barrel chests, hunchbacks, and any number of the over two hundred different instances in which proportionate or disproportionate dwarfism is known to occur.[20] Miller's next logical question then becomes, what

Figure 4.3 Dwarf figurine whistle, Maya (Jaina), Late Classic (CE 600–800), ceramic with red and white pigment, H. 4 1/2 in. (11.43 cm). The Los Angeles County Museum of Art, gift of Constance McCormick Fearing, AC1992.134.20 (artwork in the public domain; photograph © Los Angeles County Museum of Art, www.lacma.org).

Figure 4.4 Dwarf figurine whistle, Maya (Jaina), Late Classic (CE 600–800), ceramic with red and white pigment, H. 3 13/16 in. (9.53 cm). The Los Angeles County Museum of Art, gift of Constance McCormick Fearing, AC1992.134.21 (artwork in the public domain; photograph © Los Angeles County Museum of Art, www.lacma.org).

Figure 4.5 Dwarf wearing a deer headdress and holding a mirror, Maya (Jaina), Late Classic (CE 600–800), ceramic, H. 6 1/8 x W. 3 3/16 in. (15.6 x 8.1 cm). Ethnologisches Museum, Berlin/SMB, IV Ca 50146 (photograph by the author).

possible function did these objects perform? To answer this question, scholars of the ancient Americas utilize a number of different resources, including the formal analysis of artworks, ethnographic analogy, and the eyewitness accounts of indigenous practices as recorded by Europeans.

Divining disability 67

The most direct points of access into native life are the population surveys and ethnographic inquiries compiled by the conquistadors and Spanish and mestizo priests following the Conquest (c. 1521).[21] These chronicles present a rich vision of pre-Hispanic belief systems and social organization, including the structure of ritual practice, calendrical observations, linguistic behavior, and dietary habits—observations now indispensable to the study of pre-Columbian peoples. None of these sources is without bias, though, as most of these inquiries were commissioned by the Spanish Crown or the Holy Roman Church for purposes of religious conversion and economic exploitation.[22] Additionally, many of the chronicles incorporate the inconsistencies of earlier works, making them as problematic as they are invaluable.[23] Finally, while these writings at times wonderfully corroborate our understanding of Aztec art, there are doubts whether that same information can be extrapolated to gain insight into the creative endeavors of people living centuries, even millennia, prior to the Aztecs.

When the Spanish conquistadors arrived in Tenochtitlan (modern-day Mexico City) in 1519, they delighted in the Aztec ruler Moctezuma's impressive retinue of musicians, comedians, and other palace performers. As in many European royal courts of the time, this motley troupe of players was comprised of high-flying acrobats, stilt-walkers, contortionists, and clowns—many of whom were said to exhibit clear signs of physical impairment.[24] As the soldier Bernal Díaz recalls of his time in the king's court, "Sometimes some little humpbacked dwarfs would be present at [Moctezuma's] meals, whose bodies seemed almost to be broken in the middle."[25] Elsewhere, the Dominican friar Diego Durán relates that, upon the death of Lord Tizoc in 1486, "Many slaves and hunchbacks and dwarfs were killed . . . so that not one was left and so they would accompany the king to serve him in the otherworld. All his jewels and wealth were buried together with his ashes."[26] These two brief but descriptive accounts of Aztec religious and courtly life reveal important details regarding the ambivalent social standing of disabled bodies just prior to the Conquest.[27]

Primarily, the preceding passage suggests that individuals with markedly different bodies held a social (and perhaps penal) status akin to that of slaves. Commander in charge Hernán Cortés recounts:

> There was also in this house a room in which were kept men, women and children who had, from birth, white faces and bodies and white hair, eyebrows and eyelashes. . . . There was yet another house where lived many deformed men and women, among which were dwarfs and hunchbacks and others with other deformities; and each manner of monstrosity had a room to itself; and likewise there were people to look after them.[28]

Segregated from society yet "looked after" by others, it seems that "monstrosity" (as Cortés termed it) was not necessarily a damnable condition among the Aztecs but was nevertheless deserving of quarantine—or at least close supervision. A comparable ambiguity is revealed by Durán's account, in which similar bodies are entrusted with the responsibility of conveying the king's body to the afterlife, along with all his worldly riches. Expected to sacrifice their own lives so that they might continue as his eternal companions, dwarfs faced a journey at once perilous and honorable.[29]

If the preceding accounts are to be believed, then dwarfs and hunchbacks were clearly figures of importance in Aztec political and religious thought. Furthermore, given the long-standing fascination with dwarfs in the Spanish royal court at this time, it is unsurprising that the chronicles would include mention of them.[30] Nevertheless, it is impossible to know whether the people described in the preceding passages truly exhibited the characteristics of dwarfism we recognize today. After all, Díaz was a soldier of fortune with very little formal education, so his intellectual integrity and investigative rigor are by no means unassailable. Durán's story of the funeral procession is similarly problematic in its reliability, as it was penned nearly a century after the death of Tizoc, and thus neither he nor his informants were ever witnesses to such an event. Additionally, without any standardized definition of dwarfism available in the sixteenth century, it is difficult to know whether any of the parties involved—the Spaniards or their native informants—were speaking about (that is, intended) the same bodies at the same time.

The colonial accounts thus found wanting, scholars next endeavor to illuminate the curiosities of the past through ethnographic analogy, which posits that correlations exist between the ethnographic reality of modern-day peoples and the archaeological remains of their ancestors.[31] Much like the colonial sources, ethnographic analogy smacks of what ethnohistorian Louise M. Burkhart and others refer to as an "ethnographic present." Burkhart notes:

> The use of colonial sources to reconstruct pre-Conquest culture is symptomatic of a general tendency within anthropology to place other cultures into an "ethnographic present" in which they are described as static, self-perpetuating systems. . . . Living societies, with whom an investigator has had extensive personal contact, are made to seem removed in time and space, objectified; the investigator's dialogue with individual people becomes his or her monologue about the "culture," now presented as a homogeneous unit.[32]

For example, if the modern-day Maya or Nahua (Aztec) peoples believe that dwarfs function as guardian earth spirits, can one reasonably assume the same was true of their ancestors so many centuries ago? To infer that level of correspondence between the past and present would require us to assume a great deal of ideological unity among ancient and contemporary peoples—a unity too tenuous to be reliable.[33]

When ethnographic accounts assume too much, and the colonial texts are problematic, art historians next turn to the morphological analysis of objects in order to draw productive conclusions concerning their function or meaning. A foundational method of the field, visual analysis helps to unlock something of the how and why of Native expression by disentangling the structural logic of a particular artwork, often to startling degrees. Yet the problem with formal analysis is that it is a highly subjective and profoundly speculative mode of inquiry.[34] Certainly this is the case in some instances of Mesoamerican scholarship, for it emboldens scholars to make great, classificatory leaps, or to claim, for instance, that the physical characteristics of dwarfism are more or less accurately portrayed. Using visual (formal) analysis, scholars may go so far as to assert that certain works function as examples of portraiture. But to make such a claim, as scholars, we must then argue that Mesoamerican artists had initially based their depictions on historical individuals. As it stands, however, no anthropologist has ever had the opportunity to examine the physical remains of a Mesoamerican dwarf because no such skeleton is known archaeologically.[35] And without these remains, neither the indigenous depictions, nor colonial accounts of dwarfs can be definitively proved.[36]

Acknowledging such discrepancies, many more pressing questions come to the surface. For example, can a uniquely Mesoamerican concept of the human organism—including its form, function, and any ritual meanings that indigenous peoples may have attached to it—be made to abet a scientific (and decidedly Western) mode of inquiry? When are these two approaches to the work of art commensurate, and who gets to decide their appropriateness? It is important to note that the scholars who harbor such claims are not themselves medical experts. As anthropologists, archaeologists, and art historians, they have neither the degree, nor experience, to recognize or classify the characteristics symptomatic of impairment, be it social, cultural, or physical.[37] Yet this is oftentimes their defined objective: to identify those peculiar traits among the ancients that, from their contemporary points of view, appear "diagnostic" of an alleged disorder.

Among the early artistic traditions of the Olmec civilization, anthropologist Carson Murdy has identified a class of congenital idiosyncrasies that he believes are partially, although not completely, explained by the so-called were-jaguar motif of Olmec art.[38] Developed in the 1960s, the theory of the were-jaguar was based on pioneering archaeologist Matthew Stirling's (1955) discovery of three large, yet highly fragmentary stone sculptures made by the Olmec peoples of coastal Veracruz.[39] Interpreting these monuments as the depictions of human females copulating with male jaguars, Stirling suggested that the Olmec believed themselves the progeny of this unnatural union. For him, the existence of such a myth helped to explain why so many Olmec figures appear to be transforming into their feline alter egos. "In its extreme form," Murdy elaborates, "this were-jaguar motif consists of a round baby-like face, often with a cleft forehead, characterized by an open mouth with fleshly lips turned down at the corners and canine teeth sometimes shown as protruding fangs."[40] As this Middle Preclassic (900–500 BCE) jadeite mask demonstrates (fig. 4.6), these figures usually sport slanted, slightly squinted eyes; a bifurcated brow; and a highly symmetrical scowl that together elicit the salient feline features.

While scholars do not discount the presence of human-animal hybrids in Olmec art, most no longer think these figures express an indigenous belief in some "divinely sanctioned" form of bestiality.[41] Nevertheless, Murdy and several others remain largely undeterred. Should the were-jaguar motif prove to be a fabrication of modern thought, then he is only willing to concede the alternative "natural" explanation: namely, that these statues and masks may be indicative of "a

Figure 4.6 Mask, Olmec, Middle Preclassic (900–500 BCE), jadeite, H. 6 3/4 x W. 6 5/16 in. (17.1 x 16.5 cm). The Metropolitan Museum of Art, bequest of Alice K. Bache, 1977.187.33 (artwork in the public domain; photograph © The Metropolitan Museum of Art, www.metmuseum.org).

multifactorial neural-tube defect."[42] Among the other specific impairments he enumerates, Murdy gives special attention to encephaloceles, a neural-tube condition in which areas of the brain can emerge through apertures in the skull.[43] Therefore, while Murdy may be willing to reject the interpretation of cleft lips as the vestigial traces of jaguar ancestors, he cannot relinquish the possibility that such features represent symptoms of such defects.

Having enumerated a list of "defects," as Murdy termed them, he then builds on archaeologist and epigrapher Michael Coe's identification of another type of neural-tube defect, *cranium bifida*, which causes the cranium to be vertically split.[44] A range of other physical impairments are likewise posited, such as a "phlegmonous infection (extensive carbuncles) of the face, and even the externally visible cancerous tumors of terminal metastatic carcinomatosis . . . [in addition to] acromegaly (enlargement of bones and soft parts of hands, face and feet), dwarfism, as perhaps caused by cretinism . . . or leprosy . . ."[45] The conjunction of these serious impairments thus suggests, without any examination of physical remains, that the Olmec were plagued by an almost superabundance of human physical diversity—or that Olmec artists were at the very least fixated on a few rare instances.

Divining disability 71

Yet if the (apparent) aggregation of disease and disability is to be predicated upon a well-developed, even uncanny, display of naturalism in art, then its stands to reasons that artists long ago depicted the world as they saw it, rather than as they conceived of it—which is to say, that art imitated life absolutely. Clearly, though, jade masks like those made by the Maya in the Middle Preclassic period (800–400 BCE) are more than simply reflections of reality (fig. 4.7). Through their incorporation of fantastical subjects, spontaneity of form, and a superb level of finish, such works testify to the tremendous imaginative abilities of their creators.

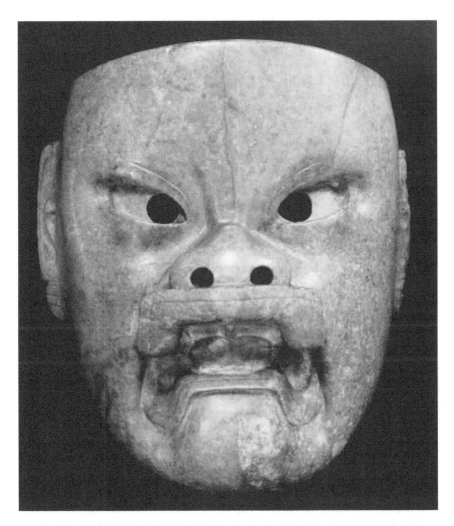

Figure 4.7 Mask, Olmec, Middle Preclassic (800–400 BCE), jadeite, H. 8 1/8 x W. 7 x D. 4 1/4 in. (20.64 x 17.78 x 10.8 cm). The Dumbarton Oaks Research Library and Collection, PC.B.020 (photograph © Dumbarton Oaks, Pre-Columbian Collection, Washington, DC).

Undoubtedly grounded in references to natural phenomena, works like these nonetheless take flight above and away from any primordial foundation and endeavor instead to depict something supernatural.

The suggestion that nature forms an inescapable referent for a people's art calls into question whether the diagnoses mentioned in the preceding pages have perhaps overlooked a key element of art itself. As the philosopher Martin Heidegger once lamented, "Art-historical study makes the works the objects of a science. Yet in all this busy activity do we encounter the work itself?"[46] In the case of pre-Columbian art especially, I would argue, visual analysis too often functions as the handmaiden of scientific inquiry, and art as simply the illustrative evidence of archaeological conjectures. To understand why this should be the case, a review of the origins of New World antiquity is perhaps instructive.

Science and the humanities: brothers or distant cousins?

The study of antiquity began during the Italian Renaissance as a humanistic pursuit. Spurred by the "rebirth" of classical art, literature, and philosophy, sixteenth-century enthusiasts began seeking material remains in and of the earth in the hopes of fleshing out, supporting, and giving credibility to the great texts of history. Hence, what we call "archaeology" today was originally conceived of as a sort of philological diversion, wherein sculptural fragments, coins, and architectural ruins served as fodder for imaginative reconstructions of the past. Ancient monuments were regarded, consequently, as simply the more durable and intrepid bedrock of the otherwise superior arts of poetry, philosophy, and drama.[47]

When introduced to the Americas in the eighteenth century, the new science was necessarily modified to accommodate the realities of a very different world. Not only were there no great Native American monuments then known (or recognized as such) by the American people, there were also no literary works against which to compare such treasures. It was not until former president Thomas Jefferson, referred to as the "Father of American Archaeology," famously conducted an archaeological exploration of an Indian burial mound in the Piedmont region of Virginia that the distinctly American flavor of archaeology was developed.[48] Although Jefferson discovered only human remains, other amateur archaeologists soon began unearthing all manner of bones, pottery, and tools left behind by former Native American communities. These physical remains were then collected and scrutinized in ever more professional manners as time progressed.

The earliest findings were organized either by typology (series of objects associated with particular traditions) or stratigraphy (estimation of age based on relative position in the earth), and soon archaeologists were able to propose broad ranges of dates with which to classify these remnants.[49] Encouraged by their findings and yearning for more facts about the composition of social hierarchies and economics, the first archaeologists sought to exploit works of art "as sources of information rather than as expressive realities," according to art historian George Kubler.[50] Thus, the "science" of archaeology eventually parted ways with the humanities and began to seek fraternity in the social and natural sciences, particularly in the

Divining disability 73

fields of anthropology, sociology, linguistics, and eventually biology. Over time, philology was no longer useful and so was left by the wayside.[51]

Believing the material remains of the ancient Americas to be largely undecipherable, as indigenous peoples lacked written or alphabetic records, scholars working in the nineteenth century were often confounded by ancient modes of expression.[52] And since these objects could not be deciphered using historical documents, their interpretations freely made use of the same scientific trends being employed then in archaeology. As a result, Kubler noted, "Today an archaeological report on an American site is a 'scientific' production of graphs, statistics, and impersonal language purporting to reach proven and repeatable conclusions."[53] Such a state of affairs is lamentable, I contend, because it makes a humanistic approach to ancient American art secondary to the archaeological and scientific view of things; and, as a result, the tools and technologies of the latter have, at times, come to dominate the discussion to a disproportionate degree.[54] As such, the divide between science and humanism has become muddled, resulting in what I call the "pathology of sculpture": the practice by which apparent (or alleged) "medical maladies" are classified through examples of their artistic expressions. Carried to its extreme, I believe that such an approach has the potential not only to medicalize artistic expression but also contribute to the historical oppression of disabled people—the fuller ramifications of which I discuss at length elsewhere.[55]

Returning to our initial question of how representations of so-called dwarfs and other figures with distinctive bodies are identifiable as such, it should come as no surprise that physical impairment has frequently fallen under the purview of biology and epidemiology, rather than aesthetics. Interestingly, some very promising studies have been produced in recent years that attempt to fight fire with fire—that is, to use science against science. For example, Carolyn Tate (art historian) and Gordon Bendersky (pediatric cardiologist–cum–medical historian) have recently sought to correct previous taxonomies of dwarfism in Olmec art.[56] Through many comparisons of head-to-body ratios and their analysis of specific bodily contortions routinely applied by Olmec artists, they have been able to recast many figures as belonging to a new typology of sculpture reportedly depicting the embryonic or fetal state—a subject previously unknown in art of the ancient world (fig. 4.8). As the authors note:

> In terms of specific abnormalities portrayed in the fetus sculptures, agnathia or micronathia (chinlessless) is the most obvious. Since fetuses normally have a large head relative to the body, all the images have relatively large heads; however, macrocephaly is probably depicted in several pieces. These abnormalities may be symptomatic of the congenital anomalies that led to the premature births and deaths of the fetuses.[57]

To really drive home the validity of their claim, the authors took the additional step of inviting a group of eleven experts in the field, whose members included an embryologist, as well as obstetricians, gynecologists, neonatologists, and perinatologists; the specialists were asked to independently examine photographs of the sixteen sculptures.[58] These specialists concluded that the sculptures corresponded so

74 *William T. Gassaway*

Figure 4.8 Diminutive figurine resembling purported "fetal typology," Olmec, Middle Preclassic (1000–800 BCE), volcanic stone, dimensions unknown. Museo Nacional de Antropología, Mexico City (photograph by the author).

strongly to the appearance of human fetuses or newborns that they could estimate gestational age and identify characteristics suggestive of pathological symptoms.[59] These findings, consequently, call for the reinterpretation of the corpus, as they suggest a new manner of conceiving these bodies—one not limited by the anachronistic reasoning needed to defend the sculptures as images of dwarfs. At the same time, however, I take issue with Tate's and Bendersky's claims because they continue to capitulate to the opinion that these are primarily objects of medical importance, as opposed to representations that do not necessarily reflect material reality. As such, any assertion regarding the significance of these dwarfs-cum-infants must be problematically argued and maintained using a voluminous body of medical experts for whom the "artfulness" of these particular pieces is of relatively minor concern.

Conclusions

It is encouraging that art historians seek recourse in the opinions of those who are assumedly qualified to give them (e.g., archaeologists and other trained scientists). Nevertheless, there is something precarious and somewhat degrading about relying on an assortment of doctors, tools, instruments, apparatuses, and theories to analyze objects of such obvious aesthetic sensibility. Indeed, it seems a rather mechanistic way of treating a peoples' art—not to mention the individuals whom these artworks purportedly depict.

The goal here, then, is not to drive a stake between the scientific and more humanistic study of American antiquity. Such hubris would only serve to impoverish the interpretive possibilities inherent to each approach. Rather, historians of science and of art are equally implored to recognize better the particular acuity of their respective methodologies—as well as their limitations. To paraphrase Michel Foucault, history really is "made for cutting," and the deliberate, artificial divisions scholars make among objects and people across time must be recognized as choices that serve particular, often predetermined, ends.[60]

Regarding Murdy's theory of neural-tube defects, Tate observes that his argument "did not address the format of the objects . . . or [their] possible functions. . . . Instead, it selected those images that fits its purpose and ignored the rest."[61] In this way, Tate draws attention to the fact that the cuts in history made by anthropologists, while at times complementary and illuminating to studies of art, are nevertheless different than those made by art historians.[62] Thus, while the conclusions afforded by the sciences are by no means incommensurable with those of the humanities, the recognition of their intrinsic limitations is critical to understanding their full (yet particular) importance within the study of the past.

In not making such distinctions more apparent, interpretation can sometimes overstep its bounds, and allowing art-historical inquiry to masquerade as science gives the latter free rein to practice as art history. But when scholars are forthright about the arbitrary ruptures and conjunctions under which the different disciplines operate, history is then able to reveal truth more effortlessly. In a way, the object is thus better able to "push back" against us, and even to protect itself from the harm sometimes inflicted upon it with all our poking and prodding.

Stated in general terms, the purpose of these objects—as with all art perhaps—is, as art historian Esther Pasztory notes, "to deal with problems on a symbolic level that cannot be dealt with on a practical level."[63] By seeking always to encapsulate art within a socio-scientific context, or to explain it away as merely imitative or illustrative, historians actually deprive art of its elegance, spontaneity, and affinity for abstraction.[64] To be sure, science has its place, and its involvement in the arts of Mesoamerica has sparked a wonderful dialogue between the two. But when enormous collections of instruments, institutions, DNA samples, and medical jargon become perpetually necessary to juggle and keep aloft these otherwise fragile diagnoses of the past, then something of the point of art has been lost.

In the future, it may benefit historians and scientists to consider whether other theories might explain why ancient peoples depicted particular bodies as shorter, less "proportionate," or more magical than others. For example, perhaps the characteristics of what is today called "disability" were for Mesoamericans the only proper way of depicting the more numinous (and personified) forces of sun, rain, corn, and so on. In this way, the focus is placed on the religious and sociopolitical context in which a body arises or subsists, rather than on any inherent pathology of that body—although, in either case, the subject of investigation remains essentially the same. The difference between the two perspectives is quite subtle: Did ancient Americans consider a body to be supernatural because it was disabled? Or did the mystical, erudite depth of a particular courtier, advisor, or priest consequently render it "deformed" in the work of art alone—as if, perhaps, that were the only appropriate way of rendering such supernatural power? When this latter question becomes the point of departure, then the congenital and acquired conditions most relevant to the disability studies discourses are conferred an ontological status that both encompasses and exceeds the medical model of disability. That is to say, physical impairments such as dwarfism, amputation, and kyphosis (hunched back) are not discussed simply as medical conditions but as the deterministic markers of supernatural forces and divine personhood.

Notes

1 Versions of this chapter were presented at the annual graduate symposia of the Graduate Center at the City University of New York and the Princeton University Department of Art and Archaeology. I am grateful to my fellow panelists as well as to the attendees for their thoughtful insights and questions.
2 The term "deformation" is problematic for a number of reasons, not least of which for its frequently pejorative and disparaging connotations (whether intentional, or not) in both Euro-American colonialist and modern popular treatments of non-Western cultures. Elsewhere, I analyze the usage of such terminology within the Spanish conquistadors' accounts of New World cultures, and trace its trajectory through Victorian-era perceptions of the "macabre" and "grotesque" in pre-Columbian art ("Extraordinary Bodies: The Art of Deformation in Postclassic Art," PhD diss., Columbia University, forthcoming). At the same time, however, I qualify my own usage of the term as a protean and pragmatic means of discussing artists' deliberate manipulations of different materials—for example, the "bending into (or out of) shape" of ceramic and stone—in their depictions of human- and god-bodies: practices which were performed according to unique cultural understandings of material plastics, anatomy, and metaphysics. In this way, I attempt to engage with "deformation" as one of several dialectical modes useful in explicating non-Western artistic activity, particularly insofar as the former helps to explain the historical and religious motivations of the latter on a material level. (Other modes include "the unformed," a term used to describe those artifacts that were deliberately disarticulated and dispersed, and "the *informe*" [or formlessness], typically used to discuss modern conceptual-artistic practices.) For a selection of relevant

literature on this topic, see Michael D. Coe, *Mexico* (New York: Praeger, 1962), 85; Virginia E. Miller, "The Dwarf Motif in Classic Maya Art," in *Fourth Palenque Round Table, 1980*, ed. Merle Greene Robertson and Elizabeth P. Benson (San Francisco: Pre-Columbian Art Research Institute, 1985), 141–153; and Carson M. Murdy, "Congenital Deformities and the Olmec Were-Jaguar Motif," *American Antiquity* 46, no. 4 (1981): 861–871.

3 A few of the more explicit sources include Hasso Von Winning, *Portrayal of Pathological Symptoms in Pre-Columbian Mexico* (Carbondale, IL: The Pearson Museum, Southern Illinois University School of Medicine, 1987), and Eduardo Matos Moctezuma, *Parálisis facial prehispánica*, Departamento de Investigaciones Antropológica, vol. 25 (México: Instituto Nacional de Antropología e Historia, 1970).

4 As discussed later, scholars of Mesoamerican culture commonly use the term "dwarf" in a monolithic, universalizing sense to describe the depictions of short-statured individuals generally. As a result, "little people" (a perhaps more appropriate or humanistic term, something that little people might call themselves or reclaim) remains altogether absent from the literature, both at large and, correspondingly, in the present chapter.

5 Iconographic and historical evidence confirms that the Aztecs, like other Mesoamericans, believed men of diminutive size called *tepictoton* were responsible for initiating (or depriving) rainfall, and that the god of war was identified by his small, damaged foot. Archaeological investigations further reveal that individuals with bone lesions and tooth decay were routinely sacrificed to the gods of rain and wind. See Juan Alberto Román Berrelleza, "A Study of Skeletal Materials from Tlatelolco," in *To Change Place: Aztec Ceremonial Landscapes*, ed. Davíd Carrasco (Boulder: University Press of Colorado, 1991), 14–15.

6 As ethnohistorian Louise Burkhart offers, "The Nahua gods punished wrongdoers with blindness, crippling, and paralysis as well as sickness, filth and poverty . . . [and] the 'merit' of the bad ruler was blindness and paralysis as well as rags and refuse." Burkhart, *The Slippery Earth: Nahua-Christian Moral Dialogue in Sixteenth-Century Mexico* (Tucson: University of Arizona Press, 1989), 176.

7 Activist Simi Linton's appeal to move beyond a "corrective" or "medicalized" approach toward disability articulates most eloquently the need for an epistemological approach toward the sociopolitical and cultural construction of the phenomenon. Linton, *Claiming Disability: Knowledge and Identity* (New York: New York University Press, 1998).

8 A notable exception is art historian Rebecca R. Stone's recent work concerning pre-Columbian shamanistic practices among the Moche culture of Peru (see chapter 3 in this volume). In an unpublished conference paper ("Disability as Divine: Special Bodies in Ancient American Art," presented at the Ninety-fifth Annual Conference of the College Art Association, New York, February 2007), Stone concludes: "Special bodies were represented in many ancient American cultures not in terms of disability but in terms of moderate to high status accorded to the transformative wounded healer as a spiritual connection with the divine. Bodily anomaly apparently predisposed certain individuals to take on a sacred responsibility to transcend the norm." For criticisms of the medical model of disability, see, for example, Paul Abberley, "The Concept of Oppression and the Development of a Social Theory of Disability," *Disability, Handicap & Society* 2, no. 1 (1987): 5–19; Steven E. Hyler, Glen O. Gabbard, and Irving Schneider, "Homicidal Maniacs and Narcissistic Parasites: Stigmatization of Mentally Ill Persons in the Movies," *Psychiatric Services* 42, no. 10 (1991): 1044–1048; and Michael Oliver, "The Social Model in Context," in *Understanding Disability* (London: Macmillan Education, 1996), 30–42.

9 Alison Kafer, *Feminist, Queer, Crip* (Bloomington: Indiana University Press, 2013), 5. While Kafer offers an insightful summary of the social/medical model binary, the broader relevance of her work lies in its juxtaposition of feminist and identity politics alongside environmental ethics and reproductive justice. Her formulation of a

completely new model of disability theory, which is predicated upon a feminist/queer/crip alliance, provides a useful paradigm for the integration and/or transcendence of the disciplinary divisions discussed in the present work.

10. For example, see Cecelia Klein, "None of the Above: Gender Ambiguity in Nahua Ideology," in *Gender in Pre-Hispanic America*, ed. Cecelia Klein, 183–253 (Washington, D.C.: Dumbarton Oaks Research Library and Collection, 2001), and Sharisse D. McCafferty and Geoffrey G. McCafferty, "Alternative and Ambiguous Gender Identities in Postclassic Central Mexico," in *Que(e)rying Archaeology: The 15th Anniversary Gender Conference*, (Calgary: University of Calgary, 2009), 196–206.

11. See, for example, Michael J. Asplan, "Dwarfism as Indicative of Shaman Status," *Ancient American: Archaeology of the Americas before Columbus* 14, no. 89 (Dec. 2010): 41–44; and Carolyn E. Tate, "The Colossal Fetuses of La Venta and Mesoamerica's Earliest Creation Story," in *Imagining the Fetus: The Unborn in Myth, Religion, and Culture*, ed. Vanessa R. Sasson and Jane Marie Law (Oxford; New York: Oxford University Press, 2009). A report by the Mayo Clinic offers the following definition of dwarfism: "Dwarfism is short stature that results from a genetic or medical condition. Dwarfism is generally defined as an adult height of 4 feet 10 inches (147 centimeters) or less. The average adult height among people with dwarfism is 4 feet (122 cm)," Mayo Clinic Staff, "Diseases and Conditions: Dwarfism," last modified September 2014. http://www.mayoclinic.org/diseases-conditions/dwarfism/basics/definition/con-20032297.

12. Susan Milbrath, *A Study of Olmec Sculptural Chronology* (Washington, D.C.: Dumbarton Oaks, Trustees for Harvard University, 1979), 15; Karl A. Taube, "The Olmec Maize God: The Face of Corn in Formative Mesoamerica," *RES: Anthropology and Aesthetics* 29/30 (Spring–Autumn 1996): 53.

13. Karl A. Taube, *Olmec Art at Dumbarton Oaks* (Washington, D.C.: Dumbarton Oaks Research Library and Collection, 2004). Although Richard A. Diehl, *The Olmecs: America's First Civilization* (London: Thames & Hudson Ltd, 2004), Fig. 14, refers to the banded element supported by the dwarfs as "the upper jaw of the Olmec Dragon," most scholars recognize it as the Mesoamerican "sky band" motif. Another pair of similarly arranged dwarfs is found on San Lorenzo Monument 18 (Taube, *Olmec Art*, Fig. 32a).

14. Archaeologist James A. Doyle provides an enlightening discussion of the representation of dwarfs, mirror-bearers, and other typically diminutive figures seen throughout Maya courtly art in his conference paper "Un mundo desaparecido: Materiales perecedores y una pieza olvidada de los mayas de la época Clásica," presented at the Museo Nacional de Antropología, Mexico City, November 13, 2014.

15. Mary E. Miller and Karl Taube, *The Gods and Symbols of Ancient Mexico and the Maya: An Illustrated Dictionary of Mesoamerican Religion* (London: Thames & Hudson Ltd, 1993), 82.

16. See, for example, Stephen D. Houston, "The Name Glyph for Classic Maya Dwarfs," in *The Maya Vase Book: A Corpus of Rollout Photographs of Maya Vases*, vol. 3, eds. Barbara Kerr and Justin Kerr (New York: Kerr Associates, 1992), 546.

17. For example, see Asplan, "Dwarfism," 41–44.

18. In a recent publication, Carolyn E. Tate, *Reconsidering Olmec Visual Culture: The Unborn, Woman, and Creation* (Austin: University of Texas Press, 2012) reevaluates a number of Olmec sculptures previously referred to as dwarfs that she now believes represent large-scale depictions of embryos, fetuses, and newborns. If true, Tate contends that these pre- and postnatal sculptures would represent the oldest known examples of "medical illustration" in history. See also Gordon Bendersky, "Tlatilco Sculptures, Diprosopus, and the Emergence of Medical Illustration," *Perspectives in Biology and Medicine* 43, no. 4 (2000): 477–501.

19. Miller, "Dwarf Motif, 141.

20. Although Miller notes there are around one hundred distinct types of dwarfism, a recent report by the Mayo Clinic Staff, "Diseases and Conditions," identifies more than twice

that number. Significantly, this latter report groups dwarfism under the heading of "Diseases," defining it as "short stature that results from a genetic or medical condition."
21 Franciscan friar Bernardino Sahagún's *General History of the Things of New Spain*, ed. J.O. Anderson and Arthur C. Dibble (Santa Fe: School of American Research, 1950–82) is regarded as the most comprehensive colonial-era account of pre-contact Mexico. To read more about the native informants Sahagún employed in the compilation of his chronicle, see Jeanette Favrot Peterson, "The 'Florentine Codex': Imagery and the Colonial 'Tlacuilo'," in *The Work of Bernardino de Sahagún: Pioneer Ethnographer of Sixteenth-Century Aztec Mexico*, ed. J. Jorge Klor de Alva, H. B. Nicholson, and Eloise Quinones Keber (Albany: Institute for Mesoamerican Studies, University of Albany, and State University of New York, 1988), 272–293.
22 Michael E. Smith, *The Aztecs*, 2nd edition (Malden, MA: Blackwell Publishing, 2003), 15.
23 Eduardo Matos Moctezuma, *The Great Temple of the Aztecs: The Treasures of Tenochtitlan* (London: Thames and Hudson Ltd, 1988), 10.
24 Miller and Taube, *Gods and Symbols*, 82.
25 Bernal Díaz del Castillo, *The Conquest of New Spain*, trans. J.M. Cohen (New York: Penguin Books, 1963), 226–230.
26 Diego Durán, *The History of the Indies of New Spain*, trans. Doris Heyden (Norman: University of Oklahoma Press, 1994), 307.
27 For Spanish accounts of dwarfs and their role in the Aztec imperial court, see Díaz del Castillo, *Conquest of New Spain*, 226–227, 230; Durán, *History of the Indies*, 295–296, 307, 356, 466, 483–489; Sahagún, *Florentine Codex*, 1978, Bk. 3:46, fn. 13; 1979, Bk. 8:30, 49; and Hernán Cortés, *Letters from Mexico*, trans. A.R. Pagden (New York: Grossman Publishers, 1971), 111.
28 Cortés, *Letters from Mexico*, 111.
29 Durán, *History of the Indies*, 295.
30 For a fascinating overview of the role of dwarfs as exotic "Others" in the history of European explorations of the non-West, see Betty M. Adelson, *The Lives of Dwarfs: Their Journey from Public Curiosity toward Social Liberation* (Piscataway, NJ: Rutgers University Press, 2005).
31 Peter Furst, "The Olmec Were-Jaguar Motif in the Light of Ethnographic Reality," in *Dumbarton Oaks Conference on the Olmec*, ed. Elizabeth P. Benson (Washington, D.C.: Dumbarton Oaks Research Library and Collection, 1968), 143, fn. 1. For examples of ethnographic analogy in practice, see Terry Rugeley, ed., *Maya Wars: Ethnographic Accounts from Nineteenth-Century Yucatán* (Norman: University of Oklahoma Press, 2001); Alan R. Sandstrom, *Corn Is Our Blood: Culture and Ethnic Identity in a Contemporary Aztec Indian Village* (Norman: University of Oklahoma Press, 1991).
32 Burkhart, *Slippery Earth*, 5.
33 Again, I would argue that this is exactly what it seems medical historians and some art historians are trying to do in their analysis of disability: to make it static throughout history. Art historian George Kubler cautions, "Ethnological analogy is an imperfect form of induction"—one that ultimately distorts the past "by pinning or imposing whole clusters of late ethnohistorical detail upon isolated fragments of very ancient symbolic behavior . . ." George Kubler, *The Art and Architecture of Ancient America: The Mexican, Maya and Andean Peoples* (Middlesex, UK; New York: Penguin Books Ltd, 1984 [1962]), 166.
34 Richard Shiff, "Regarding Art and Art History: Unexplained," *Art Bulletin* XCIV, no. 3 (2012): 339–343.
35 Archaeologists William Haviland and Hattula Moholy-Nagy note: "If members of the important lineages tended to intermarry, then they would have constituted an endogamous caste. Hints to this effect are afforded by the presence of a dwarf in a North Acropolis tomb [at Tikal], the fact that certain vertebral anomalies as presently known were confined to the elite, and the fact that wormian bones—for which a genetically set potential may be involved—appear more often in these people than in others. Taken

together, these might suggest congenital anomalies showing up in a family line through time.... If the practice of polygyny was a royal prerogative, as this implies, we have found no archaeological evidence at Tikal to confirm it." William A. Haviland and Hattula Moholy-Nagy, "Distinguishing the High and Mighty from The Hoi Polloi at Tikal, Guatemala," in *Mesoamerican Elites: An Archaeological Assessment*, ed. Diane Z. Chase and Arlen F. Chase (Norman: University of Oklahoma Press, 1992), 58–59. It should be noted, however, that Haviland revealed to Miller ("Dwarf Motif," 141) that the supposed "dwarf" skeleton was actually found in a poor state of preservation and thus could not be confirmed as such.

36 Of course, part of the problem may be that we are seeking reliable proof rather than analyzing a historical form of disability representation. Factual or not, these representations reflect the society's beliefs about disability at the time of their creation. Thus the difficulty of the historian's task is that she must simultaneously keep in mind both their reality and hers, as well as where the two might overlap. In her analysis of the Spanish chronicles, historian Mercedes da la Garza perhaps clarifies this point better: "[The] colonial books ... are a most useful guide for the person attempting to reach an understanding of the codices and of the pre-Hispanic material remains, which are generally full of complex symbols. At the same time, the remains serve to confirm or invalidate the data in the written sources. Both sources are indispensable to a study of the pre-Hispanic peoples." Mercedes de la Garza, "Time and World in Maya and Nahuatl Thought," in *Cultural Relativism and Philosophy: North and Latin American Perspectives*, ed. Marcelo Dascal (Leiden: E. J. Brill, 1991), 108.

37 Art historian Esther Pasztory, "Still Invisible: The Problem of the Aesthetics of Abstraction for Pre-Columbian Art and Its Implications for Other Cultures," *RES: Anthropology and Aesthetics* 19/20 (1990/1991), 112, elaborates on the two distinct, yet complementary, approaches to the pre-Columbian past—the humanistic and scientific—by noting: "[The] scientific metaphor and model is very much the product of Western civilization and as such is not, by any means, value free. Nevertheless, the analysis of beings other than humans has allowed natural scientists a degree of detachment less available to anthropologists and historians."

38 See Murdy, "Congenital Deformities," 861–871. For an extensive reference list of images depicting the so-called "crouching chinless dwarf" motif, see Taube, *Olmec Art*, 57.

39 Matthew W. Stirling, "Stone Monuments of Rio Chiquito, Veracruz, Mexico," *Bureau of American Ethnology Bulletin* 157 (1955): 1–23.

40 Murdy, "Congenital Deformities," 861.

41 There is increasing evidence that the "were-jaguar" motif was a product of twentieth-century inference and speculation rather than an idea originally held by the Olmec. Circulated for many years among anthropologists working in the Gulf Coast region, it was successively defended and codified over the next several decades by a litany of noted scholars before being largely dismissed in the 1990s. Other influential early explications of the motif include George Metcalf and Kent Flannery, "An Olmec 'Were-Jaguar' from the Yucatan Peninsula," *American Antiquity* 31 (1967): 109–111; and Nanette Pyne, "The Fire-Serpent and Were-Jaguar in Formative Oaxaca: A Contingency Table Analysis," in *The Early Mesoamerican Village*, ed. Kent V. Flannery (New York: Academic Press, 1976), 272–280. For a critical refutation of the were-jaguar proposition, see Whitney Davis, "So-Called Jaguar-Human Copulation Scenes in Olmec Art," *American Antiquity* 43, no. 3 (1978): 453–456.

42 Murdy, "Congenital Deformities," 862.

43 Murdy, "Congenital Deformities," 863. Neural-tube defects result in impairments of a range of severity. For example, the incomplete fusion of the spinal column, spina bifida, is an impairment with which many people live; however, neural-tube defects may also result in much more serious issues, such as an underdeveloped brain and skull.

44 Murdy, "Congenital Deformities," 863; see also Coe, *Mexico*, 85.

45 Murdy, "Congenital Deformities," 862.

46 Martin Heidegger, "The Origin of the Work of Art," in *Poetry Language Thought*, trans. Albert Hofstadter (New York: Harper & Row, 1971), 40.
47 For an illuminating compendium on the historiography of New World archaeology, see Joanne Pillsbury, ed., *Past Presented: Archaeological Illustration in the Ancient Americas* (Washington, D.C.: Dumbarton Oaks Research Library and Collection, 2012).
48 "Jefferson's Excavation of a Burial Mound," *The Jefferson Monticello*, accessed June 1, 2015, https://www.monticello.org/site/research-and-collections/jeffersons-excavation-indian-burial-mound.
49 Archaeologist George Vaillant was the first to establish a broad chronology of ancient Mesoamerican cultures based on the use of stratigraphic data. For a discussion of Vaillant's findings in particular and stratigraphic analysis generally, see George Kubler, "Period, Style, and Meaning in Ancient American Art," *New Literary History* 1, no. 2 (Winter 1970): 142.
50 Kubler, *Art and Architecture*, 33.
51 See James Lockhart, "Introduction: Background and Course of the New Philology" (2007), http://whp.uoregon.edu/Lockhart/Intro.pdf.
52 For instance, as Linda Schele and Mary E. Miller describe: "By the end of the [nineteenth] century, the notion of a peaceful Maya civilization had begun to grow because little progress had been made in determining the meaning of the carved monuments and inscriptions . . . [These] inscriptions seemed to be abstract, beautiful texts to be admired but perhaps never to be read. The dates were clear evidence of the arithmetical and calendrical skills of the Maya, and this gave rise to the idea that they were philosophers of time and numbers." Linda Schele and Mary E. Miller, *The Blood of Kings: Dynasty and Ritual in Maya Art* (Fort Worth: Kimbell Art Museum, 1986), 20–21.
53 Kubler, *Art and Architecture*, 33.
54 Whereas the discourse concerning Mesoamerican visual culture by U.S. scholars frequently blends humanistic investigations with social-scientific concerns—a fact readily evidenced by the high number of advanced degrees awarded each year in the fields of pre-Columbian art history and archaeology—Latin American universities and scholarly publications, for example, frequently regard "pure" aesthetics as secondary to anthropological, ethnological, and nationalistic concerns. Indeed, within these latter nodes of pre-Columbian scholarship, the ontological "presence" of the object so popular within American and European studies is discussed far less often.
55 Gassaway, "Extraordinary Bodies," forthcoming.
56 Carolyn Tate and Gordon Bendersky, "Olmec Sculptures of the Human Fetus," Precolumbian Art Research Institute (PARI) Online Publications, no. 30 (1999), http://www.mesoweb.com/pari/publications/news_archive/30/olmec_sculpture.html (no pagination). See also Gordon Bendersky, "Tlatilco Sculptures, Diprosopus, and the Emergence of Medical Illustration," *Perspectives in Biology and Medicine* 43, no. 4 (2000): 477–501.
57 Tate and Bendersky, "Olmec Sculptures of the Human Fetus," no pagination.
58 Tate and Bendersky, "Olmec Sculptures of the Human Fetus," no pagination.
59 Tate and Bendersky, "Olmec Sculptures of the Human Fetus," no pagination.
60 Michel Foucault, "Nietzsche, Genealogy, History," in *The Foucault Reader*, ed. Paul Rainbow (New York: Pantheon Books, 1984), 88.
61 Tate, *Reconsidering Olmec Visual Culture*, 28.
62 George Kubler, "Science and Humanism among Americanists," in *The Iconography of Middle American Sculpture*, ed. Dudley T. Easby (New York: Metropolitan Museum of Art, 1973), 272–280.
63 Esther Pasztory, *Teotihuacan: An Experiment in Living* (Norman: University of Oklahoma Press, 1997), 72.
64 James Elkins, "The Question of the Body in Mesoamerican Art," *RES: Anthropology and Aesthetics* 26 (1994): 113–124.

5 Difference and disability in the photography of Margaret Bourke-White

Keri Watson

A seminal figure in the history of twentieth-century photography, Margaret Bourke-White is well known for her scenes of modern industry, of the Great Depression, and of political and social movements.[1] In 1929, she became the first staff photographer employed by *Fortune* magazine, covering Germany, Russia, and the Dust Bowl, and in 1936 she was one of the founding photographers of *Life* magazine, contributing the cover image to the inaugural issue in 1937.[2] Over the course of her career, she was active in the relief effort to aid those affected by the Spanish Civil War, documented the liberation of the Nazi concentration camps, photographed an imprisoned Mahatma Gandhi, and covered South African labor exploitation.[3] Committed to using her work for social justice, Bourke-White was a member of the American Artists' Congress, the American League for Peace and Democracy, and the American Youth Congress. Although her life and work have received significant attention, her photographs of people with disabilities have not.[4] This chapter examines Bourke-White's images of people with disabilities found in her 1937 bestselling photo-book *You Have Seen Their Faces*, as well as those taken in 1934 at Letchworth Village, a state residential institution for people with disabilities that operated in Thiells, New York between 1911 and 1996. I argue that these photographs, some of which feature impoverished people with visible physical disabilities and some of which depict institutionalized people with intellectual or developmental disabilities, both challenged the anxiety that surrounded the disabled body as signifier of the Great Depression and opened up discursive spaces for the deconstruction of raced, gendered, and abled identities.[5] By comparing Bourke-White's images to other photographs, films, and literature of the period, and by using disability studies to contextualize these images historically, I will demonstrate that her photographs of Letchworth Village provide sympathetic portraits that challenge the efficacy and beneficence of institutionalization, and that her photographs for *You Have Seen Their Faces* included images of people with physical disabilities in order to challenge the exclusivity of New Deal programs, to critique the moral imperative of work, and to argue for expanded federal protections that would address systemic oppression.

During the 1930s, people with disabilities faced segregation and oppression. Considered by the medical and political establishments as "unfit" for normal roles in society, disabled people were excluded from jobs provided by the New Deal's

Works Progress Administration (WPA) programs, which, according to the WPA Workers' Handbook, were reserved for "able-bodied" Americans who were "certified by a local agency."[6] "Ugly laws," which made it illegal for people with visible disabilities to be seen in public, were passed across the country, and many were not repealed until the mid-1970s.[7] Twenty-eight states adopted statutes that sought sterilization, marriage restriction, and institutionalization of the disabled, and eugenicists advocated euthanasia for disabled infants.[8] People with disabilities were systematically incarcerated, as well as subject to deportation under immigration law.[9] Following the increased demand for segregated housing brought on by prejudicial medical diagnoses and public discrimination, states began building residential institutions, such as Letchworth Village, at a rapid pace.

Established in 1911 as New York's preeminent school for the "feeble minded," Letchworth Village was a model example of the cottage plan.[10] Developed in the late nineteenth century, and often situated in a rural setting, the cottage, or colony, plan replaced the large multi-use asylum with a campus of smaller separate buildings that segregated patients by gender and type of disability. Letchworth's 2,084 acres were planned by leading landscape architect Frederick Law Olmsted, and its numerous dormitories, recreation spaces, and administrative buildings were designed in the neoclassical style.[11] Although conceived of as "a practical expression of the will of the people of the State of New York to lead in an enlightened policy of State care and training for mental defectives," it was the subject of controversy from the time of its opening.[12] The legislature never allocated enough funds to fully support the institution, and it was included in Albert Deutsch's 1948 harsh critique of residential institutions, *Shame of the States*.[13] Although reports of overcrowding and improper care of residents—including neglect, abuse, and rape—date to the 1920s, the New York State Office for People with Developmental Disabilities maintains that Letchworth Village was a progressive institution that provided a caring and sympathetic home to its patients.[14] Today, Letchworth has been replaced by the Hudson Valley regional office for the New York State Office for People with Developmental Disabilities, which provides community-based services to people with cognitive and physical impairments.

In 1932, Letchworth trustee Mary Averell Harriman hired Bourke-White, who was at the time well known for her commercial work, to photographically document the effectiveness of Letchworth's programs.[15] The board of directors, along with Superintendent Charles S. Little, advocated that with education and job training, many of Letchworth's patients could be rehabilitated and paroled, and Letchworth's promotional materials were designed to demonstrate the institution's beneficence, self-sufficiency, and success.[16] Bourke-White was commissioned to create photographs to illustrate and visually corroborate these assertions, and her images, primarily posed close-up portraits, appear to support the image the board was attempting to create, as they were featured in several of the institution's annual reports.[17] As sociologist and disability studies scholar Robert Bogdan has argued, Bourke-White's photographs "show clean, well-dressed inmates happily engaged in labor," which "promoted the message that if institutionalized, possibly dangerous and certainly incapable people with disabilities could be tamed, even trained."[18] Although quite different from Irving Haberman's sensational photographs of Letchworth taken in the late 1940s, which reveal naked and neglected patients crowded into day rooms, Bourke-White's photographs, which feature working girls and boys, seem to present the institution in a positive light, but if one looks closely, there is an element of subversion to her images.[19] I contend that her photographs of Letchworth Village offer important insights into the ways in which people with physical and cognitive disabilities were systematically marginalized and oppressed, as well as providing evidence of Bourke-White's commitment to social justice.[20]

Bourke-White's photograph of patients receiving new boots illustrates this point (fig. 5.1; 1933). Ostensibly staged to showcase the generosity of the state and the appreciation of Letchworth's grateful residents, the photograph appears to fulfill the needs of Letchworth's board of directors, but the way Bourke-White has lined up the girls exposes many large holes in the stockings they wear. Moreover, Bourke-White has pushed the girls close together so that they spill out of the photograph's cropped frame and hint at the fact that Letchworth was horribly overcrowded, the result of poor planning and increased demand. Although the girls smile, their dresses appear dated, dirty, and ill fitting, with uneven hems and makeshift belts made of ropes. Bourke-White's use of artificial lights increases the photograph's contrast, making every wrinkle in the rough-hewn texture of

Figure 5.1 Margaret Bourke-White, *Girls Lined Up without Shoes, Letchworth Village*, 1933. Photo © Estate of Margaret Bourke-White/Licensed by VAGA, New York, NY.

the girls' dresses visible. Moreover, Bourke-White has arranged the girls in three distinct lines, and the girls all have the same pageboy haircut, alluding to the regimented nature of institutional life. At Letchworth, patients, or inmates as they were called, were segregated by gender and degree of disability, ranging from "infirms" to "high-grades."[21] Bourke-White's photograph emphasizes the ways in which this partition further reinforced patients' conformance to medically prescribed, socially limited, and discredited roles.

Superintendent Little argued that it was critical that patients labeled "medium- or high-grades" spend the majority of their time working "a minimum of mental with a maximum of hand work."[22] Regardless of interest and ability, girls and women were expected to clean bathrooms, trim hedges, work in the laundry, and weave, whereas men and boys engaged in farming, animal husbandry, and mining.[23] Working conditions at Letchworth were strenuous, a point demonstrated by Bourke-White in a close-up of two men holding hoes over their shoulders (fig. 5.2; 1933). Shown walking shoulder to shoulder, the man on the right wears a slight grin, and a light breeze has tousled the other man's hair. At first glance the scene may appear cheerful, but on closer inspection the men's shirts are dirty and stained, and the field through which they walk appears rocky, barren, and difficult to traverse. Bourke-White's use of artificial lighting increases the photograph's contrast and emphasizes the contours of the landscape. Letchworth is sited along the Minisceongo Creek, which cuts the property in two. To the east is a ridge, and patients were responsible for farming this uneven terrain, where they grew

Figure 5.2 Margaret Bourke-White, *Men with Hoes, Letchworth Village*, 1933. Photo © Estate of Margaret Bourke-White/Licensed by VAGA, New York, NY.

86   *Keri Watson*

the majority of their own food and tended to chickens, pigs, and cows.[24] As Little argued, "There is no reason why men and women not needed in the routine of an institution should not be busy out-of-doors, raising everything, if possible, that is consumed by this segregated community."[25] In this they were successful, as Letchworth residents not only raised their own food, but they produced a surplus. According to the New York State Office of Mental Retardation and Developmental Disabilities, during the 1930s, Letchworth's farm produced over one million dollars' worth of crops.[26]

Rather than engage in play, educational activities, or meaningful vocational training, residents worked, without any compensation beyond room and board. In addition to agricultural tasks, jobs assigned to the male patients included loading thousands of tons of coal into storage facilities and building roads.[27] Young children were not released from hard manual labor either, as seen in a photograph of boys digging ditches (fig. 5.3; 1933).[28] The tools seem as large as some of the boys who struggle with the pickaxes and shovels, as they attempt to move the hard earth. Although Bourke-White was hired to create celebratory photographs of Letchworth and its residents, and some of her photographs feature images of patients in clean uniforms, many of her photographs, such as the ones discussed here, reveal Letchworth's less-than-ideal circumstances and dependence on unremunerated labor. Moreover, Bourke-White's photographs of Letchworth's residents expose the oppression of institutional life, betray her sympathy for her

Figure 5.3 Margaret Bourke-White, *Boys Digging in a Trench, Letchworth Village*, 1933. Photo © Estate of Margaret Bourke-White/Licensed by VAGA, New York, NY.

subjects as individuals, and differ considerably from other representations of people with disabilities common at that time.

During the 1930s, visual and popular culture reinforced discrimination against people with disabilities. Most notably, the photographs taken under the auspices of the Farm Security Administration ignored those with impairments.[29] Established in 1935 as the Resettlement Administration and reorganized in 1937 as the Farm Security Administration (FSA), this New Deal program was designed to help the country's poorest farmers, but its most lasting legacy is its extensive file of photographs amassed by Historical Section director Roy Stryker and taken by now-famous photographers, including Arthur Rothstein, Ben Shahn, Dorothea Lange, Walker Evans, and Marion Post Wolcott.[30] Their mission was to educate the nation about the rural poor and to promote New Deal programs, and as literary historian James Guimond notes in *American Photography and the American Dream*, "FSA photographers seemed to have avoided photographing people who looked strange or grotesque."[31] Even Lange, who had polio as a child, ignored the disabled, and often celebrated non-disabled bodies in her photographs, presenting viewers of *An American Exodus* (1939) with images of strong hands and brawny backs.[32] For instance, in *Spring Plowing*, the muscled naked back of a laborer fills the frame (fig. 5.4; 1937). His faceless body is illustrative of Lange's work, as she regularly presented an ennobled body part that represented the whole of the working class.[33] Typical of FSA photographs, this image exemplifies Stryker's mandate that his photographers present either views of women and children to elicit sympathy or of "men at work" that reinforced the effectiveness of WPA programs and supported the American ideologies of utilitarianism, liberal individualism, and "the moral imperative of work."[34]

Although people with disabilities were ignored by the FSA, popular films and literature often reinforced stereotypes by portraying people with disabilities as depraved villains or dependent victims.[35] For example, Lon Chaney starred in a series of roles in films, such as *The Blackbird* (1926) and *Tell It to the Marines* (1926), where bodily difference signaled interior derangement. Similarly, writers, including William Faulkner and John Steinbeck, used disabled characters as ciphers for economic hardship. As literary historian Thomas Fahy has argued, Depression-era writers made "the damaged body a metaphor for unbearable loss—a tangible sign for the eroding impact of unrelenting poverty, hunger, and unemployment."[36] In *The Sound and the Fury* (1929), Faulkner employed Benjy, a black man with an intellectual disability, to tell the story of the Compsons' demise.[37] Benjy's disability operates as a metaphor for the family's and the Old South's decline. As sociologist Allison C. Carey has argued, "The poor were associated with feeblemindedness," and "stereotypes of both feeblemindedness and racial and ethnic minorities combined to reinforce the negative image of the feebleminded person."[38] Drawing on the conflation of race, poverty, and disability in the popular imagination, in *Of Mice and Men* (1937) Steinbeck used Lennie, Crooks, Candy, and their disabilities as symbols of the nation's economic frustration. Steinbeck compared Lennie, a white developmentally disabled man, to an animal and described him as "dragging his feet a little, the way a bear drags his paws . . . [drinking] with long gulps,

Figure 5.4 Dorothea Lange, *Spring Plowing. Guadalupe, California. Cauliflower Fields*, March 1937. FSA-OWI Collection, Prints and Photographs Division, Library of Congress.

snorting into the water like a horse."[39] Lennie's disabled mind and animal-like body prevent him from attaining a better life. Similarly, Crooks, a black character with a stooped back (the result of being kicked by a horse when he was young), was limited by both physical disability and race, which kept him trapped in an oppressive environment, unable to move to another town and build a better life for himself.[40] Likewise, the elderly and disfigured white character Candy is isolated from the other workers because he is one-handed. His physical disability incites the fears of the other ranch hands, who see their usefulness and self-worth bound to their bodies.

Unlike Lange, Chaney, Faulkner, and Steinbeck, Bourke-White challenged the traditional politics of bodily display and provided viewers with sensitive portrayals of people with disabilities. Rather than following the formulas of the period, her photographs of Letchworth Village provide sympathetic portraits that critique institutionalization, and, as I will demonstrate, her photographs for *You Have Seen Their Faces* included images of people with physical disabilities, not as metaphors, but in order to challenge systemic oppression.

During the summer of 1936 and the spring of 1937, Bourke-White traveled with writer Erskine Caldwell and took photographs for one of the best-known and commercially successful photo-books of the Great Depression, *You Have Seen Their Faces*.[41] At the time of its publication, Caldwell was famous for two best-selling and controversial novels of life in the South, *Tobacco Road* (1932) and *God's Little Acre* (1933), but with *You Have Seen Their Faces*, he took "the camera to Tobacco Road . . . [to] show the authenticity of the people and conditions about which he wrote."[42] His agent, Maxim Lieber, introduced him to Bourke-White, then an associate editor and staff photographer for *Fortune* magazine, and they collaborated on the project, which for the next two decades was considered an exemplary photo-textual portrayal of rural poverty.[43] Dissatisfied with photo-books of the 1930s that culled their photographs from the FSA's file, Bourke-White and Caldwell wanted to reveal the devastating physical and emotional consequences of poverty. As literary scholar Natalie Wilson notes, "[Caldwell] harnessed the jolting power of the grotesque in a mode similar to Upton Sinclair and in doing so revealed that the politicized grotesque is conducive to fiction and non-fiction alike."[44] For her part, Bourke-White called upon her advertising background and photographic expertise to create compelling visuals. The photographs and text combine to illustrate how the capitalistic plantation system encouraged racial discord and endemic poverty, and it offers solutions, including interracial cooperation, education, unionization, and, most importantly, government-subsidized entitlements. Of its seventy-five photographs, ten feature people with visible disabilities, but whereas *You Have Seen Their Faces* has received significant scholarly attention, its inclusion of images of disability has not. Although *You Have Seen Their Faces* was a bestseller in 1937, since the 1960s, it has been derided as presenting a patronizing, clichéd view of the South.[45] As pointed out by literary historian Alan Trachtenberg in the preface to the 1995 reissue of the book, "Caldwell's prose now seemed simplistic and callous, and against the stern eye of Walker Evans, Bourke-White's photographs looked excessively theatrical and manipulative."[46] Although Bourke-White has been criticized for overdramatizing her subjects, her Letchworth images demonstrate her aptitude for subtlety and her ability to meet her patron's expectations while also imbuing her photographs with subversive connotations. Moreover, all photographs are constructions, and Bourke-White was not alone in her staging of documentary images, as it was a common practice at the time. In fact, as literary historians James Curtis and Miles Orvell have shown, Walker Evans, Arthur Rothstein, and Dorothea Lange all composed or manipulated their "documentary" photographs to varying degrees.[47] Comparing Bourke-White's photographs for *You Have Seen Their Faces* to her images of Letchworth Village reveals the ways in which she thoughtfully and consciously composed her images to convey a message. This is not to say that she did not take advantage of her position of power and privilege as a white, professional artist in order to take these photographs, only that through them, she was able to destabilize viewers' preconceptions about disabled people, as well as to draw attention to society's role in and responsibility for the care of others. In this, she was progressive for her time.

Evidencing her commitment to social justice, with *You Have Seen Their Faces*, Bourke-White demanded that viewers "see the faces" of the poor and to confront the economic hardships and physical suffering of the nation's most vulnerable citizens. As such, several of the photographs included in *You Have Seen Their Faces* feature people with visible physical disabilities. For instance, one of the last images in the book shows a woman holding a baby (fig. 5.5; 1937). It appears that she is missing her left leg, there is a mark of some sort on her right cheek, and the left side of her face appears pinched by paralysis. As she had in her Letchworth portraits, Bourke-White employed strobe lights to create harsh contrasts of dark and light that destabilize the environment and visually project the trauma of poverty and disability onto the subjugated bodies of the young woman and her child. Emphasizing the degree of the family's economic need, the ticking is coming out of the mattress and the clapboard wall is splintered. Everything in this richly textured image indicates extreme hardship, but the woman's love for her young child is evident, and Bourke-White has composed the image to evoke the Christian symbolism of the Madonna and Christ Child. The caption, "Happy Hollow, Georgia. 'Sometimes I tell my husband we couldn't be worse off if we tried,'" demonstrates the subject's lack of control over the circumstances of her life, even as it references the importance of the nuclear family group.[48] Rather than shy away from these types of images, Bourke-White focuses her lens on them and forces viewers to see her disabled subjects and to acknowledge the physical consequences of discriminatory policies.

Just as she constructed sympathetic portraits of Letchworth's residents, Bourke-White applied her extensive knowledge of innovative formal photographic techniques to create compelling images for *You Have Seen Their Faces*, as seen in this photograph of a young girl and her brother in Belmont, Florida (fig. 5.6; 1937). The boy reclines in a homemade rocking chair, his atrophied arms and legs peeking out of his too-big jeans and sweater. His eyes appear focused on the ceiling and his paralysis is emphasized by two flies that have alighted on his face. His sister stands behind him, her left hand resting protectively and lovingly on the back of his chair. The rough-hewn room is papered with newspapers, and the hem of a tattered curtain blows out the open, glassless window. The caption, ostensibly the voice of the little girl, informs the reader, "Little brother began shriveling up eleven years ago." Both a reference to the eroded land and a symbol for all who were broken by the southern agrarian system, the materiality of the little boy's disabled body reminds the viewer of the limits of governmental work-relief programs. To highlight the disparity between wealth and poverty and ability and disability, Bourke-White has orchestrated the scene to include emblems of

Figure 5.5 Margaret Bourke-White, *Happy Hollow, Georgia, You Have Seen Their Faces*, 1937. Photo © Estate of Margaret Bourke-White/Licensed by VAGA, New York, NY.

Figure 5.6 Margaret Bourke-White, *Belmont, Florida, You Have Seen Their Faces*, 1937. Photo © Estate of Margaret Bourke-White/Licensed by VAGA, New York, NY.

consumer culture. The walls of the room are papered with magazines and newspaper advertisements, creating a startling juxtaposition of disability to the slick world of advertising. As Bourke-White remembers:

> As we penetrated the more destitute regions of the South, I was stuck by the frequent reminders I found of the advertising world I thought I had left behind. Here the people really used the ads. They plastered them directly on their houses to keep the wind out. Some sharecropper shacks were wrapped so snugly in huge billboard posters advertising magic painkillers and Buttercup Snuff that the home itself disappeared from sight.[49]

Hawking products such as Camel Cigarettes, Prince Albert Pipe Tobacco, and cure-alls like 666, Bromo Quinine, and Grove's Chill Tonic, these signs are also reminders of consumerism, of the medicalization of disability, and of the pharmaceutical industrial complex. The result of using these questionable remedies is seen in the accompanying images that show malnourished and disabled bodies.

Take, for instance, this image of an elderly couple and young child (fig. 5.7; 1937). The man holds a walking stick, possibly alluding to blindness, and sits above and to the right of a woman and small boy. The woman, barefoot and wearing a tattered dress, has a tumor protruding from the left side of her neck, and the young boy, clothed only in an oversized shirt, rubs his eyes, perhaps indicating trachoma, or sandy blight. Trachoma, which was common in impoverished communities during the 1930s, is a bacterial infection that causes blindness. Pushed to the foreground and filling the frame of the darkened doorway, the family group is captioned, "Sweet Fern, Arkansas. 'Poor people get passed by.'" Although the New Deal may have overlooked these families, Bourke-White did not. As she wrote in her autobiography, "Here were faces engraved with the very paralysis of despair. These were faces I could not pass by."[50] Through dramatic lighting and framing, Bourke-White brings the viewers' attention to this iconic family grouping. These figures are without agency. None of them are able-bodied; they are either old and disabled or young and dependent, but together they exemplify the power of bodily representations to expose the physical effects of poverty compounded by disability. The accompanying caption, constructed to exaggerate their desperation, exposes the reality of lived experience, and appeals to President Franklin D. Roosevelt's policies of relief, recovery, and reform.

Although the President's New Deal was designed to assist the needy, strengthen the economy, and eradicate poverty and unemployment, people with disabilities were systematically ignored. According to the New Deal, "Social programs should enhance the well-being and security of the entire national community rather than simply providing charity to the needy."[51] Despite the rhetoric, New Deal programs excluded people with disabilities, and although President Roosevelt had impaired mobility due to childhood polio, he kept his disability largely hidden from public view except as testament to his ability to overcome adversity.[52] The physicality of the body and its ability to move were paramount during the Great Depression, as millions of farmers were forced from their homes to find either temporary

SWEETFERN, ARKANSAS. "Poor people get passed by."

Figure 5.7 Margaret Bourke-White, *Sweet Fern, Arkansas, You Have Seen Their Faces*, 1937. Photo © Estate of Margaret Bourke-White/Licensed by VAGA, New York, NY.

jobs as migrant workers or to secure employment as factory workers in cities. Bourke-White's photographs for *You Have Seen Their Faces* put social inequality in material terms by including images of bodies disfigured by poverty, those unable to move or to work. Through their inclusion, she confronts the national anxiety exacerbated by the Great Depression and challenges the moral imperative of work, as well as the normalization of economic and physical independence as appropriate gauges of personhood. Although her photographs may seem dramatic, contrived, or even exploitive by today's standards, she focused on people with disabilities at a time when many, including the photographers of the federally sponsored FSA, ignored them. Rather than taking advantage of her subjects as many scholars have argued, I contend that she used her photographs to magnify the limits of social policy and to illustrate the ways in which poverty is written on and through the body.[53]

In 1933 Bourke-White was hired to create promotional materials for Letchworth Village. She completed the commission to the satisfaction of her patron, but she also managed to include a subtle critique of the institution and its policies. Just as she imbued these images with subversive connotations, she emphasized the corporeality of her subjects in *You Have Seen Their Faces* to emphasize the need for expanded federal relief programs. During a period when people with disabilities were consistently hidden from public view, when even the president of the United States concealed his disability, Bourke-White put people with disabilities front and center and showed them as daughters and sons, as mothers and fathers, as sisters and brothers, as caregivers and family members, and as part of an interdependent community of people worthy of consideration. As a pioneer in photojournalism and an advocate of the rhetorical power of the photo-essay to incite social reform, Bourke-White's work has had a profound influence on the history of photography and opened the door for others, including W. Eugene Smith, Stephen Shames, and Danny Lyon, to focus their lenses on those marginalized by normative culture.

Notes

1. S. L. Harrison, *Twentieth Century Journalists: America's Opinion Makers* (New York: University Press of America, 2002), 176. Margaret Bourke-White has been the subject of several monographs, biographies, and an autobiography. See: Susan G. Rubin, *Margaret Bourke-White: Her Pictures Were Her Life* (New York: Abrams, 1999); Vicki Goldberg, *Margaret Bourke-White: A Biography* (New York: Harper & Row, 1986), and Margaret Bourke-White, *Portrait of Myself* (New York: Simon and Schuster, 1963).
2. Sean Callahan, *Margaret Bourke-White: Photographer* (Boston: Bulfinch Press, 1998), 11 and 19.
3. Goldberg, *Biography*, 158–159 and 208.
4. For more on Bourke-White's images of poverty see Maren Stange, *Symbols of Ideal Life: Social Documentary Photography in America, 1890–1950* (Cambridge: Cambridge University Press, 1989); Winfried Fluck, "Poor Like Us: Poverty and Recognition in American Photography," *Amerikastudien/American Studies* 55, no. 1 (2010): 63–93; Robert E. Snyder, "Erskine Caldwell and Margaret Bourke-White: *You Have Seen Their Faces*," *Prospects* 11 (1986): 393–405; Tom Jacobs, "Poeticizing the Political Image: Caldwell, Bourke-White, and the Recasting of Phototextual Expression," in

Reading Erskine Caldwell: New Essays, ed. Robert L. McDonald (Jefferson: McFarland and Company, 2006), 92–113; and Carol Shloss, "The Privilege of Perception," *Virginia Quarterly Review* 56, no. 4 (1980): 596–611. For more on representations of disability in visual culture see: Robert Bogdan, *Picturing Disability: Beggar, Freak, Citizen, and Other Photographic Rhetoric* (Syracuse: Syracuse University Press, 2012); Ann Millett-Gallant, *The Disabled Body in Contemporary Art* (New York: Palgrave Macmillan, 2010); Rosemarie Garland-Thomson, *Extraordinary Bodies: Figuring Physical Disability in American Culture and Literature* (New York: Columbia University Press, 1997), and *Staring: How We Look* (New York: Oxford University Press, 2009).

5 Although Bogdan discusses Bourke-White's Letchworth photographs, he does not discuss her images for *You Have Seen Their Faces*.
6 Works Progress Administration, *WPA Workers' Handbook* (1936).
7 Paul K. Longmore and David Goldberger, "The League of the Physically Handicapped and the Great Depression: A Case Study in the New Disability History," *Journal of American History* 87, no. 3 (December 2000): 894.
8 Longmore and Goldberger, "League of the Physically Handicapped," 894.
9 Allison C. Carey, *On the Margins of Citizenship: Intellectual Disability and Civil Rights in Twentieth-century America* (Philadelphia: Temple University Press, 2009), 52.
10 James W. Trent, Jr., *Inventing the Feeble Mind: A History of Mental Retardation in the United States* (Berkeley: University of California Press, 1994), 185.
11 Albert Deutsch, *The Shame of the States* (New York: Harcourt Brace, 1948), 132; and Trent, *Inventing the Feeble Mind*, 102.
12 Trent, *Inventing the Feeble Mind*, 102.
13 *Annual Report of the Board of Managers of Letchworth Village*, vol. 13 (1922): 10; Deutsch, *The Shame of the States*, 132–134; and Trent, *Inventing the Feeble Mind*, 258.
14 Allan Goldstein, "Letchworth's True Story on Display at King's Daughters Library this Month," *Rockland County Times*, accessed March 15, 2012. http://www.rocklandtimes.com/2012/03/15/letchworths-true-story-on-display-at-kings-daughters-library-this-month/
15 Correspondence Margaret Bourke-White to Franklin Kirkbride, January 24, 1933, Margaret Bourke-White Papers, Box 26, Folder "Letchworth Village," Special Collections Research Center, Syracuse University Libraries; and Trent, *Inventing the Feeble Mind*, 225.
16 Trent, *Inventing the Feeble Mind*, 88.
17 Bourke-White was commissioned to take photographs for the 1933 annual report, but her photographs were also included in the twenty-sixth, thirtieth, and fortieth annual reports. Margaret Bourke-White Papers, Box 26, Folder "Letchworth Village," Special Collections Research Center, Syracuse University Libraries. See also: Bogdan, *Picturing Disability*, 69; and Trent, *Inventing the Feeble Mind*, 225.
18 Bogdan, *Picturing Disability*, 71.
19 Irving Haberman (1916–2003) was a well-known twentieth-century photojournalist who worked for the CBS News Agency. His photographs of Letchworth Village first appeared in the New York daily *PM* before they were republished in Albert Deutsch's *Shame of the States* (1948). See Trent, *Inventing the Feeble Mind*, 226.
20 John Edwin Mason, "Picturing the Beloved Country: Margaret Bourke-White, 'Life' Magazine, and South Africa, 1949–1950," *Kronos* 38 (2012): 154–176.
21 Trent, *Inventing the Feeble Mind*, 88.
22 Charles S. Little, "Letchworth Village: The Newest State Institution for the Feebleminded and Epileptic," *The Survey* 27 (1912): 1872.
23 Trent, *Inventing the Feeble Mind*, 110.
24 Little, "Letchworth Village," 1869.
25 Finding Guide, Letchworth Village Records, Rare Book and Manuscript Library, Columbia University Libraries Archival Collections, MS #0771.

26 Finding Guide, Letchworth Village Records, Rare Book and Manuscript Library, Columbia University Libraries Archival Collections, MS # 0771.
27 Trent, *Inventing the Feeble Mind*, 103 and 109.
28 The thirteenth annual report lists the number of patients admitted that year. Out of 506 people, 317 were between the ages of five and sixteen, and 11 were under the age of five years. *Annual Report of the Board of Managers of Letchworth Village* 13 (Albany: J.B. Lyons Company, 1922), 15.
29 An exception is Ben Shahn's *A One-Legged Man Sitting in Front of a Building, Natchez, Mississippi, October 1935*. Still, of the some 160,000 photographs in the Farm Security Administration's collection, very few feature people with visible physical disabilities.
30 Mary Jane Appel, "The Duplicate File: New Insights into the FSA," *Archives of American Art Journal* 54, no. 1 (2015): 6. The scholarship on FSA photography is extensive. For an overview see Roy Emerson Stryker, *In This Proud Land: America 1935–1943 as Seen in the FSA Photographs* (Greenwich, CT: New York Graphic Society, 1973); Cara A. Finnigan, *Picturing Poverty: Print Culture and FSA Photographs* (Washington D.C.: Smithsonian Books, 2003); Carl Fleischhauer and Beverly Brannan, *Documenting America* (Berkeley: University of California Press, 1988); William Stott, *Documentary Expression and Thirties America* (Chicago: University of Chicago Press, 1973); James Curtis, *Mind's Eye, Mind's Truth: FSA Photography Reconsidered* (Philadelphia: Temple University Press, 1989); James Guimond, *American Photography and the American Dream* (Chapel Hill: University of North Carolina Press, 1991); John Raeburn, *A Staggering Revolution: A Cultural History of Thirties Photography* (Urbana: University of Illinois Press, 2006); and Paula Rabinowitz, *They Must Be Represented: The Politics of Documentary* (New York: Verso, 1994).
31 Guimond, *American Photography*, 120.
32 Linda Gordon, *Dorothea Lange: A Life Beyond Limits* (New York: W.W. Norton & Company, 2011), 4.
33 Dorothea Lange was one of the Farm Security Administration's most prolific photographers. Her photographs, including *Hoe Culture, Aniston, Alabama*, 1936, and *Migratory Cotton Picker, Eloy, Arizona*, 1940, zoom in on workers' hands, whereas her *Feet of Negro Cotton Hoer Near Clarksdale, Mississippi*, 1937, and *Sharecropper Boy, Chesnee, South Carolina*, 1937, feature workers' feet.
34 Garland-Thomson, *Extraordinary Bodies*, 41.
35 Longmore and Goldberger, "League of the Physically Handicapped," 895.
36 Thomas Fahy, "Worn, Damaged Bodies in Literature and Photography of the Great Depression," *Journal of American Culture* 26, no. 1 (2003): 15.
37 William Faulkner, *The Sound and the Fury*, 1929 (New York: Random House, 1984).
38 Carey, *On the Margins*, 64.
39 John Steinbeck, *Of Mice and Men*, 1937 (New York: Bantam Books, 1955), 2, 3.
40 Steinbeck, *Of Mice and Men*, 73.
41 For literature on *You Have Seen Their Faces* see James Goodwin, "The Depression Era in Black and White: Four American Photo-Texts," *Criticism: A Quarterly for Literature and the Arts* 40, no. 20 (1998): 273–307; Carol Shloss, *In Visible Light: Photography and the American Writer, 1840–1940* (New York: Oxford University Press, 1987), 181–187; Raeburn, *A Staggering Revolution*, 207–226; Guimond, *American Photography and the American Dream*, 117–120; Jeff Allred, *American Modernism and Depression* (New York: Oxford University Press, 2010), 59–91; Bill Mullen and Sherry Lee Linkon, *Radical Revisions: Rereading 1930s Culture* (Urbana: University of Illinois Press, 1996); Jane M. Rabb, *Literature and Photography Interactions, 1840–1990: A Critical Anthology* (Albuquerque: University of New Mexico Press, 1995); and Robert E. Snyder, "Erskine Caldwell and Margaret Bourke-White: *You Have Seen Their Faces*," *Prospects* 11 (1986): 248–281.
42 Bourke-White, *Portrait of Myself*, 113.

43 John Rogers Puckett, *Five Photo-Textual Documentaries from the Great Depression*, (Ann Arbor: UMI Research Press, 1984), 23–24.
44 Natalie Wilson, "Social Injustice Embodied: Caldwell and the Grotesque," in *Reading Erskine Caldwell: New Essays*, ed. Robert L. McDonald (Jefferson: McFarland and Company, 2006), 126.
45 Stott, *Documentary Expression and Thirties America*, 220, and Shloss, "The Privilege of Perception," 601–602.
46 Alan Trachtenburg foreword to Erskine Caldwell and Margaret Bourke-White, *You Have Seen Their Faces* (Athens: University of Georgia Press, 1989), vii.
47 James Curtis, *Mind's Eye, Mind's Truth: FSA Photography Reconsidered* (Philadelphia: Temple University Press, 1989); Errol Morris, *Believing Is Seeing (Observations on the Mysteries of Photography* (New York: Penguin Press, 2011); and Miles Orvell, *The Real Thing: Imitation and Authenticity in American Culture, 1880–1940* (Chapel Hill: University of North Carolina Press, 1989).
48 Happy Hollow is a real place located about thirty miles northeast of Atlanta. Caldwell and Bourke-White, *You Have Seen Their Faces* (New York: Modern Age Books, 1937).
49 Bourke-White, *Portrait of Myself*, 127.
50 Bourke-White, *Portrait of Myself*, 111.
51 Carey, *On the Margins*, 94.
52 Longmore and Goldberger, "The League of the Physically Handicapped," 893.
53 Scholars who have argued that Bourke-White exploited her subjects include Stott, *Documentary Expression and Thirties America*, 220, and Shloss, "The Privilege of Perception," 601–602.

6 Representing disability in post–World War II photography

Timothy W. Hiles

In the post–World War II era, photographic representation of individuals with disabilities shifted markedly from portrayals that reinforced hierarchical preconceptions and stereotypes to those that questioned the dominance of the representative "normal." Accompanying this change was a departure from representing disabled people within a visual construct of medical anomaly to presenting them as provocateurs through which to question the prevailing structure. In concert with increased photographic awareness of other prejudicial constructs in American society, these images represent a broader shift in perception that increasingly took into account individual experience and usurped a predetermined theatrical narrative. As disabilities studies scholar Rosemarie Garland-Thomson has demonstrated, photographic content has significant impact on our perception of disabled people.[1] This study, which is steeped in art historical methodology, will focus on how formal characteristics—the visual language used in presentation—impact the reading of content. Specifically, it will identify three distinct visual constructs that embody isolation, integration, and ultimately an expansive view of the disabled "other," which coincides with an increased awareness of difference in what has become known as the Civil Rights Era.

The first construct embodies separation, which contributed to a hierarchical structure that sustained the privileged position of the abled normal. In the Foucauldian sense, reality here is submerged within an isolating, socially constructed visual language.[2] The second construct discards these traditional portrayals of disability and represents a more inclusive view of disabled individuals within a normative structure. The result is a more egalitarian representation of the disabled "other" but one that continues to sustain the structural hierarchy of the collective normal. The third construct redefines normal by representing difference as a legitimate aspect of society. This construct presents disabled people as provocateurs through which to question the dominance of the representative normal, expanding our understanding of disability beyond the medical model of deficiency. By portraying the disabled individual as a real and integral part of a multifaceted society, rather than as an artificially constructed outsider, these photographs contributed to an expanded understanding of society whereby disability becomes a part of a more inclusive normal. Together, these visual constructs can be interpreted as representing a progression of sorts toward a more inclusive presentation of people with disabilities. As we will see, however, embedded within each of these constructs lies a complex play of cultural biases that, for better or worse, continue to represent and affect our perception of disabled people.

Isolating the "other" through visual structure

In 1977, Robert Bogdan and Douglas Biklen, scholars in the emerging field of disability studies, recognized the concept of disability as largely a social construct, rather than as a signifier of an objective state of impairment.[3] They brought to the fore prejudicial and discriminatory treatment and called attention to certain assumptions and stereotypes that had relegated those outside the privileged state of physical "normal" to a station of inferiority.[4] Photographs of disabled people in the decades immediately following World War II provide visual cues that support Bogdan and Biklen's premise that preconceptions and stereotypes encouraged separation and unequal treatment of those who were physically or mentally outside of the perceived mainstream. The visual language used in these photographs can be understood in terms of linguist and semiotician Ferdinand de Saussure's relational concept of binary opposition, a structuralist notion whereby the conventional meaning of a concept is determined by its relation to other concepts. In this visual construct, the concept of disability is defined by its distinction from its opposite, or what was considered the able-bodied normal.[5] Of equal importance to our comprehension of this construct is the philosopher Jacques Derrida's expanded understanding of oppositions as inherently carrying an encoded hierarchy. If normal, for example, defines itself in opposition to abnormal, it would also assume a hierarchy where the group doing the defining (the "normal") devalues the "other." This devaluing, according to disability studies scholars Mairian Corker and Tom Shakespeare, is essential to our understanding of the hierarchical social construct concerning disability and its visual representation.[6] Also important to our comprehension of these photographs is a recognition of what philosopher Michel Foucault termed "bio-power," whereby the established top of the hierarchical structure, the average normal, accounts for aberrations by defining them as problems and categorizing them, a process that sustains the "normal" by subjugating the "abnormal."[7] Photographs, in this sense, can legitimize that subjugation by substantiating it through the illusion of verity—"real" depictions that actually adhere to predetermined notions of disabled people.

Photographs within this construct portray disabled individuals in a manner that sustained their status as "other" and reinforced the prevalent perspective of the abled "normal." Ralph Morse's photographs for a 1951 *Life* magazine article on P.S. 135, a Manhattan school developed specifically to help integrate children with cerebral palsy, are a case in point as they contribute to a singular perception of separation rather than integration.[8] In the initial uncaptioned, full-page image that appears to illustrate the article title, "Cerebral Palsy: Once Considered Helpless, Its Victims Now Can Make Adjustment to Normal Life," a darkened form dominates the photograph; his tense body is silhouetted by the light of the window before him (fig. 6.1). Emphasized is not his face, which would undoubtedly

Figure 6.1 Ralph Morse, *Nine-Year-Old Neil Koenig, Who Has Cerebral Palsy, Walking Unassisted*, 1950. Published in *Life* magazine, April 30, 1951, p. 85. Getty Images.

individualize and humanize him, but his exaggerated arching back, unstable bent legs, and straining arms and hands—those characteristics that visually define him as "abnormal." The low angle of the camera and straining limbs exaggerate and distort his form to the point where it becomes nearly overwhelming, reminiscent of those iconic monsters that appeared in films of the 1930s and '40s.[9] The image, coupled with the article's emphasis on adjusting to "normal life," establishes the individual shown as an outsider, someone who is visually abnormal. The threatening nature of the image is particularly noteworthy, for here the different body becomes an oddity, in a sense, an aberration that threatens the identity of the constructed modern world based upon normalization.[10] Through compositional devices, the viewer becomes an observer from a particular pre-constructed "normal" perception. The photograph, to make a verbal analogy, presents the individual as a largely preconceived and well-defined noun rather than a living and transitional verb. The child with cerebral palsy, nine-year-old Neil Koenig, becomes merely a tool in a trope.

Of course, the verity inherent in the photographic process plays an essential role in our reading of this image. The photograph does, after all, capture a visual moment in time, and thus there is always an element of reality in it. But in our analysis, it is important to recognize that what we see is not the disabled individual, but a photograph of the disabled individual, a visual construction that fulfills the photojournalist's assignment to distinguish the normal from the abnormal, and appeals to our predetermined desire to define, categorize, and subjugate. To continue the verbal analogy, the photograph here becomes a meaningful opposition noun that sustains our understanding of normal while negating the most significant element of human identity—the predicate, or moment of individual becoming. Living is removed as the individual becomes a simulacrum of reality, merely an image through which to reinforce the collective normal.

This objectification and subjugation is more literally evident in an untitled photograph by Morse from this 1951 article that shows, according to the caption, "normal pupils" watching "their handicapped classmates" through a one-way window (fig. 6.2).[11] Here, the viewer's perspective is that of the "normal" children. We see the backs of their heads, as though we are in a theater seat, as they watch the children with cerebral palsy. By virtue of this viewpoint, we become a part of the collective normal, draped in a unifying darkness while watching a theatrical presentation of the other, or subnormal, play out before us. The visual effect is that of sustaining the hierarchical role of "normal" children by allowing them to become accustomed to those who are categorized as "crippled," thus undergirding the hierarchical structure implied in the article, which states: "The teachers do want the children to realize that they may never be quite like other kids. Consequently, most of P.S. 135 is occupied by normal schoolchildren who mingle and form friendships with their less fortunate classmates. . . ."[12]

My purpose here is not to belittle the good intentions of those who sought to integrate P.S. 135; indeed, its establishment was to address concerns by many interested citizens, including parents, therapists, and doctors, who sought to consider issues such as those expressed by Dr. William Cooper, an orthopedic surgeon

Disability in post–World War II photography 103

Figure 6.2 Ralph Morse, *Normal Pupils Watching Their Handicapped Classmates through a One-Way Window*, 1950. Published in *Life* magazine, April 30, 1951, p. 89. Getty Images.

involved with the Cerebral Palsy Institute in 1950, who acknowledged: "We often forget that we are dealing with people and not merely an aggregate of disabilities or deformities. These children have ideals and emotions like other children, and like them need a sense of self-worth and accomplishments."[13] Notwithstanding the altruism of this expanded approach toward disability, it is important to consider the point made by disability theorist Chris Drinkwater, who demonstrated that inclusion may also be seen as an aspect of maintaining a power structure through increasing normalization, and homogenization, reflecting a broader desire to fix society.[14] While isolation, the traditional manner of handling abnormalities, sanitized society through removal, integration, despite its benevolence, can be seen as extending a power structure through absorption. This theory is supported by these photographs, which contain a visual language that maintains traditional structural isolation and sustains the hierarchy of the normal through separation from the abnormal.

In a post-war society increasingly driven by the photographic image, visual language played an important role in reinforcing cultural stereotypes. As

Garland-Thomson has noted, photographs both recapitulate and perpetuate cultural ideas about disability.[15] The attendant consequences of sustaining such a power structure were recognized by Foucault, who theorized that subjugated individuals tend to identify with the social structure constructed by the normal.[16] Ironically, while the article on P.S. 135 attempts to explain the benefits of integration, the photographs remain steeped in a visual language of separation. As psychologist Beatrice White recognized nine years later in her groundbreaking study *Physical Disability—A Psychological Approach*, such separation, even within integration, encouraged the binary oppositions of normal and abnormal, "good and bad," leading to feelings of inferiority and difference and contributing to delayed emotional and intellectual development.[17] The psychological effect of this type of self-awareness on the disabled child was vividly described by contemporary writer Raymond Goldman, who had experienced the socio-psychological effects of polio:

> Now I became fully aware of the fact that I was not like other children. I knew now that legs should be stout and shapely and that mine were skinny and deformed. I knew that I should walk and could not. I learned indeed that I was a cripple, a pariah among the strong and straight, an object of pity to grown-ups and of scorn to children.[18]

The contribution of photography to this phenomenon is particularly noteworthy, for the viewer has a propensity to see it as truth. It therefore can be a powerful representation of cultural bias by representing it as reality. The visual language of Morse's photographs reinforces the social construct about which Bogdan and Biklen were so concerned and, indeed, reveals to some extent a hidden aspect of sincere attempts at integration. Despite efforts to normalize, distinctions become more salient, particularly through the visual image which either substantiates a pre-existing stereotype or, in some cases, creates an entirely new identity that conforms to preconceptions.[19]

Visual language: integrating the "other" and the open form

In 1956, Australian novelist Alan Marshall, who had contracted infantile paralysis (poliomyelitis) at a young age, made this astute observation about social constructs: "Suffering because of being crippled is not for you in your childhood; it is reserved for those men and women who look at you."[20] Marshall, as a young child, had accepted his difference as reality. Having friends place him in a pram and pull him along roads was as natural as helping a younger child over a fence. Being "crippled" was an objective state. "Suffering" was equated with this state, not by the young Alan, but by adults, who problematized his condition. He came to be defined by stereotypes, assumptions, and pre-existing perceptions associated with the problem. Marshall's comments reflect an increasingly acute awareness of the negative effects of these preconceptions. That same year, in a 1956 report on the Cerebral Palsy Units, of which P.S. 135 in Manhattan was one, it was determined that inclusion and integration had been a benefit not only to the "handicapped" child, but also to the "non-handicapped" child, who became accepting of difference beyond classification within a simple rubric of ability and behavior, and aware that each child had a role to play as one among many.[21] By the mid-1950s, individual perception beyond stereotypical representation also became an important aspect of photographs of disabled individuals. This move toward an independent language is part of a larger avant-garde trend in photographic imagery that might be identified as a more open form of visual normality that invites a dialogue with the viewer. This open form avoided the encoded message of difference that had depended upon theatrical representations. It relied less on a moment of recognition and pre-established meaning and more on the banality of everyday vision.

Within the broader field of photography, the open-form photograph became more prominent after the *Family of Man* exhibition of 1955, the culmination of the more direct, culturally constructed image. This momentous, era-defining exhibition, held at New York's Museum of Modern Art, presented more than five hundred photographs that conveyed a single editorial theme of international unity—what its curator Edward Steichen would describe as "a mirror of the essential oneness of mankind throughout the world."[22] The exhibition was a significant attempt to help heal a world torn by two world wars. Henceforth, however, many photographers began to reject the notion of photographing to fit someone else's editorial construction, and instead emphasized their unique individual contribution to a growing visual language. The most notable example of this is apparent in the work of Robert Frank, who departed from a predetermined editorial narrative structure and presented instead a more personalized approach to photography. In his book, *The Americans* (1959), Frank presented images that were less theatrical, and stereotypical, in nature.[23] The initial reaction to these photographs is banality—one has difficulty finding a cultural reference point from which to read the images. Pointedly, these photographs have become associated with novelist and poet Jack Kerouac and the Beat movement for their lack of a definitive predetermined representation or narrative, relying instead upon an ever-becoming moment of transition that defies stereotypes or editorial preconceptions.

In images of disabled people published within a photo-journalistic context, this form represents a shift away from predetermined meaning and theatricality and presents new opportunities for visual integration. Early examples can be seen in Cornell Capa's images that accompanied a 1954 *Life* magazine article entitled "Retarded Children," which verbally describes attempts to integrate the "helpless and submerged population of the mentally retarded."[24] Although earnest in its stated intention to have an "open discussion," the verbal essay portrays disabled children, as did the article on P.S. 135, conventionally as a problem to be solved, rather than as difference to be embraced. Visually, however, Capa departs from the structure of Morse by presenting photographs that belie the notion of problem and embody a distinct integration where individuals are thoroughly absorbed within the hierarchical normal rather than used as a binary prop to define it through opposition. In one image by Capa from this 1954 article, a disabled boy holds the hand of his brother as the two walk comfortably across an expanse of grass (fig. 6.3). Pictorially, little

Figure 6.3 Cornell Capa, *Sunday Visit*, published in *Life* magazine, October 18, 1954, p. 121. Magnum Photos.

distinction is discernable between the disabled boy and his brother. The distance from which they were photographed deemphasizes anomalies and instead contributes to a sense of unity and harmony in the park-like setting. Those differences in dress and mannerisms that are apparent could easily be attributed to age and maturity. It is only after reading the caption that one begins to attribute those differences to disability. In another photograph by Capa for the same article, a disabled child is shown with her family at the dinner table (fig. 6.4). Photographed from a high vantage point, she is compositionally assimilated into the family unit with no perceptible dissimilarity between the child and other family members. Unlike the photographs by Morse, references to stereotypical, predetermined structures are here avoided. The images appear uneventful, lacking a theatrical punch. Visually, the subjects of the article are absorbed into the mainstream, or "normal," through both content and form. In fact, one would be hard-pressed to make a distinction between Capa's image of the dinner table and other images of a family around the table, such as a photograph by Myron H. Davis of a family at a lunch table published in *Life* earlier that same year.[25] In both instances, the family is integrated through a composition that brings them together rather than isolates individuals. The commonality apparent in these compositions is accentuated if one compares the images to the language of their captions, which maintains a verbal differentiation through

Figure 6.4 Cornell Capa, *Eileen and Her Family*, published in *Life* magazine, October 18, 1954, p. 124. Magnum Photos.

binary oppositions by describing differences between the "normal" and constructed "abnormal" child. Under the image of the brothers walking is the description "Sunday Visit by Joseph (left), 15, one of Charles's three normal brothers, enables him to enjoy a ramble across Letchworth Village's 2,100-acre grounds"; while the caption below the dinner-table photograph states "Eileen and her family eat dinner together. Eileen, sitting next to her normal sister Judy, 11, can use knife and fork. But meat must be precut for her."[26] In both instances, clear verbal distinctions are made between the disabled child and his or her "normal" sibling. We are directed verbally by a predetermined code as to how to read the photograph in contradistinction to Capa's integrative visual language. Charles is distinguished from his "normal" brother, who "enables" him to enjoy a ramble across the grounds. Eileen is differentiated from her "normal" sister by pointing out that her meat must be precut for her.

The effectiveness of this verbal distortion of visual language is readily apparent in Capa's photograph from the same article of Eileen sitting on her bed, staring up at the heavens in what appears to be a moment lost in thought (fig. 6.5). Visually, one might interpret this image as representing a theatrical moment of sanity and conviction. This reading, however, is altered, and indeed negated, by the caption which reads: "Mentally Retarded Eileen Sundheimer Stares Emptily Out

Figure 6.5 Cornell Capa, "Mentally Retarded Eileen Stares Emptily Out into Space, Lost in Her Own Infantile World," published in *Life* magazine, October 18, 1954, p. 123. Magnum Photos.

into Space, Lost in Her Own Infantile World." These are powerful words indeed, which could transform what might be considered a moment of courage and conviction into one of unintelligible emptiness. Similarly, when the caption is placed under Capa's image, it encourages a stereotypical reading of the disabled child that is not immediately apparent in the photograph.

It should be noted, of course, that Capa's form, although less directed than Morse's, embodies a visual code of its own—that of a perceived normality. One might compare this photographic language to contemporary promotional images that reflect stereotypes of a common "normal" in American life. An example of this is the staged photograph of famed African American baseball player, Jackie Robinson, by Nina Leen from 1949 that was created to counter the pervasive racism that obstructed his reception into the American pasttime (fig. 6.6). Here, Robinson sits comfortably on the front steps of what is presumably his home signing

Figure 6.6 Nina Leen, *Jackie Robinson Signs Autographs*, 1949. Getty Images.

his autograph. His wife, Rachel, stands beside him. Lined up in front of him are three white children who wait in eager anticipation for Robinson to sign his name. Robinson's child, Jackie Jr., sits on a tricyle compositionally within the group of boys, forming a picture of racial harmony. Considered within this context, the visual code continues to be troublesome because it attempts to absorb difference into the fold of the "normal," maintaining the prevailing bio-power structure.

Expanding the *normal:* deconstructing the "other" and the provocateur

As we have seen, a formal reading of Capa's photographs without captions reveals the photographer's presentation of the "other" within the visual structure of what was considered "normal." The year 1954 was Capa's last with *Life* magazine and marks a notable moment in his career when he increasingly recognized the value of photographs that were not staged and existed independent of a constructed written narrative. This interest, which he would later promote in a broader context through the Fund for Concerned Photography and the International Center of Photography, led him to encourage photographers to visually present a statement independent of predetermined editorial narratives.[27] Toward this end, he promoted a consideration of the photograph as embodying a visual language that is distinct from written language. For Capa, photographs constituted "visual writing," which at its best could be independent of and as powerful as the written word.[28] This interest in a stand-alone visual language was shared by other photographers such as W. Eugene Smith, who rejected attempts to control photographs to fit an editor's preconceived idea, and Robert Frank, who expressed an interest in moving away from the *Life* magazine narrative approach to photography.[29] This turn—where according to Capa the photographer becomes a "witness-artist" and takes responsibility for the visual impact of his or her image—is part of a new approach to photographing that encouraged photographers to move beyond the paradigmatic cultural structure apparent in the written language.[30]

Among the photographers who embraced this independent-language approach is Bruce Davidson, who consciously avoided images that conveyed predetermined messages, or as he put it "preached," and instead allowed the viewer to find meaning.[31] In his photographs of Jimmy Armstrong, a man with dwarfism employed by the circus as an entertainer and curiosity, Davidson avoids a visual structure that would situate Armstrong within a pre-established cultural identity as "other" and focuses rather on a presentation that allows the viewer to relate to common human experiences. Thus the viewer is not so much directed to a particular reading as invited into a dialogue with the image. In *USA, Palisades, New Jersey, The Dwarf* (in restaurant) 1958 (fig.6.7), Mr. Armstrong is seated in a restaurant eating a sandwich. His weariness is betrayed by eyelids which, half closed, hang heavy over his eyes, and the disheveled look of his shirt and tousled hair reveal perhaps a day of labor. All of this is amplified by the harsh light on his face which, coming from above, throws his eyes into deep shadow and accentuates the profound age lines. The photographer's viewpoint from slightly higher than and across the table from

Disability in post–World War II photography 111

Figure 6.7 Bruce Davidson, *USA, Palisades, New Jersey, The Dwarf* (in restaurant), 1958. Magnum Photos.

Mr. Armstrong, the restaurant setting, and even the toasted sandwich convey an ordinary, one might even say normal, scene. They are recognizable and easily associated with a similar experience the average viewer may have had in a restaurant. A viewer may also identify with the man's weary gaze, which seems to be without focus or intention. The ordinariness of the scene, however, is disrupted by the man to the left, who stares with a combination of bemusement and curiosity that one might associate with an audience member at the circus. The stare here provides a reference point for our perception of difference without resorting to conventional visual stereotypes. It conveys a common human reaction to difference—staring. It also invites us to do our own staring, which with the photograph we can do for as long as we like without social consequences.[32] In this open form, the photographer emphasizes his personal perception, while encouraging the viewer to bring his or her own experience toward understanding the image, rather than to be directed toward a predetermined meaning. This nuanced approach, based upon a pictorial language of normality, is prevalent within Davidson's work after the mid-1950s, which captures subgroups such as circus performers, a Brooklyn teenage gang, and residents of East 100th St. in New York. It allows us to be aware of the photographer's perspective without being directed by cultural norms.

The distinction from the isolating form with which we began this chapter is readily apparent if we compare Davidson's photograph from 1958 of Jimmy Armstrong smoking a cigarette outside the circus tent (fig. 6.8) with the image by

Figure 6.8 Bruce Davidson, *USA, Palisades, New Jersey, The Dwarf*, 1958. Magnum Photos.

Morse of the boy with cerebral palsy (fig. 6.1). In the latter, Morse presents the boy from a very low camera angle, emphasizing the darkened, monstrous, and anonymous form of the child awkwardly moving away from us; the former presents a frontal view of Mr. Armstrong from above, or what one might consider a "normal" height. Thus the effect is not to enfreak Mr. Armstrong by emphasizing his small stature, but rather to present him as one might expect to experience him. The view is empathetic in that it presents an individualized perspective that invites interpretation rather than a predetermined and editorial view that operates through the binary opposition of normal/abnormal. This is not to say that his role as a performer and curiosity is denied; indeed, it remains salient in the outfit and clown's mask that he wears.[33] What Davidson captured was his own initial reaction to Jimmy Armstrong, which he described as visual repulsion and attraction.[34] But the position of the figure, the emphasis on the cigarette held to his lips and the intensely far-away look in his eyes convey a moment of human existence rather than a defined cultural stereotype. We are invited to multiple readings within the realm of "normal" behavior. This bridge between normal and abnormal rejects the binary opposition model of approaching the photograph. In Davidson's photograph we bring meaning; in Morse's image the meaning is directed.

Despite the turn toward a more open dialogue with visual language, dependency on the concept of the "normal" remained an important aspect of photographic language. Just as Morse's images of P.S. 135 emphasized physical abnormality, representing difference in order to rectify as much as possible the "problem" so that we might return to a state of normalcy, Capa and Davidson embraced a visual language that ascribed normality to the disabled individual through a visual representation of the everyday. Dissimilarity becomes normal. During the 1960s and early '70s this approach increasingly recognized the provocative nature of the disabled body. It accepts the reality that, like race, disability defies correction.[35] Because these photographs portray disabled individuals as markedly different, even to the point of spectacle, they can be interpreted as serving to further isolate and segregate disabled people by continuing the freak show tradition of representing them as curiosities.[36] But unlike the traditional image associated with enfreakment, which isolated difference for purposes of entertainment, these photographs integrate the disabled individual within the context of "normal" society. Within this new visual language, the genre that has come to be known as "street photography" plays an essential role.

In Garry Winogrand's photograph, *American Legion Convention, Dallas*, 1964 (fig. 6.9), a man without legs pulls himself through the streets within a busy urban setting. His position within the conventional golden section (two-thirds/one-third) composition of the photograph places him clearly as the focal point. This role is reinforced by his stare, which is met by the reciprocal stare of the viewer. Although captured as one among many figures in a common street setting, the disabled man is not absorbed into a visual normal. In fact, his difference is emphasized to the point where he becomes a provocateur. Disability studies scholar David Hevey has interpreted this type of image by Winogrand as a representation of the enfreakment of the disabled individual in a consumerist society.[37] Hevey

Figure 6.9 Garry Winogrand, *American Legion Convention, Dallas*, 1964. © The Estate of Garry Winogrand, courtesy Fraenkel Gallery, San Francisco.

also notes that Winogrand's portrayal of the disabled person leaves unquestioned the issue of oppression. While these are important interpretations to consider, we should also take into account that it is the unquestioning that gives these images their power of inclusion. The disabled man's difference is captured in a matter-of-fact way, as though it is an inevitable aspect of the human community. Despite his disability, he becomes a part of the normal state of affairs—one more individual on a busy urban street filled with unique people. This is not to say that Winogrand discounts difference; rather, he seems to relish it. The disabled man remains distinct, even within the everyday setting. He becomes a visual provocateur, but as part of the multiplicity of figures within a city street. His presence expands our understanding of the human community as varied.[38]

As in Davidson's image of Jimmy Armstrong at the restaurant, the stare contributes to our understanding of difference, but in Winogrand's photograph the stare is confrontational and disquieting, provocative because it comes from the "other." It intensifies our recognition of difference and invites our reciprocal and prolonged stare. As has been noted, the viewer's stare can be interpreted as an outward manifestation of exclusion, a form of isolation and reinforcement of a hierarchical structure that has the potential to diminish the disabled person.[39] Contrarily, the invitation to stare at a figure in a photograph can be seen as a call for recognition and acceptance of difference. Winogrand forces a confrontation and acknowledgment. The disabled man is not isolated or representative of an opposition to help

Disability in post–World War II photography 115

define the normal, nor is he absorbed into the normal; rather, his role as provocateur references a larger context of diversity. Moreover, Winogrand's photograph offers a wealth of dissimilitude. To the left of the disabled man walks an African American man in a youthful and comfortable gait. In contrast, facing him is an older man with a cane. By his cap, we assume he is a member of the American Legion, or at least associated with that subgroup, as are three other men who form a rhythm of similitude in contrast to the multiplicity of the many figures. Behind the legionnaire stands an older woman, and behind her a young man whose confident posture and demeanor invite a reciprocal stare as well, as does the older man smoking a cigarette in the right foreground. In fact, all three men through their stares invite our acknowledgment of their difference. The disabled man becomes, then, one of many.

Also embracing multiplicity within a unified setting are the photographs of Paul McDonough. In *Blind Man, Old Woman, Hari Krishnas, NYC* 1972, for example, a blind man, an elderly woman, and four Hari Krishnas are brought together formally in a compositional semicircle. The blind man's tilted-back head leads to a group of three Hari Krishnas visible through the building window. A fourth Hari Krishna to the left is separated from the others by the corner of the building. Distinctive by his shaved head and traditional robes, he steps forward while patting his drum. Compositionally, the lines of the taxi behind him lead to the elderly woman, who leans on her cane and steps toward the camera. Despite this pictorial coherency, each person remains an individual rather than a character in a unified story. The blind man sits on a milk carton within his own space. Though he holds in his right hand a cup for alms, the scene is not about him. His head is thrown back in a position that does not imply interaction. Although the three Hari Krishna practitioners are compositionally connected to him, they are separated by two panes of glass. The Hari Krishna man to his right is separated from his colleagues, and although he is formally attached to the elderly woman, he remains distinctly separate from her. They are people, not stereotypes. Belying the notion of the freak show, within the context of others, these diverse individuals create together some semblance of what might be considered normality—difference is normal. And, as McDonough noted: "There's nothing stranger than the 'normal.'"[40]

Context and conclusion

The three visual constructs presented here form a progression in terms of a more complex and nuanced approach to photographically representing disabled individuals during the post-war period. These photographs, of course, were not created in a vacuum. They represent an aspect of a remarkable era in America when disabled people and their concerns increasingly became visible, particularly through non-profit organizations, public policy, and activism. President Franklin D. Roosevelt, who contracted polio as a young man, helped set the tone for seeing disability beyond stereotype. Although, as has been well documented, a willing press and aggressive Secret Service greatly controlled the release of photographic representations of President Roosevelt in his wheelchair or on crutches, many articles were published that described his condition.[41] Moreover, the March of Dimes fundraising efforts of his organization, the National Foundation for Infantile Paralysis (1938), placed images of disabled children in nearly every town and city in America for the next thirty years. Concurrently, other non-profit organizations—such as the National Foundation for Cerebral Palsy (1948, became United Cerebral Palsy the following year), the Muscular Dystrophy Association (1950), and the National Association for Retarded Citizens (1950)—contributed to an awareness of the need for re-evaluation of how those outside of the considered "normal" were understood and treated. In 1962 the Special Olympics, founded by Eunice Kennedy Shriver, expanded this awareness considerably by embracing disabled athletes in what would become an international event by 1968. Although governmental contributions to this awareness were more measured, steps were taken during this era toward addressing social and institutional isolation of the physically and mentally disabled. Government became an important voice to promote training and employment of the disabled, as evidenced by the numerable Vocational Rehabilitation Amendments, which culminated in the equal access clause of the Rehabilitation Act of 1973. President John F. Kennedy, in tribute to his sister Rosemary's mental disability, established the President's Panel on Mental Retardation in 1963. In 1966, under President Lyndon B. Johnson, the President's Committee on Mental Retardation sought to raise awareness by issuing several important public service announcements. Political activism for civil rights also played an important role in the recognition of discrimination and its effects. In 1963, Ed Roberts protested the University of California at Berkeley's decision to reject his admission due to his polio-related limited physical abilities. His efforts led to the Independent Living Movement, which to this day provides support for millions of disabled individuals throughout the country. In 1970, protests were held in many American cities when President Richard M. Nixon vetoed the Rehabilitation Act, leading ultimately to a congressional override. And it was once again protests that led to the ultimate implementation of Section 504 of the Rehabilitation Act that prohibited federal employment discrimination based upon physical or mental handicap in 1977.

This is to say that the pictorial transformation presented here took place in a post-war era of increased recognition of the oppressive nature of a societal structure built on the misconception of a homogeneous idea of what is "normal." From the validation of stereotypes that categorized and subjugated the disabled person in the immediate post-war era, to attempts to absorb disabled individuals into the visual everyday and the ultimate recognition of a more expansive and diverse population, the notion of what is normal was continually challenged. Like any language, photography is a complex form of communication built upon the conveyor's intention, the receiver's experience, and the societal structure through which meaning is discerned. Distinct to this medium, however, is the assumed veracity of the photographic process. Even in the most manipulated of images, a latent sense of reality accompanies the photograph. It is an awareness of this aspect of the photograph that is so important to its analysis, for as we have seen, the photograph has the potential to represent society's biases, reinforce them, and contribute to their deconstruction.

Notes

1 Rosemarie Garland-Thomson, "Seeing the Disabled: Visual Rhetorics of Disability in Popular Photography," in *The New Disability History: American Perspectives*, ed. Paul K. Longmore and Lauri Umansky (New York: New York University Press, 2001), 335–374.
2 The term "Foucauldian" refers to the concepts and ideas proposed by philosopher and social theorist, Michel Foucault (1926–1984). Specifically, I am referring here to that aspect of Foucault's thoughts that considers how power relationships affect and help define those outside of the considered normal. Most notably, Foucault addressed these issues in *Madness and Civilization* (1961); *Birth of the Clinic* (1963); *Discipline and Punish* (1975); and *The History of Sexuality* (3 volumes; 1976, 1983, 1984).
3 R. Bogdan and D. Biklen, "Handicapism," *Social Policy* 7, no. 5 (March/April 1977): 14–19.
4 For a discussion of the distinction between impairment and disability, see Michael Oliver and Colin Barnes, *The New Politics of Disablement* (New York: Palgrave Macmillan, 2012), 20–27.
5 Ferdinand de Saussure (1857–1913) was a Swiss linguist and semiotician who analyzed language as a formal system of relational and differential signs, whereby the sign is only understood in relation to other signs. The sign in my application here is "disability," which would be defined by what it is not, able-bodied or "normal."
6 See Jacques Derrida, *Writing and Difference*, trans. A. Bass (London: Routledge and Kegan Paul, 1990); Mairian Corker and Tom Shakespeare, *Disability/Postmodernity: Embodying Disability Theory* (London: Continuum, 2002), 7.
7 Shelley Tremain, "Foucault, Governmentality, and Critical Disability Theory," in *Foucault and the Government of Disability*, ed. Shelley Tremain, 2nd edition (Ann Arbor: University of Michigan Press, 2015), 3–7.
8 "Cerebral Palsy: Once Considered Hopeless, Its Victims Now Can Make Adjustment to Normal Life," *Life*, April 30, 1951, 85–91.
9 I am referring specifically here to the tense and threatening hands of Bela Lugosi's Count Dracula in *Dracula* (1931); the stiff legs and arms, and gnarled hands of Boris Karloff's Frankenstein in *Frankenstein* (1931) and *Bride of Frankenstein* (1935); and Lon Chaney's portrayal of the clawed werewolf in *The Wolf Man* (1941).
10 See Maarten Simons and Jan Masschelein, "Inclusive Education for Exclusive Pupils: A Critical Analysis of the Government of the Exceptional," in *Foucault and the Government of Disability*, ed. Shelley Tremain (Ann Arbor: University of Michigan Press, 2005), 208–228.
11 "Cerebral Palsy: Once Considered Hopeless . . .," 89.
12 "Cerebral Palsy: Once Considered Hopeless . . .," 89.
13 Dr. Cooper refers to P.S. 135 in his comments. William Cooper, "The Clinic School," in *Proceedings: Cerebral Palsy Institute, November 1950* (New York: Association for the Aid of Crippled Children, 1950), 37.
14 Chris Drinkwater, "Supported Living and the Production of Individuals," in *Foucault and the Government of Disability*, ed. Shelley Tremain (Ann Arbor: University of Michigan Press, 2005), 229–244.
15 Rosemarie Garland-Thomson, "Seeing the Disabled: Visual Rhetorics of Disability in Popular Photography," 336.
16 See Tremain's application of Foucault's analysis of power structure to disability in Tremain, "Foucault, Governmentality, and Critical Disability Theory," 6–7.
17 Beatrice A. Wright, *Physical Disability—A Psychological Approach* (New York: Harper & Brothers, 1960): 144–148.
18 Raymond Leslie Goldman, *Even the Night* (New York: Macmillan, 1947), 38–39.
19 Davide Sparti, "Making Up People: On Some Looping Effects of the Human Kind—Institutional Reflexivity or Social Control?" *European Journal of Social Theory* 4, no. 3 (2001): 331–349.

20 Alan Marshall, *I Can Jump Puddles* (London: Secker & Warburg, 1956), 73.
21 *The Cerebral Palsy Program of the New York City Schools* (New York: Coordinating Council for Cerebral Palsy in New York City, 1956), 29, accessed Hathi Trust Digital Library, February 15, 2015, http://catalog.hathitrust.org/Record/001578963.
22 *The Family of Man*, prologue Carl Sandburg and intro. Edward Steichen (New York: Museum of Modern Art, 1955), 5.
23 Robert Frank, *The Americans* (New York: Grove Press, 1959).
24 "Retarded Children," *Life*, October 18, 1954, 119–127.
25 See Myron H. Davis, "Lunch in the Kitchen," *Life*, January 4, 1954, p. 8.
26 "Retarded Children," 121, 124.
27 One of the chief promoters of this shift in emphasis toward a visual language distinct from concepts associated with the written word was Cornell Capa, who would establish the Fund for Concerned Photography in 1966 and begin to publish photographers' work in his *Concerned Photographer* series of books in 1968 (Grossman Publishers, New York). He would also found the International Center of Photography in 1974.
28 *The Concerned Photographer 2*, ed. and intro. Cornell Capa (New York: Grossman Publishers, 1972): intro. See also the Capa interview in James Danziger and Barnaby Conrad III, *Interviews with Master Photographers* (New York: Paddington Press, 1977), 66–67.
29 W. Eugene Smith, "Photographic Journalism," *Photo Notes* (June 1948): 4–5; James Guimond, *American Photography and the American Dream* (Chapel Hill: University of North Carolina Press, 1991), 219.
30 *The Concerned Photographer*, ed. Cornell Capa (New York: Grossman Publishers, 1968), intro.
31 *The Concerned Photographer 2*, 2.
32 Timothy W. Hiles, "Shifting Perception: Photographing Disabled People during the Civil Rights Era," *Review of Disability Studies: An International Journal* 10, no. 3/4 (2014): 33–38.
33 Amanda Cachia, "Composing Dwarfism: Reframing Short Stature in Contemporary Photography," *Review of Disability Studies: An International Journal* 10, no. 3/4 (2014): 10–11.
34 Bruce Davidson, *Circus* (Göttingen, Germany: Steidl, 2007), 5.
35 See David T. Mitchell and Sharon L. Snyder, *The Body and Physical Difference: Discourses of Disability* (Ann Arbor: University of Michigan Press, 1997), 3, for a discussion of this issue of disability.
36 For the "freak show" tradition see *Freakery: Cultural Spectacle of the Extraordinary Body*, ed. Rosemarie Garland-Thomson (New York: New York University Press, 1996).
37 Hevey, *The Enfreakment of Photography*, 65–67.
38 Tobin Siebers, *Disability Aesthetics* (*Ann Arbor: University of Michigan Press, 2010*), 3. See Siebers's contention that "disability enlarges our vision of human variation and difference, and puts forward perspectives that test presuppositions dear to the history of aesthetics."
39 Rosemarie Garland-Thomson, *Staring: How We Look* (Oxford: Oxford University Press, 2009).
40 Guy Anglade, "In Conversation: An Interview with Paul McDonough," *Visura Magazine.com*, July, 2011, accessed March 10, 2015, http://www.visuramagazine.com/interview-paul-mcdonough.
41 See Matthew Pressman, "Ambivalent Accomplices: How the Press Handled FDR's Disability and How FDR Handled the Press," *The Journal of the Historical Society* 13, no. 3 (September 2013): 325–359.

7 The disabled veteran of World War I in the mirror of contemporary art

The reception of Otto Dix's painting *The Cripples* (1920) in Yael Bartana's film *Degenerate Art Lives* (2010)

Anne Marno

This interdisciplinary art history and disability studies chapter discusses the influence of art of World War I on contemporary art by the example of the motif of the disabled veteran in Otto Dix's painting *The Cripples* (1920) and Yael Bartana's film *Degenerate Art Lives* (2010).[1] The chapter investigates how the image of the disabled veteran is constructed in each case, which attributions he receives by the artists and in contemporary discourses, and how the interpretation changes. Whereas the motif of the disabled veteran in Dix's painting still refers to World War I and is an expression of critique of the society of Weimar Republic around 1920, it shifts from this historical context in Bartana's film, in which the figure of the war veteran can be related to the terror and violence in the Gaza War. But Bartana goes far beyond a critique of sociohistorical events in Israel. In the film, she mobilizes the disabled veterans from Dix's painting to become a collective force; the film thus strongly asserts the power of modern art against the Nazi's defamation.

Otto Dix's painting *The Cripples*, in which he depicts injured war veterans on a street, critiques the glorification of war. Dix himself knew the horrors of war very well. Born to a working-class family in 1891 in Gera-Untermhaus (Thüringen), he was inducted into military service in 1914, during his studies at the arts and crafts school (Großherzoglich-Sächsische Kunstgewerbeschule) in Dresden.[2] For almost four years, Dix was a leader of a machine gun troop on both the western and eastern fronts. He served in the trenches in numerous battles, including the Second Battle of Champagne in autumn 1915 and the Battle of the Somme in Flanders (1916–1917).[3] After the war, Dix returned to Dresden, studying there at the Academy of Arts, and lived temporarily in Düsseldorf and Berlin. In the year 1927, he was appointed Professor at the Academy of Arts in Dresden. With the rise to power of the Nazi party, Dix was removed from office and denounced as a degenerate artist; his works were presented in exhibitions of degenerate art throughout Germany. Dix went into internal exile in South Germany, where he first lived in Randegg, and from 1936 on in Hemmenhofen on Lake Constance. He has become well known for his artistic works relating to World War I, which were created in the 1920s, far beyond the borders of Germany.

In Dix's painting *The Cripples* (1920),[4] uniformed veterans with severe facial injuries and/or amputated limbs are the central motif. Dix depicts men who, by means of prostheses or in the absence of them, have difficulty coping with everyday life. The veterans in *The Cripples, Prague Street*, and *The Skat Players* from 1920 were described as "cardboard characters" and "puppets of hooray-patriotism."[5] These works are closely related to Dix's dealings with the Berlin Dadaists. Here he uses the collage technique, pasting various materials onto the oil-painted canvas.[6] In *The Cripples*[7] (fig. 7.1), Dix depicts a sort of parade of four veterans, miserably battered by the war, who move with difficulty assisted by crutches and in one case a cart. Thereby he distorts the presentation in a Dadaist way: the artistic style is not at all realistic and implies exaggeration. The man on the left side appears dwarfish, since both of his legs (and one of his arms) are amputated, and his peg-leg prostheses are not as long as his own legs would have been. His involuntarily grin results from a face injury, which appears to have torn away the left side of his mouth. Dix depicts the second person from the left as a war neurotic: the irregular contour of his face and arm points to his shivering, which was a characteristic symptom of this condition.[8] Because his prosthetic leg is much too short in comparison with his intact leg, he is only able to move forward with an inclined upper body. The third man is sitting in a cart: his left arm and both legs have all

Figure 7.1 Otto Dix, *The Cripples*, 150 × 200 cm, oil on canvas, 1920, in: Beck, Rainer. *Otto Dix 1891–1969: Zeit, Leben, Werk.* Konstanz: Stadler, 1993, 69, fig. 114. Permission source: Artist Rights Society, New York. © 2015 Artists Rights Society (ARS), New York / VG Bild-Kunst, Bonn.

been amputated, evidently leaving him with only a torso; he wears a patch over one eye. The veteran on the right pushes the cart forward. He wears a prosthetic leg that is hyperextended strangely, and his oversized artificial eye gazes at the viewer. His mandibular prosthesis—probably a model of "Dix Brand"—appears to be screwed onto his face from the outside.[9] The four veterans seem to move mechanically, as if they are automatons or puppets.[10] Despite their repellent visual appearance, the first three men proudly display their medals and badges, including an Iron Cross worn by the veteran on the left. In the background is a facade of houses with two windows, with a self-portrait of Otto Dix in profile on a pilaster between them.[11] A sign with the inscription "Schuma" ("shoema"), which is cut off by the right border, points to a business, of which the men would now have little need (shoemaking), because they mainly move on peg-legs.

This work displays essential features of contemporary artistic discourse. Between 1910 and 1915, illness and disability were favorite subjects of the Expressionists. In visual arts of World War I and in the post-war period, issues such as war injuries and disability were widely represented in works of art. In visual arts (and in literature) of the Weimar Republic, the war-disabled body became an object of a discourse with specific goals and characteristic attributes. In addition to Dix, numerous artists created works presenting this motif, including Max Beckmann,[12] George Grosz, Heinrich Hoerle, Ernst Ludwig Kirchner,[13] Erich Heckel,[14] Max Pechstein,[15] and Karl Schmidt-Rottluff. Their pictures were often created to express pacifist ideas. In many works by progressive or politically left-oriented artists, the artistic representation of war disability functioned as an accusation of the capitalist system and militarism in Germany.[16] The disabled individual with crutches, whose leg or legs were amputated, became an especially iconic motif in Weimar art.[17] Besides serious bodily or psychological injuries, artists emphasized the social distress of the disabled veterans, who often are presented as beggars—reduced to a very low socioeconomic state—to attack the military system, which produced this misery.[18] Moreover, the presentation of disabled veterans by many visual artists and writers served to accuse the veterans themselves:[19] the artists present them cynically as unteachable and close to the militarists, industrialists, and the agents of the bourgeoisie, who were responsible for the war and the social disorder.[20]

At the time Dix painted *The Cripples*, and in the years before, the atrociously mutilated and psychologically traumatized veterans were part of the everyday street scenery at an unprecedented scale.[21] Already during the war, the amputee veteran was the focus of social welfare, with the objective of social reintegration after elaborate surgical procedures and hospital stays.[22] Attention was given especially to reintegration into employment, and also to keep pension claims low.[23] Because of their extensive injuries, disabled veterans had to endure countless reconstructive and disciplining measures (such as drills and gymnastic exercises) on their bodies; in addition to more major surgical interventions—for example, for initial amputations following injury—they underwent countless follow-up operations. These interventions and the equipment with appropriate prostheses should have not only secured survival and produced a bearable health status, but also served to optimize the usefulness of the veterans in everyday life and at work.[24]

122   *Anne Marno*

Despite the previously mentioned measures of surgical reconstruction, the attempt to reintegrate the disabled veterans into society and in the workforce failed in many cases. Because of their impairments and their frightening appearance, many war veterans were not able to work regularly and were socially marginalized. Thus the veterans of World War I with facial and traumatic brain injuries played a special role in the process of reintegration.[25] They were not suitable for the Tayloristic vision of the steel man ("Vision vom 'stählernen Menschen'").[26] In Germany, the war veterans were disregarded and devalued because they made the defeat of the country visible.[27] In his painting *The Cripples*, Dix focuses on veterans with amputated limbs as well as those with head injuries as socially excluded outsiders of the Weimar society.[28]

The Cripples, which was the prototype for an etching, is today presumed lost. Although the large-format picture was prominently displayed at the international Dada fair in Berlin in 1920, the press ignored it.[29] The Stadtmuseum purchased the painting, but it disappeared in 1924 in the "Depot," which was also called "chamber of horrors" ("Schreckenskammer");[30] in 1933, together with Dix's painting *The Trench*, it was shown in all exhibitions of degenerate art as an example of the mockery of heroic life by a malignant artist, hostile towards the people.[31]

The Israeli artist Yael Bartana's film *Degenerate Art Lives* (2010) is a contemporary reinterpretation of Dix's *The Cripples*. Taking up the motif of the disabled veteran from Dix's paintings the film opens a new perspective on this work. Bartana (born 1970 in Israel) works mainly as a film and video artist. She lives in Tel Aviv and Amsterdam.[32] Her work focuses on the complex relationship between the individual and society against the background of her country of origin.[33] Thereby she substantially problematizes cultural identity: in her photographs, films, and installations, she explores critically the struggle for the identity of Israel.[34] Bartana's "'Jewish Renaissance Movement in Poland' (JRMiP)," in which she demands the return of 3.3 million Jews to Poland, is her best-known multimedia project in Germany.[35] In contrast to Dix, Bartana witnessed combat operations in the Gaza War only as a civilian. However, like almost every woman in Israel, she received military training.

In her film *Degenerate Art Lives*, Bartana animates the war veterans from Dix's painting *The Cripples* (figs. 7.2–7.4).[36] She created this work while living in Israel.[37] In the film, which includes contrasting sequences, the composition is held together by the monotonous background sound (reminiscent of metal noises) as well as by recurring motifs such as clouds of smoke, prosthetic hands, headpieces, and so on. Bartana makes the veterans more present for the viewer than Dix does: she augments the sensual perception of their presence by showing more and more veterans and by producing more noise, culminating in the appearance of a collective event—the figures from Dix's painting finally form a sort of army of disabled veterans.

The arrangement of the figures as a parade in the painting is the key component of the composition of the film. The film starts with the appearance of these figures on the screen, entering in a gray field from the right. Presented as silhouettes, the figures appear abstract, as if translated into a distant world. By staging

The disabled veteran of World War I 123

Figure 7.2 Section from Yael Bartana, *Degenerate Art Lives* (*Entartete Kunst Lebt*), 2010, video still, courtesy of Annet Gelink Gallery, Amsterdam, and Sommer Contemporary Art, Tel Aviv.

another series of veterans in front of the first series, then of a series closer to the front, a three-dimensional space is created. As the figures multiply, they lose their silhouette-like appearance and details become visible, so that they become recognizable as figures from Dix's painting the closer they are to the front—as if the phenomenon is concretized and therefore also is brought into the present. The scene becomes more immediate and at the same time more collective. The spatial concentration corresponds with the extension of the perspective by the view from above, which strengthens the three-dimensionality of the events and makes them more insistent than in the painting. The impression of a strange bumpy movement, intensified by accompanying rattling noises, increases, when the figures are seen from above: they appear as machine people, comparable with the figures in Dix's painting. Single movements, such as the blink of an eye and exhalation of smoke, appear mechanical.

A general view of the scene, which finally appears endless, is contrasted by the close-up view of the body fragments of the disabled persons, showing details including medals on their uniforms. In the close-up view, the noises are intensified; they imitate the scrunching sound of the wheels of the cart and the rasping

Figure 7.3 Section from Yael Bartana, *Degenerate Art Lives* (*Entartete Kunst Lebt*), 2010, video still, courtesy of Annet Gelink Gallery, Amsterdam, and Sommer Contemporary Art, Tel Aviv.

sounds produced by the peg-legs and the soles of the shoes. The design of changing perspectives makes the viewer aware of the separation of the individual, and also his or her integration in a collective event.

The setting is the gray, abstract area, which on the one hand removes the events to a time when a richly coloured media presentation was not yet possible. On the other hand, the scene receives timeless and placeless dimensions by eliminating the facade of the houses, which Dix presents in the background of the painting. With this design, the work develops an ambivalent effect at different levels: although memories of World War I and of bodily injuries and traumas, caused by this war, are evoked, the film also relates to contemporary issues. Moreover, Bartana points out another horizon of meaning in the title of the work (*Degenerate Art Lives*), which is shortly before the end of the film indicated, formed by the veterans themselves, who are seen from above: in this perspective the viewer sees the heads/headgears of the veterans from a wide distance. They appear in light and dark color, only as small "points," and these "points" form the terms "Entartete Kunst lebt" in block letters. By this Bartana refers to the historical stigmatization of this kind of art.[38]

Figure 7.4 Section from Yael Bartana, *Degenerate Art Lives* (*Entartete Kunst Lebt*), 2010, video still, courtesy of Annet Gelink Gallery, Amsterdam, and Sommer Contemporary Art, Tel Aviv.

The work has been the subject of debate and public response, especially on the Internet. The following positions are predominant and demonstrate important interpretations. The film *Degenerate Art Lives* is viewed as an act of revitalization ("Akt der Wiederherstellung")[39] of the painting of Dix, which makes possible new readings ("Lesarten").[40] It is interpreted as a criticism of false ideals, patriotism, nationalism, and heroism ("Kritik an falschen Idealen, Patriotismus, Nationalismus und Heldentum"),[41] as they are expressed in Dix's paintings of war veterans (1920). Thereby Bartana intends to clarify, according to these interpretations, that works of art of the past remain active in present time.[42] It is argued in this sense that Bartana's film allows Dix's figures to go further: "In Bartana's work Dix's cripples produce their own form of 'degenerate art.' Beaten, injured and exhausted they proudly declare their victory: the victory of art."[43] Other viewers claim that Bartana wants to raise public awareness about disabled war veterans or rather disabled people in general.[44] Some reviewers argue from a biographical standpoint and accentuate the overall context of Bartana's work. According to them, she belongs to a generation socialized in globalization, one that wishes that the borders for people were as open as they are for money and goods; they argue that she aims to overcome obsolete stereotypes ("Festschreibungen") on the basis of race, religion, sex, and nationality, which have caused the oppression of minorities throughout history.[45] The reception shows the variety of possible understandings, which can be explained by the fact that the film itself is complex and open to various interpretations.

Moreover, not addressed in public response but also relevant as a context for the interpretation is the long-standing trauma discourse in Israel.[46] This trauma discourse takes place through professional discourse in psychology and psychiatry, but is also linked with social and political developments, and is in a sense representative of the way Israeli society deals with war, terror, and traumas.[47] The Israeli trauma discourse is not only about the suffering of concerned individual veterans, but also a national trauma—the suffering of the war veterans has been extensively politicized.[48] The discourse can be traced back to the response to traumatic experiences of the soldiers in the Yom Kippur War; in this war in 1973, Israel was unexpectedly attacked by Egypt and Syria.[49] Only then was the mental trauma of the Israeli soldiers noticed in public life.[50] Since the second Palestinian Intifada, a strong discourse has developed, in which collective violence and the notion of resilience play central roles.[51] In this discourse, heterogeneous elements flow together: the struggle for identity in Israel in context with the historical past of the Holocaust,[52] actual social and political developments, and influences from abroad. Against the background of this context, Bartana's work can be interpreted as a critique of war in general—similar to Dix—and moreover as a critique of the Gaza War in particular.

But Bartana goes far beyond a critique of sociohistorical events in Israel.[53] In a comparison of the presentation of bodily injuries and disability in Dix's painting and in Bartana's film, it is evident that in Dix's work, the representation still has a historical reference to World War I and its veterans, whose bodies showed the effects of violence. In Bartana's film, by contrast, the war veteran is to a large extent severed from historical references. In her film, the original historical reality of World War I is only implicitly addressed, as well as the related life experiences of the veterans. From Dix's painting, Bartana draws only the series of the four veterans and fades out the historical location. She doesn't replace it with a scene of daily life in Israel around 2010. Instead, the restaging happens in the anonymous, timeless field of a gray area—this makes the update and modification of the message possible. The gray area stands for an indefinite, generic place, appropriate for new interpretations, which could be anywhere in the world. This area is not at all nationally, temporally, or structurally defined. Are the war veterans Israelis or Palestinians? Or is the human being in general and his or her vulnerability represented? The film doesn't show specific individuals, as Dix's painting does, but—especially due to the duplication of the figures—rather prototypes, patterns of physical or mental destruction, which have occurred perennially in history and will occur in future, but in new forms and manifestations. Instead of individuals, Bartana presents a phenomenon of the masses.

In the transition from the painting to the film, the medium and technique changed drastically: Dix created his painting *The Cripples* as a Dadaist collage and therefore experimented with different materials. Today, not the painting itself, but the preserved photograph shapes our idea of this work, and in this photograph, the original materiality and artistic technique are hardly discernible. In the film, the presentation obtains new dimensions, which also include the animation of the figures, a three-dimensional room and the sound (but not the color). The production of sound in the film causes an expanded form of perceptibility. Thereby interactions happen between the visual and the acoustical experiences.

Why did Bartana choose Dix's painting *The Cripples* as a basis for her film, and not Dix's corresponding etching with the same motif (in which the figures proceed in the opposite direction) or the paintings *The Skat Players* or *Prague Street* from 1920, which are extant? One reason for this was that the painting was the object of an unprecedented proscription by the Nazis, and it no longer exists.[54] By taking the figures not from the painting itself, but from a preserved photograph, she makes the viewer aware of this historical destruction.

The comparison of Dix's painting and Bartana's film makes the following aspects clear: the critique of war articulated in Dix's painting—comparable with other contemporaneous artworks—from today's viewpoint alternates between a critique of the military authority; a critique of the veterans themselves, who were complicit in the structures of war; and (in context with Dix's other paintings of disabled veterans from 1920) a critique of capitalism. In the Nazi era the work was outlawed as degenerate art, because of its negative take on the myth of the heroic soldier. Against this background and the practice of euthanasia, which aimed to eradicate physically disabled human beings, the full extent of this suppression of Dix's painting becomes understandable.

Like Dix's *The Cripples*, Bartana's film can be understood generally as a critique of war and of every form of violence that destroys the human body and/or psyche. Like Dix, Bartana doesn't clearly take sides: she avoids siding with the Israeli society or the opposing Palestinians, which have inflicted serious injuries on each other. In context with Bartana's complete body of work, it could be assumed that she wants to focus on the suffering of the disabled war veteran, and more generally on the traumatized human being, in Israel. The disabled veteran in this work could be interpreted in this sense as a kind of symbolic figure for the trauma suffered by herself, her family, and the Israeli people, which reaches into the past (the Holocaust) and continues in the present.[55] In context with the long-standing trauma discourse in Israel, the mobilization of disabled veterans to a mass appearance in the film can also be taken as an expression of resistance against enduring violent impacts and the struggle for the identity of Israel.

Bartana aims to go much further: giving the film the title *Degenerate Art Lives*, she opposes the historical proscription of the painting by the Nazis in an artistic act, which on the one hand expresses solidarity with Dix as an artist persecuted by the Nazis, and on the other hand contests every form of discrimination against and marginalization of individuals and social groups because of their bodily appearance, religion, race, and so on, as was practiced by the Nazis. Thereby, it was her significant concern to demonstrate that Dix's painting asserted itself in history: although only the photograph is preserved, the painting remains still active until the present times, not only because of its original intention, but also because of its history.[56]

Notes

1 Disability will be in the following understood according to the new Disability Studies as a construct rather than as a medical problem; see Anne Klein, "Wie betreibt man Disability History? Methoden in Bewegung," in *Disability History: Konstruktionen von Behinderung in der Geschichte. Eine Einführung*, ed. Elsbeth Bösl, Anne Klein, and Anne Waldshmidt (Bielefeld: Transcript, 2010), 45; see also Rosemarie Garland-Thomson, "Andere Geschichten," in *Der (im-) perfekte Mensch: Metamorphosen von Normalität und Abweichung*, ed. Petra Lutz (Köln: Böhlau, 2003), 418–425.
2 See Otto Conzelmann, *Der andere Dix. Sein Bild vom Menschen und vom Krieg* (Stuttgart: Clett-Cotta, 1983), 254.
3 See Conzelmann, *Der andere Dix*, 68; see also the military passport of Otto Dix, Deutsches Kunstarchiv, Nachlass Dix, Otto, I, A-2.
4 The discriminating term "cripples," which Dix uses in the title of the artwork, was criticized already during World War I; see Maren Möhring, "Kriegsversehrte Körper: Zur Bedeutung der Sichtbarkeit von Behinderung," in Disability Studies, *Kultursoziologie und Soziologie der Behinderung: Erkundungen in einem neuen Forschungsfeld*, ed. Anne Waldschmidt and Werner Schneider (Bielefeld: Transcript, 2007), 177.
5 "Pappkameraden," "närrische Marionetten des Hurrahpatriotismus," Hanne Bergius, "Im Laboratorium der mechanischen Fiktionen: Zur unterschiedlichen Bewertung von Mensch und Maschine um 1920," in *Die Nützlichen Künste: Gestaltende Technik und Bildende Kunst seit der Industriellen Revolution*, ed. Tilmann Budensieg and Henning Rogge (Berlin: Quadriga-Verl., 1981), 292; see also Matthias Eberle, *Der Weltkrieg und die Künstler der Weimarer Republik* (Belser Chr., 1992), 46.
6 See Jung-Hee Kim, "Frauenbilder von Otto Dix: Wirklichkeit und Selbstbekenntnis" (PhD diss., University of Hamburg, 1994), 21.
7 Another title of the painting was *45% Fit for Work* (*45% erwerbsfähig*).
8 Reasons for this condition were often traumatic experiences, for example, an explosion or gas poisoning.
9 In Dix's painting *The Skat Players*, a comparable prosthesis has the inscription "Dix Brand" ("Marke Dix").
10 See Bergius, "Im Laboratorium der mechanischen Fiktionen," 292; see also Eberle, *Der Weltkrieg und die Künstler der Weimarer Republik*, 46.
11 See Dietrich Schubert, "Krüppeldarstellungen im Werk von Otto Dix nach 1920," in *Krieg und Utopie: Kunst, Literatur und Politik im Rheinland nach dem Ersten Weltkrieg*, ed. Gertrude Cepl-Kaufmann Gerd Krumeich, and Ulla Sommers (Essen: Klartext-Verl., 2006), 298.
12 For example, see Max Beckmann's lithographs *The Way Home* (*Nachhauseweg*), and *The Street* (*Die Straße*), part of his cycle of lithographs *The Hell* (*Die Hölle*), 1919, in Carol Poore, *Disability in Twentieth-Century German Culture* (Ann Arbor: Univ. of Michigan Press, 2010), 22.
13 See for example Ernst Ludwig Kirchner's *Self-Portrait as a Soldier* (*Selbstporträt als Soldat*) (1915), which presents the artist with an injured right arm; Poore, *Disability in Twentieth-Century German Culture*, 20 f.
14 See Erich Heckel's etching *Street in Ostende* (*Straße in Ostende*), 1915, which presents two war veterans with crutches, and his wood-cuts *Two Wounded* (*Zwei Verwundete*) and *Wounded Sailor* (*Verwundeter Matrose*), both 1915; and the lithographs *Mad Soldier* (*Irrer Soldat*) and *Cripple at the Seaside* (*Krüppel am Meer*), both 1916, Poore, *Disability in Twentieth-Century German Culture*, 20 f.
15 See Max Pechstein's drawing of an amputee with the title *The Gardener, Somme IX* (*Der Gärtner, Somme IX*), Poore, *Disability in Twentieth-Century German Culture*, 20 f.
16 Poore, *Disability in Twentieth-Century German Culture*, 20.
17 See Poore, *Disability in Twentieth-Century German Culture*, 20.

18 In fact, the state supported the majority of the disabled war veterans, Poore, *Disability in Twentieth-Century German Culture*, 20. These works widely disregard the fact that already since the foundation of the Weimar Republic in Germany, self-help groups were formed by disabled people, for example, the "Selbsthilfebund der Körperbehinderten (1919–1931)," Petra Fuchs, "Von der *Selbsthilfe* zur Selbstaufgabe: Zur Emanzipationsgeschichte behinderter Menschen (1919–1945)," in *Der (im-) perfekte Mensch: Metamorphosen von Normalität und Abweichung*, ed. Petra Lutz, Thomas Macho, Gisela Staupe, and Heike Zirden (Köln: Böhlau, 2003), 436.
19 See Poore, *Disability in Twentieth-Century German Culture*, 28.
20 Poore, *Disability in Twentieth-Century German Culture*, 29. Characteristic examples are Dix's works *The Cripples, The Skat Players*, and *Prague Street* (1920). By the presentation of the medals and badges, and even more clearly by the flyer with the inscription "Jews out!" ("Juden Raus!") in *Prague Street*, Dix alludes to the political context, as well as to the right-wing nationalist political conviction of the disabled veterans, Brigitte Reinhard, "Dix—Maler der Tatsachen," in *Otto Dix: Bestandskatalog, Gemälde, Aquarelle, Pastelle, Zeichnungen, Holzschnitte, Radierungen, Lithographien*, ed. Johann-Karl Schmidt (Stuttgart: Cantz, 1989), 15. For the satirical works of George Grosz see also Poore, *Disability in Twentieth-Century German Culture*, 29.
21 See Möhring, "Kriegsversehrte Körper," 177.
22 See Sabine Kienitz, *Beschädigte Helden: Kriegsinvalidität und Körperbilder 1914–1923* (Paderborn et al.: Schöningh, 2008), 157.
23 See Peter Riedesser and Axel Verderber, *"Maschinengewehre hinter der Front": Zur Geschichte der deutschen Militärpsychiatrie* (Frankfurt a. M.: Fischer-Taschenbuch-Verl., 1996), 92.
24 See Kienitz, *Beschädigte Helden: Kriegsinvalidität und Körperbilder 1914–1923*, 153.
25 See Sabine Kienitz, "Beschädigte Helden: Zur Politisierung des kriegsinvaliden Soldatenkörpers in der Weimarer Republik," in *Der verlorene Frieden: Politik und Kriegskultur nach 1918*, ed. Jost Dülffer and Gerd Krumeich (Essen: Klartext, 2002), 204 ff.
26 Michael Hagner, "Verwundete Gesichter, verletzte Gehirne: Zur Deformation des Kopfes im Ersten Weltkrieg," in *Gesichter der Weimarer Republik: Eine physiognomische Kulturgeschichte*, ed. Claudia Schmölders and Sander Gilman (Köln: DuMont, 2000), 85.
27 See Schubert, "Krüppeldarstellungen im Werk von Otto Dix nach 1920: Zynismus oder Sarkasmus?", 294; a differentiated view on the body of the injured of World War I is to be found in Sabine Kienitz, "Der verwundete Körper als Emblem der Niederlage? Zur Symbolik der Figur der Kriegsinvaliden in der Weimarer Republik," in *Kriegsniederlagen: Erfahrungen und Erinnerungen*, ed. by Horst Carl, Hans-Henning Kortüm, Dieter Langewiesche, and Friedrich Lenger (Berlin: Akad. Verl., 2004), 341. To this text section see Anne Marno, "Otto Dix Radierzyklus *Der Krieg* (1924): Authentizität als Konstrukt" (PhD diss., University of Düsseldorf, Petersberg: Imhof, 2015), the section 2.1.7, S. 50–65.
28 The exclusion and discrimination of the disabled veteran becomes especially clear in Dix's painting *The Match Seller* (1920), where the passers-by move away from the veteran and a dachshund urinates on him.
29 See Andreas Strobl, *Otto Dix: Eine Malerkarriere der zwanziger Jahre* (Berlin: Reimer, 1996), 40.
30 Löffler does not explain this term and he does not mention, since when the "Depot" was called "Schreckenskammer." But it is probable, that in this depot Dix's painting *The Cripples* and artworks of other artists were hidden from the public until the Nazis collected together all these works, to present them in the exhibitions of degenerate art.
31 "Beweisstück für die Verhöhnung 'heldischen' Lebens durch einen bösartigen, 'volksfeindlichen' Künstler," Fritz Löffler, *Otto Dix: Leben und Werk* (Dresden: Verl. der Kunst, 1960), 35, 39; see also Schubert, "Krüppeldarstellungen im Werk von Otto Dix nach 1920," 298 f. Löffler writes that the painting *The Cripples* was confiscated in 1937 and probably destroyed in Berlin in 1942, see Löffler, *Otto Dix 1891–1969: Oeuvre der Gemälde* (Aurel Bongers KG: Recklinghausen, 1981), fig. 8 (in the catalogue).

130 *Anne Marno*

32 See Isabella Marte, *documenta 12: Katalog, Documenta Kassel, 16.06–23.09 2007* (Köln: Taschen, 2007), 332.
33 See Marte, *documenta 12*, 332.
34 See "Yael Bartana, Biography," accessed April 21, 2015, http://www.annetgelink.com/artists/5-yael-bartana/biography/.
35 In context with this project Bartana presented 2001 posters and videos on the Biennale in Venedig and organized a congress afterwards, Catrin Lorch, "Leben und arbeiten in Berlin: Die Künstlerin Yael Bartana macht Kunst aus Propaganda und politischen Symbolen," *Süddeutsche Zeitung*, Nr. 43, February 21, 22, 2015, 22.
36 "Entartete Kunst Lebt (Degenerate Art Lives), 2010," accessed March 3, 2015, http://www.annetgelink.com/artists/5-Yael-Bartana/works/video/12510/. Bartana studied at the Bezalel Academy of Arts and Design in Jerusalem, at the School of Visual Arts in New York, and at the Rijksakademie in Amsterdam. Her work was shown in numerous leading museums and at biennales. It is part of the collections of, for example, the Centre Pompidou in Paris, the Guggenheim Museum and the Museum of Modern Art in New York, the Stedelijk Museum in Amsterdam, and the Tate Modern in London.
37 Yael Bartana in discussion with the author, July 6, 2015. The film was shown in 2014 in the exhibition "Les Gueules Cassées. Narben des Ersten Weltkrieges in der zeitgenössischen Kunst" in the Art Gallery at Mainz (Kunsthalle Mainz), Markus Schinwald and Thomas D. Trummer, *Les Gueules Cassées: Narben des Ersten Weltkrieges in der zeitgenössischen Kunst, 27.2.–8.6.14*, Kunsthalle Mainz, program; see also the exhibition: Crossings Dance Festival, Cologne, Germany, 2011, "Entartete Kunst Lebt (Degenerate Art Lives), 2010;" the exhibition "Tür an Tür" in the Martin Gropius Bau in Berlin.
38 During the Nazi dictatorship in Germany, the term "Entartete Kunst" ("Degenerate Art") was propagated for artworks and cultural trends, which did not reconcile with the art appreciation and ideal of beauty of the Nazis; for example, it was used for artworks of Expressionism, Dadaism, Cubism, and Fauvism.
39 Besides, it is assumed that Bartana wants to thematize the relevance of the conservation and reconstruction of a destroyed visual object by new technologies, "berlinale forum 2011," accessed March 4, 2015, http://www.berlinale.de/external/de/filmarchiv/doku_pdf/20116216.pdf.
40 "Entartete Kunst lebt: Ein Animationsfilm," accessed February 26, 2015, http://www.din-a13.de/index.php?id=48; "Geführter Rundgang *Kunst ohne Grenzen*. tanzhaus nrw düsseldorf," accessed March 4, 2015, http://tanzhaus-nrw.de/main_pages/gefuehrter-rundgang-kunst-ohne-grenzen; "berlinale forum 2011."
41 "Vot ken you mach? Kunst, Filme, Konzerte, Lesungen, Gespräche, Comics zu jüdischen Identitäten in Europa heute," accessed March 4, 2015, http://votkenyoumach.de/artist/yael-bartana/.
42 See "Vot ken you mach?"
43 "In Bartanas Werk erschaffen Dix' Krüppel ihre eigene Form von 'entarteter Kunst'. Geschlagen, verwundet und erschöpft erklären sie stolz ihren Sieg: die Macht der Kunst," "Entartete Kunst lebt: Ein Animationsfilm;" see as well "berlinale forum 2011."
44 See "Entartete Kunst lebt: Ein Animationsfilm;" "Geführter Rundgang *Kunst ohne Grenzen.*"
45 Kolja Reicher, "Entartete Kunst lebt! Europa wird überwältigt sein: Die israelische Künstlerin Yael Bartana fordert die Rückkehr von 3,3 Millionen Juden nach Polen," *Die Welt*, January 6, 2012, accessed March 4, 2015. http://www.welt.de/print/die_welt/kultur/article13800937/Entartete-Kunst-lebt.html.
46 In this conflict it is mainly about four manifestations of extreme collective experiences of violence: war, military occupation, popular uprising, and terror; see José Brunner, *Die Politik des Traumas. Gewalterfahrungen und psychisches Leid in den USA, in Deutschland und im Israel-Palästina-Konflikt* (Berlin: Suhrkamp, 2014), 195.

47 See, for example, Brunner, *Die Politik des Traumas*, 230 f; for the role of media see ibid. S. 250 f; see also Sandrine Brenner Dijan, "Vom individuellen zum kulturellen Trauma: Terror und Trauma in den israelischen Tageszeitungen von 1993 bis 2003" (Master-diss., University of Tel Aviv, 2004).
48 See, for example, Keren Friedman-Peleg and Yoram Bilu, "From PTSD to *National Trauma*: The Case of the Israel Trauma Center for Victims of Terror and War," *Transcultural Psychiatry* 48, no. 4 (2011): 416; in relation to the construction, representation, and coping with suffering due to war, see also Yoram Bilu and Eliezer Witztum. *War-Related Loss and Suffering in Israeli Society: A Historical Perspective* (Bloomington: Indiana Univ. Press, 2000).
49 See Brunner, *Die Politik des Traumas*, 212.
50 See Brunner, *Die Politik des Traumas*, 215.
51 See Brunner, *Die Politik des Traumas*, 274.
52 See Sara McDowell and Máire Braniff, *Commemoration as Conflict. Space, Memory and Identity in Peace Processes* (Basingstoke et al.: Palgrave Macmillan, 2014), 104, 112.
53 See Bartana's intention of social criticism, which she articulated in an interview: "I make art in order to challenge and question society and I believe that is certainly the responsibility of an artist. I think creative work can open opportunities and change things on a small scale. It is a strong tool with which to undermine the status quo," http://www.aestheticamagazine.com/blog/interview-artist-yael-bartana/.
54 Yael Bartana in discussion with the author, July 6, 2015.
55 See Bartanas Kunstaktion in Köln: Holocaust für alle, http://www.taz.de/!118800/.
56 The artist told me in the interview from July 6, 2015 that it was her central intention to "bring back" the painting of Dix and to make possible an "experience of the painting in a new way."

8 Disabling Surrealism
Reconstituting Surrealist tropes in contemporary art

Amanda Cachia

Disabled and non-disabled artists have explored what happens when the fantastic, non-rational context of Surrealism rubs up against disability aesthetics. The politics that emanate from Surrealism are at times useful for and at other times in conflict with the politics of disability art. The iconography of Surrealist artists Hans Bellmer, Jacques-André Boiffard, Brassaï, and André Masson takes on new meaning when juxtaposed with performances, sculptures, and photographs by contemporary artists Lisa Bufano, Chun-Shan (Sandie) Yi, and Artur Żmijewski. The works of the Surrealists and these contemporary artists share some critical characteristics, as they each execute lively imagery exploring human and non-human body parts in various guises, such as the praying mantis, the mannequin, and the doll. Specifically, Bufano's animal-like performances with props and prosthetics have an uncanny physical and metaphorical similarity to the praying mantis depictions in Masson's paintings, and Yi's photographs of her two-fingered toes and feet demand and call for a reconsideration of the infamous, stark depiction of hands, feet, and other body parts in the Surrealist photography of Boiffard and Brassaï. The cocktail of Żmijewski's amputee and non-amputee bodies in his photographs evokes Bellmer's *Poupée* sculptural constellations of limbs and flesh, and his work may represent antagonism towards the very disability politics that I seek to promote in this chapter. The work of Bufano, Yi, and Żmijewski simultaneously enhances and destabilizes Surrealism's tropes and iconography, because these contemporary artists grapple with psychoanalysis and ideas of the non-rational in more complex, corporeal forms. While it is the image of disability that interested the Surrealists, the languages of disability and Surrealism have rarely been conflated within both the fields of art history and disability studies. Utilizing Surrealist tropes ultimately empowers disabled people, because they wield agency over how their own bodies are being portrayed, rather than being objectified from a distanced gaze. For this reason, contemporary representations of disability by disabled and non-disabled artists can shake up and destabilize the very radical efforts of Surrealism itself, as this was a period of art history that, to my knowledge, was predominantly composed of non-disabled artists, or artists who did not identify as disabled or have intimate familiarity with disability.

Surrealists embraced Freudian psychoanalytic theories about sexuality, eroticism, perversity, dream interpretation, the uncanny, hysteria, the death drive, trauma, shock, and castration.[1] The Surrealists' interest in psychoanalysis produced presentations of the marvelous, through convulsive beauty, the game of the exquisite corpse, and more. Given their interest in how the body might be presented as unruly, deviant, and strange, it makes sense that it was also the Surrealists who were responsible for the imaginative constructions in which the inanimate, mechanical human form, such as the magical doll or mannequin, might be conflated with the human body, especially through the work of Bellmer, Breton, Dali, and others.

How might imagery from Surrealism be reconstituted in the contemporary moment, in order to wield a more politicized function, yet simultaneously retaining its erotic, violent edge? The Surrealists frequently conflated images of the unsettling with constructions of the freak, because this most often summoned associations of disability. The mainstream often perceived that a disabled person inhabited the very characteristics of a freak, prompting visceral affective reactions in others, such as fear, curiosity, and wonder. The Surrealists were very attracted to these contradictory and mysterious qualities, and thus they utilized them prolifically. Given this, the rendering of disabled corporeality ended up being extraordinarily limited, biased, and strained. Rather than immediately reject the work of the Surrealists, by pointing out how much their work diverged from the reality of lived experience of disability and was potentially exploitative, I uncover the nuanced vocabulary of Surrealism and demonstrate its productive use in disability art.

British visual studies scholar Marquard Smith feels that despite the Surrealists' anti-bourgeois political radicalism, they never really engaged critically with psychoanalysis, "to challenge it, to transform it, to tear it asunder."[2] But Surrealist-influenced art by contemporary disabled and non-disabled artists does critically engage with psychoanalysis—the uncanny and the fetish—by virtue of a more confrontational and personal approach to disabled bodies, and through their lived experience. Picking up where the original Surrealists left off, contemporary disability art shows how Surrealism can be simultaneously enhanced and destabilized. Indeed, the works of the contemporary artists discussed in this chapter seem like familiar and yet unfamiliar forms of Surrealism. Art historian Hal Foster states that "the estrangement of the familiar that is essential to the uncanny in the very etymology of the German term: *unheimlich* (uncanny) derives from *heimlich* (homelike) . . ."[3] In the context of my chapter, I read "uncanny" to mean a body that is atypical in form and ability, and which is ghettoized within the mainstream, but is no less human than any other ostensible natural or normal corpus. The word "uncanny" has become somewhat of a synonym for "freak" in popular culture, given that both terms emerge from the world of the supernatural, the eerie, or the extraordinary, where it is inhabited by characters like Frankenstein or the Hunchback of Notre Dame. It is no coincidence that these characters share similar physical atypical attributes to the shape and form of real disabled bodies. If disabled bodies have so regularly been portrayed in fictionalized, mysterious, and scary forms in the media, the mainstream immediately assumes that real disabled people share these similar strange attributes. The Surrealists were seeking to illustrate a strangeness within our everyday lives through their artwork. Thus, if Surrealism attempted to make the familiar strange, or uncanny, I hope to make the familiarity of Surrealism's tropes more strange through the ostensible strangeness of disability itself. Psychoanalysis has also had a long-standing historical and medical interest in the uncanny; thus it was and still is, in many cases, the disabled body that comes under examination and study within this field.

The praying mantis, the exquisite corpse, and Lisa Bufano

The Surrealists turned to particular forms in culture and in nature that had potent qualities that, for them, could be utilized in ways that illustrated their politics and their vision. For instance, the praying mantis was attractive to the Surrealists for its mating ritual, in which the female eats the male during or after coitus. Art historian William L. Pressly states that "the Surrealists found this cannibalistic nuptial a compelling image of the potential for erotic violence."[4] The praying mantis embodied the most negative female archetype, the "castrating woman" who represents cannibalism, sex, and death. The mantis, then, became a metaphor for the Surrealists and their alternative, dream-like world, given its ability to embody contradictory qualities, such that it could be simultaneously attractive and repulsive. The Surrealists were also very interested in metamorphosis, as it could challenge reality and reach into an alternative, sensorial world.[5] The mantis was important here too, because this insect is able to camouflage itself through color, and the Surrealists admired the mantis's need to become one with nature and trick her mates. Because the mantis has anthropomorphic and metaphorical qualities, especially in the sexual unease she creates with her mates, her activities were then easily transferred over to human behavior patterns in the minds of the Surrealist artists. Breton and Dali included the mantis in many of their artworks; Masson depicted the mantis many times. In the drawing *Le génie de l'espèce III* (1939) (fig. 8.1), Masson depicts a mantis as though it is dancing and leaping across a stage. The way that the legs of the mantis are positioned could be mistaken for the dramatic flung-out arms and legs of an energetic ballerina in mid-air glide.

These depictions are in striking contrast to how I believe the mantis appears in the work of contemporary artist Lisa Bufano. The artist uses prosthetics and props in her performance-based practice, such as by strapping Queen Anne table legs to her legs and arms, in *Home Is Not Home* (2011) (fig. 8.2). She became a bilateral, below-the-knee and total finger-thumb amputee, due to a life-threatening staphylococcus bacterial infection at the age of 21, and she sadly committed suicide in 2013 at the age of forty. She had performed all over the world and toured with AXIS Dance Company from 2006 to 2010. In an artist statement, Bufano said that in this work, she manipulates her body as a way to explore alternative locomotion, corporeal difference, her sexual identity, and the alternative use or animation of prosthetic body parts.[6] At first, Bufano's performances with props and prosthetics have an uncanny similarity to the Surrealists' depictions of the praying mantis. Indeed, Bufano's prosthetics here look very similar in shape and form to the legs of the praying mantis depicted in *Le génie de l'espèce III*.

Disabling Surrealism 135

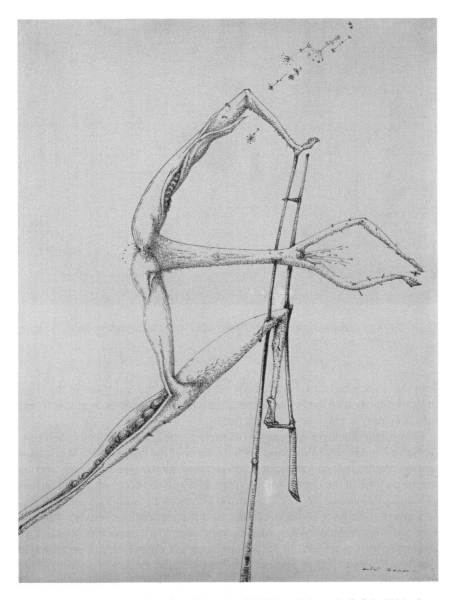

Figure 8.1 André Masson, *Le génie de l'espèce III*, 64.5 × 19.3 cm, India ink, 1939, photo © Centre Pompidou, MNAM-CCI, Dist. RMN-Grand Palais / Philippe Migeat © 2015 Artists Rights Society (ARS), New York / ADAGP, Paris.

In *Home Is Not Home*, Bufano moves across the bare stage on all fours in insect-like fashion, while a black-and-white graphic illustration of a domestic living space is projected onto a screen in the background. Like a scurrying spider or mantis, when hit by the light of the projector, her captivating form casts shadows

Figure 8.2 Lisa Bufano, *Home Is Not Home*, video still, 2011, courtesy Jason Tshantrè, photo by Jason Tshantrè.

onto the white screen, so that her body moves across the real space of the stage in synchronicity with the fictive domestic interior space in the background. These effects amplify the bizarreness of her form.

How might this literal staging of Bufano's atypical, amputee body shed light on Surrealist imagery? Beginning with the form of the mantis itself, it is important to consider Bufano's transformation and conflation between her body and the inanimate form of the Queen Ann furniture, in which she becomes animal instead of human. Because of the way that Bufano moves on all fours, face and belly-up, in a crawling fashion, it might be easy to make associations between her new form with that of many insects, such as, ants, caterpillars, or praying mantises, or arachnids, such as spiders. In her seminal essay, "Corpus Delecti," art historian Rosalind Krauss discusses Surrealist photographers as masters of disorientations of the body, and she argues that in the case of Man Ray's photographs, the nude body was revealed as beast. She writes, "[T]he body cannot be seen as human, because it has fallen into the condition of the animal."[7] The title of Bataille's very own magazine, *Minotaure*, references the man/beast. Bufano's mantis-like form falls, then, within these very essential Surrealist tropes. Bufano was also inspired by Hans Bellmer, who will be discussed in more detail later in this chapter.

Bufano's work may also be seen as the literal, instead of imaginative, embodiment of the Exquisite Corpse (fig. 8.3). This was the Surrealist popular game in which the first participant would compose part of a drawing, and then fold over

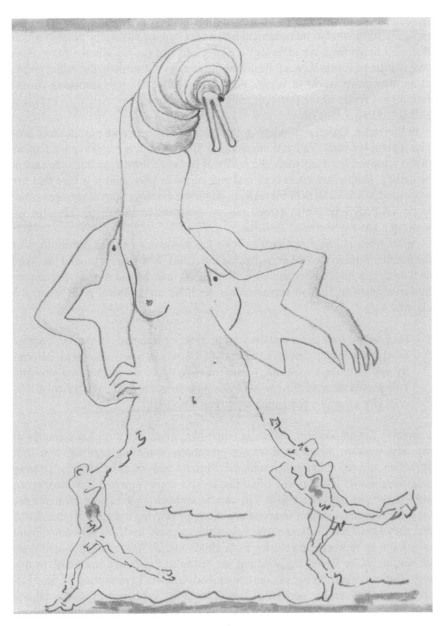

Figure 8.3 André Masson, Max Ernst, Max Morise, *Exquisite Corpse*, 20 × 15.5 cm, graphite and colored crayons on ivory wove paper, March 18, 1927, Lindy and Edwin Bergman Collection, 104.1991, The Art Institute of Chicago. Photography © The Art Institute of Chicago. © 2015 Artists Rights Society (ARS), New York / ADAGP, Paris.

the paper so that his contribution would be concealed, except for a few lines, from the next participant, who would then add to it. This would continue until all were finished, and the paper would be unfolded to reveal the completed drawing.[8] Bufano's form inhabits metaphorical Exquisite Corpse folds, as the point in which Bufano's limbs meet the table legs are suggestive of the folds in the paper. This coagulation of forms between flesh and furniture is not smooth, but rather points to an alternative world of bodies that become alive through inanimate forms. Bufano has rendered the furniture anthropomorphic, and her disjointed hybrid is a disabled Exquisite Corpse.

In this sense, Bufano's shape, her movement, and her overall performance provide a complex constellation of meaning. While her form is a creative work of art that is removed from any truth, the reality of Bufano's form as an amputee cannot be denied. Bufano's form is both real and unreal at once, and it is here that her work muddies the waters of Surrealism; while she employs Surrealist tropes in the work, her body type is also a trope and has thus been frequently used in what we understand as the Surrealist aesthetic.

Apart from physical similarities with the aesthetics and phenomenology of the mantis, Bufano also takes on its characteristics. She weaves around the stage as if casting a spell on her audience, drawing its members in through her femme fatale magnetism. Bufano explained her aesthetic and political goals when she claimed that,

> Despite my own terror and discomfort in being watched (or, maybe, because of it), I am finding that being in front of viewers as a performer with deformity can produce a magnetic tension that could be developed into strength. I attempt to channel this tension by exaggerating the mode of physical difference (for example, presenting myself on stilts).[9]

I perceive her empowering dance as witch-like, given her form has elements of mystery, wonder, danger, and magic, potentially conjuring curiosity and fear, attraction and repulsion in her audience. Bufano elaborates by saying, "[B]eing a performer with a deformity, I find that there's a gut response in audiences, an attraction/repulsion aspect to it that can be compelling."[10] These elements are what the Surrealists found so appealing about the praying mantis and other forms that they fetishized. Bufano encompasses the uncanny itself, as her embodiment might stir up repressed memories from childhood, as well as deep-rooted fears of mutilation, or becoming impaired, or "crippled," just like her body. In this way, Bufano might then also come to embody Breton's conception of "convulsive beauty," given her performance is captivating, yet her form is atypical and might embody many contradictory qualities.[11] For instance, Breton links convulsive beauty with the trauma of a railway accident, which results in a jolt, shock, or short circuit that happens to derail the rational mind.[12] Convulsive beauty is characterized by contradictory qualities, because it might contain dark desires and passions that are released after being repressed for a period of time. The beauty, then, of Bufano's performance is how she beautifully releases horror and how her

Disabling Surrealism 139

trauma simultaneously makes her beautiful as she finds freedom in expressing her form and her movement.

The ties, fingers, and toes that bind: Surrealist photography and Chun-Shan (Sandie) Yi

Analysis of the work of Chun-Shan (Sandie) Yi furthers the conversation on how a woman's body may be deformed and made strange in the work of Surrealist artists, in particular Hans Bellmer. In 1958, Bellmer took a series of black and white photographs of a female torso that was bound up in string (fig. 8.4). Unica Zürn, Bellmer's collaborator, posed for the images. Binding and bondage were recurring themes of Bellmer and Zürn's partnership, resulting in a tableau of straps,

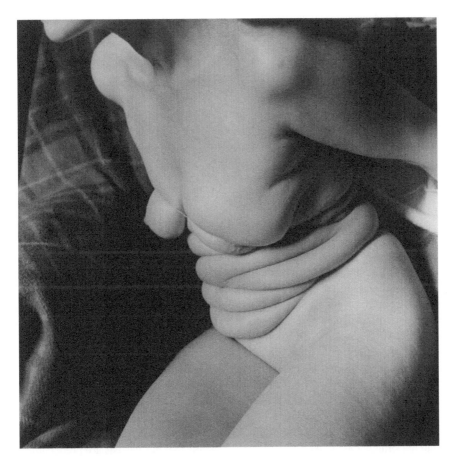

Figure 8.4 Hans Bellmer, Untitled *(Unica Bound)* 16.2 × 16.2 cm (6 3/8 × 6 3/8 in.), gelatin silver print, 1958, Ubu Gallery, New York. Photo by Joelle Jensen.

ropes, lace, and corsets, with allusions to anal penetration. Of this work, art historian Sue Taylor states,

> The bondage photographs . . . are not portraits, as Zürn's face is invariably cut off by the frame or otherwise obscured. Amid the entirely banal setting of an ordinary bedroom or parlor, these pictures render her naked torso or legs bound tightly with string, transforming her body into a series of folds and bulging mounds of flesh.[13]

Taylor believes that Bellmer created these photographs out of some desperate strategy to become closer to the female and also to the figure of the mother.[14]

While it is true that these photographs convey how the taut string across the woman's body makes her body strange, what happens when that body is already "strange," or differently bodied? Yi makes wearable art that addresses bodily and social experience and social stigma. According to her artist statement, Yi has been influenced by members of her family, who, including herself, were born with two fingers on each hand and two toes on each foot for generations.[15] Thus, Yi's work often revolves around memories of stressful and confrontational social interactions that were focused on the atpyical appearance of her body. The process of making her adornments and objects unleashes much of the artist's hidden and unconscious emotions and distress, similar to the process undertaken by the Surrealists. By using metals, fabrics, and found objects in combination with heavily handcraft-oriented techniques like metalwork, crochet, felt-making, and sewing, the artist re-examines the stereotypes and values placed on physical "deformity" and their impact on a person's well-being.[16] These stereotypes include those that consistently associate and reduce the disabled body to freak, eliciting prejudicial reactions based on fear.

Yi's series of photos, *Can I Be Sexy for Once?* (2005; fig. 8.5) depicts the artist's legs floating across a black background. She created a rock-like stone object and inserted it in the spaces between her two toes on each foot. She attached the object with string, which winds up and around each leg, where it stops halfway up her calf and is tied into a knot. The string secures the rock-like object so that it rests comfortably between the artist's toes as she moves. Juxtaposing Yi's photographs of her disability ornaments with Bellmer's photographs of the binding to which he subjected Zürn's body reveals generative intersections. The first aesthetic connection is obvious—both are using string as a type of binding, or tying up. Yet Bellmer's impulses towards the deformation of the female body may not be shared precisely by Yi, given Yi's body has an ostensible deformity to begin with. The gap between her two toes is her blank slate, and she does not need to mutate the body into something other than what it is. Rather, Yi transforms and even enhances her foot by the addition of inanimate objects, which echoes Bufano and her orange Queen Ann legs. Indeed, it seems that both artists are preoccupied with how objects might enhance or emphasize the irregularity of the body in order to challenge perceptions of beauty and perfection.

Still, this unusual shoe-like fashion piece also firmly ensconces Yi's work in the Surrealist interest in fashion and its inextricable ties to sexuality. While the ties

Disabling Surrealism 141

Figure 8.5 Chun-Shan (Sandie) Yi, *Can I Be Sexy for Once?* (no printed size), digital photo, 2005, courtesy the artist, photo by Cheng-Chang Kuo.

around Zürn's breasts and waist look uncomfortable, likely cutting off circulation, thereby hinting at violence and torture, Yi's legs look adorned. Krauss says that Surrealist fashion is "a system for rewriting the sexual organs in the register of a peculiar displacement of sexual identity," citing examples of a hat shaped in the form of female genitalia, for instance, or other ornaments like the bow tie, the garter, and so on.[17] While Yi's work deviates from Bellmer's in his interest in the possession of the female body, it is Yi who takes possession of her own body, by not only creating objects to enhance rather than diminish or hide her body, but that also act as amulets that transmit her sexiness and power as a woman. Yi's desire to look and feel attractive is demonstrated by her liberation and agency, which is channeled through her almost sadomasochistic garments. They ultimately illustrate her authoritative reclamation over both her two-toed feet. It is through Surrealist tropes that Yi finds power, and she simultaneously reconstitutes such tropes to her own politicized ends within a disability arts politics. Rather than reject the notion of physical alteration as demonstrated in Bellmer's photographs, she provides intimate and erotic bodily adornment as a tool for remapping and engaging with a new physical terrain, one imbued with personal standards of physical comfort and self-defined ideals of beauty.

I now want to juxtapose Yi's work with the infamous, stark depiction of hands and feet and other body parts in photography that the Surrealist artists found so uncanny. Krauss describes the Surrealist mechanism of rotating the axis that was "proper" to man—"his verticality, a station that defines him by separating his upright posture from that of the beasts—onto the opposing, horizontal axis."[18] The Surrealists therefore sought to reorganize these axes of orientation in order to provide dynamic new body images. They performed revisionist aesthetics, while also coining new conceptual, physiological links between seemingly quite separate parts of the body. Through innovative new arrangements of the body, the Surrealists pointed out that the human form is not always what it seems. A number of iconic photographs demonstrate that the Surrealists attempted to confuse or abstract body parts in order to make them seem strange and unfamiliar, such as Jacques-André Boiffard's series of images of big toes, like *Gros Orteil* (1929; fig. 8.6), or a close-up of fingers weaving through toes (fig. 8.8), all of which completely isolated these appendages from the rest of body. In Yi's images, which range from a close-up of the same bound-up foot that displays her disability fashion object resting in the gap between her two toes (fig. 8.7) to a close-up shot of her two-fingered hands against a red background (fig. 8.9), we detect similarities and yet marked differences between her work and that of the Surrealists.

The Surrealists and Yi both create confusion, but while the Surrealists had to search for discordant, disobedient body parts through dynamic and forced corporal commotions of the flesh, so that flesh became abstract and undefined, Yi's flesh as harbor of so-called deviancy is there to begin with. While the Surrealists searched for the uncanny to promote and fuel unconscious fears, Yi, as a person and artist who identifies as disabled, has a real body that is precisely what activates the unconscious fears of a mainstream society. If what stems from fear is the fear of castration—the idea that the vagina is a castrated version of the penis—then Yi's "missing" fingers, thumbs, and toes (or Bufano's missing legs, fingers and thumbs) might represent this very castration. But rather than a vagina suggesting the fear of castration, we see other knob-like forms of flesh on atypical bodies instead to embody what we might traditionally think of as "missing." Yi's atypical number of fingers and toes is flesh in the present, rather than conveying any kind of absent penis in the form of vagina. Yet Yi's form still offers another kind of complex erotic appendage.

Indeed, it is as if the Surrealists knew that the disabled, deformed, and castrated body is what provoked such fear, and while they searched for it and created art that became notorious for such uncanny characteristics, the disabled artist who objectifies his or her own body before a camera lens is doing something that the Surrealists could never quite attain. Surrealists made "normal" bodies into "abnormal" ones, emphasizing the power of having such fears through these bodily transformations and exaggerations. Yet, as far as I know, the Surrealists did not seek out and photograph actual disabled bodies. Yi's work, like Bufano's, demonstrates that the disabled artist therefore has the power and agency to borrow from Surrealist tropes, while at the same time providing a certain quality of complicated authenticity through the depiction of the real lived body. This is the disabled body that is absent of any rhetoric around the freak on center stage; rather, Yi shows her audience this otherness through confrontational aesthetics, removed

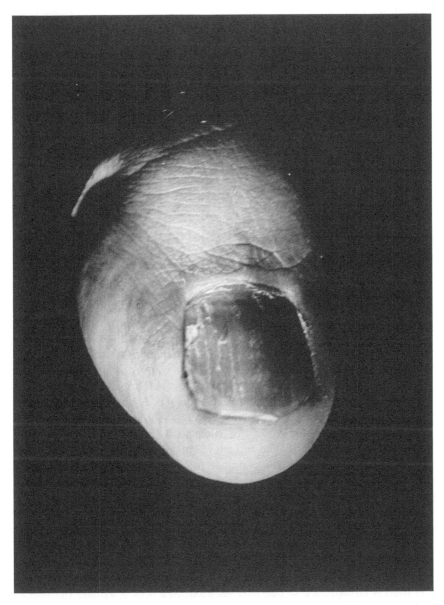

Figure 8.6 Jacques-André Boiffard, *Gros orteil*, 31 × 23.9 cm, gelatin silver print, 1929, Photo © Centre Pompidou, MNAM-CCI, Dist. RMN-Grand Palais / Philippe Migeat © Mme Denise Boiffard, © 2015 Artists Rights Society (ARS), New York / ADAGP, Paris.

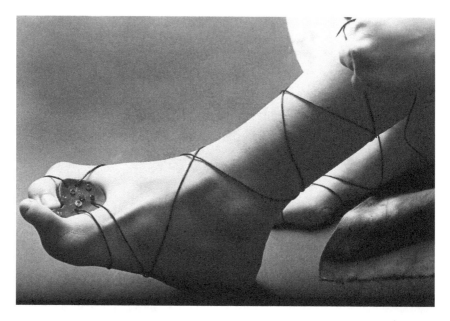

Figure 8.7 Chun-Shan (Sandie) Yi, *Footwear Close-Up* (no printed size), digital photo, 2005, courtesy the artist, photo by Cheng-Chang Kuo.

from any romantic distance that the Surrealists maintained, which kept their audiences safe from the honesty of the disabled corpus. Surrealism was based on the fantastical, evocative, and symbolic, whereas these contemporary artists use their own corporeal and conscious bodies to express real body images and experiences that are unique and personal to them.

Further, Yi's images also explicitly participate in the disorientating axes of the body that the Surrealists sought through imaginative juxtapositions, according to Krauss.[19] And yet, Yi's body is already ostensibly uncanny, according to all the characteristics already described, and made more so by employing Surrealist tropes. For instance, consider Brassaï's photograph *Nu, la poitrine* (1931–1932; fig. 8.10), juxtaposed with Yi's *Animal Instinct* (2005; fig. 8.11). Krauss notes that photographers like Brassaï and Man Ray aimed to defamiliarize the human body by "redrafting the map of what we would have thought the most familiar of terrains."[20] Rather than human and vertical, Brassaï's female body is supine and resting horizontally, which is a position that Krauss associates with the animal. Her head is thrown back so that only her elongated neck is visible. Her breasts and nipples protrude as if to suggest animal horns. Yi's position is quite unlike the female in the Brassaï photograph, because while Brassaï was trying to get the viewer to see familiar forms as sculptural objects, instead, Yi's body comes alive with agency. Yi is crouched like a cheetah, almost on all fours, in *Animal Instinct*

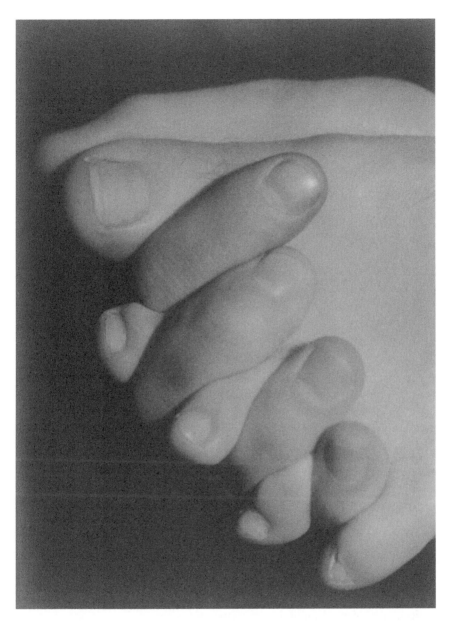

Figure 8.8 Jacques-André Boiffard, *Sans titre*, 23.8 × 17.8 cm, silver gelatine print, 1929, Photo © Centre Pompidou, MNAM-CCI, Dist. RMN-Grand Palais / Bertrand Prévost, © Mme Denise Boiffard © 2015 Artists Rights Society (ARS), New York / ADAGP, Paris.

146 *Amanda Cachia*

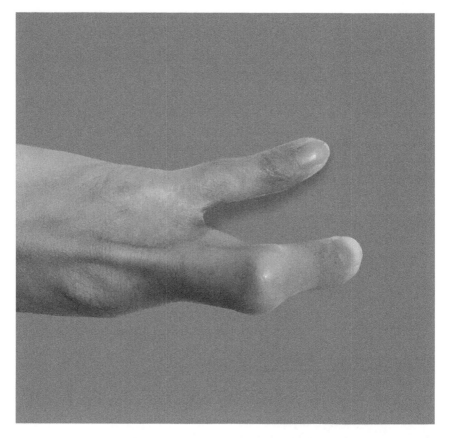

Figure 8.9 Chun-Shan (Sandie) Yi, Untitled (no printed size), digital photo, 2013, courtesy the artist, digital image edit by Shu-Ching Chou.

(2005), ready to pounce, enforcing the animalistic axis of horizontality instead of the normative standing-up verticality, to which Krauss referred.[21] Yi is nude from the waist up and proudly reveals her atypically shaped feet juxtaposed against her two-fingered hands, which are placed on her hips. Yi becomes empowered over her marginalized, objectified status, as the artist's real-life embodiment is not typically considered beautiful or attractive. However, Yi flips notions of beauty by presenting her body as attractive and seductive in this pose and under this lighting.

Yi performs as a radical activist by fitting her own corpus with a unique prosthetic toe, which has become the prosthetic claw—sharp, unfurling, and "armed." The claw sits inserted into the space between her two toes, each animal-like foot resting on tottering platform-wedged heels.

Figure 8.10 Brassaï, *Nu, la poitrine* (no known original dimensions), silver gelatin print, 1931–1932 © RMN-Grand Palais / Michèle Bellot, © Estate Brassaï—RMN-Grand Palais, © 2015 Artists Rights Society (ARS), New York / ADAGP, Paris.

Mannequins and limbs in Bellmer and Żmijewski

Another major trope the Surrealists explore is that of the mannequin or doll, and how the inanimate form of the doll becomes eerily and freakishly conjoined with the human corpus. The doll was meant to be the ultimate "emblem of castration anxiety" for the Surrealists, given that the doll was endowed with a manipulated vagina, thereby signifying a missing penis.[22] The interfusion of specifically the female mannequin or doll with the human corpus is also inevitably bound up with the commingling of technology and a fabricated sexuality. In this sense, art historian E. L. McCallum suggests that "fetishism can provide an alternative epistemological model for exploring the connections between subjects and objects, desire and knowledge."[23] Fetishism is the attribution of a special power to an object, and in psychoanalysis, the fetish was steeped within the phenomenon of substitution. In the context, we might also then read that the doll was simultaneously a penis substitute. The doll thus held a special ambiguous power for the Surrealists as a fetishistic icon. What knowledge may be gained about unconscious and repressed memories by coupling these powerful dolls with human bodies? Surrealist Hans Bellmer explored this question, producing numerous distorted, life-size female

Figure 8.11 Chun-Shan (Sandie) Yi, *Animal Instinct*, 78.7 × 55.8 cm (31 × 22 in.), digital chromogenic print, 2005, courtesy the artist, photo by Cheng-Chang Kuo.

Disabling Surrealism 149

dolls called *Poupées* and then photographing them. The dolls were often manipulated and reassembled in various combinations and poses by the artist; art historian Haim Finkelstein comments that they embodied "both total submission and subversion."[24] Indeed, Bellmer desired to have a mastery over the female figure and yet give in to its femme fatale characteristics.

It is very interesting that Bellmer's dolls end up having multiple limbs of the same kind, or sometimes no limbs at all: in the case of the image seen here (fig. 8.12), the nude mannequin lacks arms. Her genitals are very prominently exposed and her breasts protrude, blocking her head, which appears to have no neck with which to connect to her contorted torso. Bellmer took countless photographs of this same mannequin and many others in different domestic spaces, against lace backgrounds, and sometimes outdoors. Of this work, art historian Allison de Fren writes, "[T]he uncanny doubling of limbs that are often contorted or flailing

Figure 8.12 Hans Bellmer, *The Doll*, 24.1 × 23.7 cm (9 1/2 × 9 5/16 in.), gelatin silver print, 1935–1937, Samuel J. Wagstaff, Jr. Fund © 2015 Artists Rights Society (ARS), New York / ADAGP, Paris.

conveys both the disarticulation and the convulsive visuality of hysteria, with which Bellmer, like many Surrealists, was fascinated."[25] De Fren emphasizes the seemingly contradictory qualities that continued to fascinate the Surrealists so, which again had/has associations with the disabled corpus that embodies both beauty and repulsion. In the case of Bellmer's work, most often the mannequin was alone in his compositions, although sometimes Bellmer inserts himself alongside the mannequin as either its loyal companion or a mere voyeuristic observer.

The predominance of mannequins and dolls in the Surrealist imaginary warrants comparison to images of the disabled body in contemporary art practice. This raises the issue of whether there is an automatic or obvious connection between dolls/mannequins and disabled bodies in particular, or with bodies in general. For example, are the mannequins and dolls in Surrealism generally disabled, so to speak? As stated in an earlier passage, the Surrealists did not seek out actual bodies with disabilities to photograph, and instead demonstrated a desire to create these bodies. While artists, or in this case, the Surrealists, have activated their imaginations to execute works of art, the resemblance between the forms and shapes of bodies portrayed by the Surrealists in juxtaposition with real, enfleshed disabled bodies is undeniable. Why didn't the fictional disabled body and the real disabled body have a more substantial dialogic relationship? I'd like to suggest that this goes back to my previous comments around the fear, curiosity, and wonder that the disabled body has typically elicited from a mainstream, non-disabled public for centuries. Imagination is a safer refuge than having to encounter real disabled forms, and indeed, I speculate that fiction is a safe space that allows for permissible exaggeration, but also where an artist can revel in the curiosity and wonder of the "other," neatly avoiding any possibility for an oppositional gaze or affective reactions by empowered disabled subjects.

Bellmer's *Poupées* are reconstituted in the contemporary moment by bodies that are also ostensibly disarticulated. Bellmer's usage of mannequins is an act of displacement, and the mannequin becomes manipulated and appears as a fetish. Given the connection the Surrealists' work had with psychoanalysis, Bellmer's use of the mannequin as fetish feeds into the style and subject matter of the movement. Further, Bellmer's use of the mannequin as fetish ties directly to the disabled body, because the disabled corpus is always already part of a fetish subculture, where there is a subconscious desire by some to be disabled and pretend to be disabled, or to have sex with disabled people because their bodies are unique. While Bellmer may have sought to rupture the normative female form and turn it into other phallic creations as a means to reach back into his unconscious, contemporary work that explores the disorientation of bodies and body fragments may say something else about the body through the lens of a disability rhetoric.

To think about these ideas more deeply, I will look at the work of Polish artist Artur Żmijewski, who has a long-standing interest in bodily difference, but who has never identified as a disabled artist himself, as there is an absence of any mention of this in the literature that accompanies his work. In 1998 he developed the project *Oko za oko* or *An Eye for an Eye* (*An Eye for an Eye [Undressed Ib]* is seen in fig. 8.13) consisting of large-format color photographs and a video. The

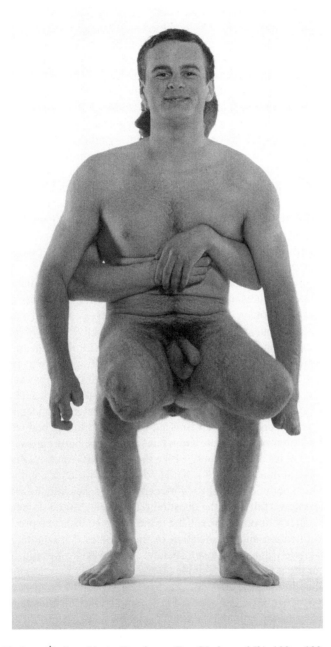

Figure 8.13 Artur Żmijewski, *An Eye for an Eye (Undressed Ib)*, 100 × 100 cm (39 3/8 × 39 3/8 in.), color photograph, 1998, courtesy the artist and Galerie Peter Kilchmann, Zurich.

photographs and video depict naked men with amputated limbs, accompanied by non-disabled people, who in the staged photographs and in the film "lend" their limbs to the amputees as they stroll, climb stairs, or bathe. The naked bodies of the protagonists were assembled by the artist in complex compositions creating bodily hybrids: the viewer will see two-headed men, men with two pairs of arms, and so on, and the appearance of new non-disabled organisms in which the "healthy" supply the amputee with substitute limbs. The title of Żmijewski's work recalls the antique rule of dispensing justice, but the artist is concerned not with the question of revenge but with that of possibility.[26] In this work, Żmijewski poses challenging questions such as whether it is possible at all for one person to "compensate" another for his or her impairments. Żmijewski's work also illustrates new ways that bodies move with and in composition with one another. His protagonists become destabilized and restabilized through their physical and emotional encounters with one another. The exchange between legs, skin, hands, arms, penises, and other body parts of the two men create new possibilities that transform concepts of mobility, immobility, pathology, and especially disability. These bodies suggest there is a need for new concepts and language around notions of "support" and insufficiency, and they are evocative of a new construction of prosthesis: where prosthesis becomes the limb of another.

All of this in juxtaposition with the work of Bellmer must be untangled, so to speak. Bellmer's figures inherently embody the markings or traces of disability, given that their forms are atypical. Indeed, the very cocktail of Żmijewski's amputee and non-amputee bodies seem viscerally evocative of the *Poupées*' constellations of limbs and flesh. His *Poupées* also reveal a more abstract quality or characteristic that represents the symbolic burden of things gone awry in the world—that is the disabling conditions of humanity, through, for example, the *Poupées* made up of grotesque features. Does Żmijewski's work seek to reproduce this quality of the disabled body suggested by Belmer's mannequins? Or is Żmijewski's work more like that of Brassaï, where the disabled body is defamiliarized through the mix of axes, as Krauss describes, and body parts are at many non-normative angles and positions?[27] Like the Surrealists' images, Żmijewski's bodies play optical illusions, for it is hard to determine which leg and which arm belongs to which body. Żmijewski's work certainly reaches into these Surrealistic tropes most powerfully, but the question remains: Is Żmijewski empowering his disabled subjects through Surrealistic tropes, or is he instead reproducing the reductive exotification and fetishization of their bodies that continues to conjure fear and anxiety in a mainstream society? Żmijewski's work illustrates how the identity of the artist creates complexity and ambiguity in representations of disabled bodies in contemporary art practices. Given that Żmijewski does not identify as a disabled artist (as opposed to Bufano and Yi), is there a difference if the artist identifies or not, and does this somehow affect the political intent of the work? Is Żmijewski watering down the agency of the disabled body, or in this case, the amputee body? Żmijewski's work straddles a precarious balance between these various zones, but it also points out how the genealogy of the Surrealists' work is alive and well in the present context in a very different form, where the association of the uncanny continues to be perpetuated, and where the disabled body is most certainly instrumentalized towards similar Surrealist tropes and metaphors. In other words, the disabled body is both subject and agent in contemporary disability art practices, and it is important to chart the fits and turns of these developments as the discourse of disability in art history is re-written and continues to evolve. Thus, Żmijewski's use of Surrealist body imagery in comparison with that of Bufano and Yi might be considered closer to a Surrealist desire to promote fear and confusion through ostensibly disabled forms and shapes in the bodies of the amputees, and yet, here, Żmijewski has used real disabled bodies in his photographs, unlike the Surrealists. He seems to be showing a genuine interest in exploring and experimenting with the disabled corpus and the artistic possibilities it can offer, but it is how he uses this interest that remains questionable. Given that Bufano and Yi directly express personal experiences of their disabled forms and shapes, Żmijewski's images can only ever be read knowing that his interpretations are in the second or even third person, which leaves them within an interpretive zone that remains strategically ambiguous. This ambivalence is possibly welcomed by the artist, and indeed, may even be part of the point, given so many contemporary artists enjoy working in this way and dislike didacticism.

Conclusion

In this chapter, I have sought to conflate the tropes of Surrealism with disability art in an attempt to complicate and layer a popular period in art history against an art movement that remains marginalized. It is my hope that Surrealism's definitions and usages of terms like eroticism, perversity, the uncanny, hysteria, narcissism, repression, trauma, shock, castration, and more will be expanded and reshaped through the careful juxtaposition of historical work by artists like Masson and Bellmer with the contemporary works of disabled and non-disabled artists, such as Bufano, Yi, and Żmijewski. Artwork about the experience of disability gets to the heart of the business within a Surrealist context; in other words, it confronts Surrealism by getting to the core of what the Surrealist artists were going for, because disability art both represents and embodies the uncanny with a twist. While the Surrealist artists sought to shock and pick at the unconscious in order to release repressed memories and other contents in the id that were often caked in fear and trauma, art that represents disability and that uses the language of disability is a different case in point. The disabled figure and/or form in contemporary art is always already ostensibly surreal in both an ontological and epistemological sense, and does not strive towards the goal of "becoming" or transforming. Rather, through exaggerating Surrealism's tropes, and by employing iconography like the praying mantis or the mannequin and doll in both traditional inanimate and animate form, the disabled artist wields great power. For the disabled body in contemporary art, the two-fingered hand or the two entwined male and female supporting bodies are absolute; they cut to the chase. Bufano's and Yi's works especially stage real corporeal bodies, rather than Surreal, symbolic ones. Their works also engage their personal experiences in and with these bodies. They have the ability to move quickly into donning these Surrealist tropes creatively, effectively, and viscerally, and then just as quickly, they can choose to shed the Surrealist trope, leg, arm, finger, or toe, so that it falls off, and away.

Notes

1 Marquard Smith, *The Erotic Doll: A Modern Fetish* (London and New York: Yale University Press, 2013), 137.
2 Smith, "Modernity's Outmodedness," 138.
3 Hal Foster, *Compulsive Beauty* (Massachusetts, Cambridge: 1993), 7. For more information, see Freud's seminal 1919 essay, "The Uncanny," in *The Standard Edition of the Complete Psychological Works of Sigmund Freud*, vol. 17, trans. and ed. James Strachey in collaboration with Anna Freud, assisted by Alix Strachey and Alan Tyson (London: The Hogarth Press, 1955), 219–252, and Ernst Jentsch's 1906 essay, "On the Psychology of the Uncanny," trans. Roy Sellars, *Angelaki* 2, no. 1 (1995): 7–16.
4 William L. Pressly, "The Praying Mantis in Surrealist Art," *The Art Bulletin* 55, no. 4 (Dec. 1973): 600.
5 Ruth Marks, "Surrealism's Praying Mantis and Castrating Woman," *Woman's Art Journal* 21, no. 1 (Spring/Summer 2000): 33.
6 http://www.body-pixel.com/2008/05/24/lisa-bufano---the-spiderwoman/, accessed June 14, 2014.
7 Rosalind Krauss, "Corpus Delecti," *October* 33 (Summer 1985): 33.
8 http://www.exquisitecorpse.com/definition/Morgue_%5Bthe_corpses%5D.html, accessed June 14, 2014.
9 http://www.body-pixel.com/2008/05/24/lisa-bufano---the-spiderwoman/, accessed June 14, 2014.
10 Allison de Fren, "Technofetishism and the Uncanny Desires of A.S.F.R. (alt.sex.fetish.robots)," *Science Fiction Studies* 36, no. 3 (Nov. 2009): 404.
11 The phrase "convulsive beauty" first appeared in André Breton's novel *Nadja* (1928) as well as in *Mad Love* (1937).
12 de Fren, "Technofetishism," 404.
13 Sue Taylor, "Transgression, Pornography, Scoptophillia," *Hans Bellmer: The Anatomy of Anxiety* (Massachusetts, Cambridge: The MIT Press, 2000), 186.
14 Taylor, "Transgression, Pornography, Scoptophillia," 186.
15 https://www.accessliving.org/375, accessed June 14, 2014
16 Cachia, "What Can a Body Do?" http://exhibits.haverford.edu/whatcanabodydo/, accessed June 14, 2014.
17 Krauss, "Corpus Delecti," 40.
18 Krauss, "Corpus Delecti," 40.
19 Krauss, "Corpus Delecti," 40.
20 Krauss, "Corpus Delecti," 40.
21 Krauss, "Corpus Delecti," 40.
22 Hal Foster, Rosalind Krauss, Yve-Alain Bois, Benjamin H. D. Buchloh, "1924," *Art Since 1900: Modernism, Antimodernism, Postmodernism Volume 1, 1900–1944* (London and New York: Thames and Hudson, 2011), 195.
23 de Fren, "Technofetishism," 411.
24 Haim Finkelstein, "The Incarnation of Desire: Dali and the Surrealist Object," *RES: Anthropology and Aesthetics* 23 (Spring 1993): 116.
25 de Fren, "Technofetishism," 412.
26 http://www.polishculture-nyc.org/index.cfm?itemcategory=30817&personDetailId=77, accessed November 20, 2012.
27 Krauss, "Corpus Delecti," 40.

9 The dandy Victorian

Yinka Shonibare's allegory of disability and passing

Elizabeth Howie

Yinka Shonibare appears, in *Diary of a Victorian Dandy* (1998), fine and fancy, charming and debonair, confident and poised, a feast for the eyes, and a fine figure of a man, at whom we have no choice but to gaze, admiringly. Master of a Victorian world of corsets and petticoats, liveried servants, mob-capped maids, billiards, and a salon, adored by all in his company, this dandy's authority and prestige are unquestionable. The *Diary*, a series of five Chromogenic photographs, each 72 × 90 inches, depicts the revels of a black dandy holding court in a luxurious nineteenth-century stately home. The dandy, in the most general sense, is a literary and social figure who, through observation and innovation, has evolved an exquisitely perfect personal style of dress and behavior, which facilitates his dazzling social ascent.[1] Dandyism is about style, with a complex relationship to class as well as to the idealization and activity of the body, and a fraught racial history, making the dandy an ideal figure on which to base an exploration of the elusiveness of identity.

In the *Diary*, Shonibare deftly manipulates the viewer's gaze as he explores the dandy's subversive and counternormative ability to trespasses class boundaries and mockingly flout social conventions.[2] Moreover, for Shonibare, a man with impaired mobility, a dandy is the perfect vehicle for the recuperation of the gaze, for an expert managing of the spectacle of disability. Challenging historical traditions about the visibility of and representation of disability, Shonibare explores the visibility of race, and in turn, the relation of visibility to identity. The relationship between visibility and identity raises themes of passing, a performance that allows for strategic slippage between social identities and transgression of social boundaries.

Of course we know that color photography was not possible during the Victorian era and that Shonibare is not a Victorian; the artist makes his deceit obvious. This photograph serves to remind the viewer that the likelihood of a black man, a black dandy, experiencing such unmitigated adulation in the Victorian era is implausible. That is a tragedy of a long history of racial oppression. Nevertheless, such a scene may now be sweetly amusing, and we can smile with a bit of disdain at the silly worshipfulness of the white figures, while admiring the dandy's tongue-in-cheek swagger. It appears to be a delightful tweak to the typical Hollywood fantasy of the Victorian era.

Much of Shonibare's work explores confluences and collisions of privilege and exploitation, otherness, cultural hybridity,[3] and the indeterminacy of meaning that results. He also frequently responds to and critiques canonical art historical and literary works.[4] He is well-known for installation works featuring beige-skinned, headless mannequins of ambiguous race dressed in elaborate historical costumes made from African wax print fabric. His interpretation of Fragonard's *The Swing* (1767), for example, replaces the Meissen-like woman of the original with a headless mannequin dressed in Dutch wax cloth.[5] The fabric is in a way passing as African, being originally manufactured in Holland, and inspired by Javanese batik. The mannequin, like others he uses, is also passing: they appear to be versions of familiar boutique figures when in fact their headlessness represents brutal violence as they fire guns, ride unicycles, or engage in scandalous sexual activity, while fully clothed. Their often exuberant postures and proper garments allow them to pass as blithely upbeat when they also carry connotations of violence and suffering and allusions to African colonization.[6] At first glance the work seems beautiful, graceful, and innocent, but Shonibare's manipulation of the original raises issues of exploitation and violence. Similarly, the images that comprise the *Diary* are charming, beautifully staged and shot, yet the visually enticing series concerns serious subject matter related to disability and race. Shonibare often explores the complexities of ambiguous appearances through a dandyish strategy of visual pleasure and seduction, and has made explicit his intention to address serious subject matter through delightful imagery.[7] He has commented, "[W]hen people see an artist of African origin, they think: oh, he's here to protest . . . but I am going to do it like a gentleman. It is going to look very nice."[8]

His exploration of disability in the *Diary* is more overt in other works; for example, *The Age of Enlightenment* (2008) features prominent Enlightenment figures with disabilities, such as using crutches or wheelchairs and having prosthetic limbs, they did not in reality possess. As disability theorist Lennard J. Davis has stated, "The visual arts have done a magnificent job of centralizing normalcy and marginalizing different bodies."[9] Shonibare centralizes difference, sidestepping normalcy. This dandy, black and disabled, is doubly marginalized; these identities have some similarities but it is their conjunction that creates a rich dialogue.

Yet the layers of meaning are far more complex. What feminist and social activist bell hooks says of African American director Oscar Michaux could apply to Shonibare as well: "Though Michaux aimed to produce a counter-hegemonic art that would challenge white supremacist representations of 'blackness,' he was not concerned with the simple reduction of black representation to a 'positive' image."[10] Similarly, Shonibare has commented that he is uninterested in revisionism, which, for him, "would come across as merely illustrative" when the work "is more about disruption and unexpectedness."[11] Nor is his work, he has said, about rediscovering a black dandy who has been lost to history. Instead, Shonibare employs the substitution of a black dandy for the conventional white one as a fulcrum with which to shift the weight of ideologies relating to race as well as to disability.

A dandy's self-invention is accomplished through his powers of observation; the dandy's keen scrutiny makes him who he is.[12] Not only is he observed (and revered), but he observes as well, and clearly the importance of looking is emphasized in the *Diary*. Yet our lingering gazes may not discern the artist's physical impairments, the evidence of which may not be immediately apparent although they are hiding in plain sight, impairments which would be incompatible with the traditional persona of the stylish and graceful dandy. That the photographs are obviously staged serves as a reminder that photography is not always truthful, however much it may appear to be, and in fact pointedly addresses the untrustworthiness of appearances in general. Shonibare's work acknowledges and explores the ways in which identities are not fixed, but instead, conditional and mutable, and that often, identity's characteristics are nonvisible, while visible characteristics have multiple meanings.[13]

Whether recovering from a late night of indulgence, pontificating in a library, placing bets on billiards, enjoying music at an intimate concert, or aloofly ignoring sybaritic behavior in the wee hours of the morning, what the dandy's handsome and fashionable mien may disguise are the visible effects of Shonibare's having contracted transverse myelitis as a teenager. This condition caused partial paralysis, leaving him at times in need of an electric wheelchair or cane and with his head tipped permanently to the right, which is very noticeable in most photographs of the artist.[14] Yet these characteristics are both visible and suggested in the images. For example, at *19.00 Hours* (fig. 9.4), he stands supported by an elegant cane, which reads perhaps as a stylish affectation. The tilt of his head has here been utilized strategically so that it emphasizes dandification, and a strong sense of superiority, thwarting a pathological reading. Many of the other figures in the *Diary* also angle their heads in ways that suggest attentive listening or looking, which makes the tilt of the dandy's head seem part of a stylized performance instead of an effect of impairment. Furthermore, Shonibare shot *03.00 Hours* (fig. 9.5) and *11.00 Hours* (fig. 9.1) from a slightly tilted point of view, as if replicating the visual experience of the artist. Rather than the paralysis with which he lives every day, Shonibare the dandy displays vigor, strength, fortitude—except for the indisposition that confines him to bed at *11.00 Hours* (fig. 9.1), necessitating the assistance of servants. Yet even that appears to be transient, followed as it is by his triumphal afternoon appearance at *14.00 Hours* (fig. 9.2).

The lone black figure in the *Diary*, Shonibare's dandy is no mere supplicant on the threshold of the white aristocracy: as cultural historian Janice Cheddie points out, Shonibare's works "are not acts of colonial mimicry on the part of the desiring colonial subject seeking to gain entry into the closed Western system of power and subjection."[15] Instead, she argues, Shonibare's work reveals the artificial and performative nature of cultural identities. His work challenges the ways visibility frames the formation of identity and subjectivity in Western culture.[16] The identification and recognition of dandyism, race, and disability are predicated on visibility, which Shonibare's work both exploits and eradicates.

Shonibare's *Diary* is a fantasy that demands examination of the history it references, including the legacy of blackface minstrelsy in Britain, and Victorian attitudes toward disability. Furthermore, it reveals ways in which perception of experience is constructed ideologically. Starting from the seeming incompatibility of a dandy performed by a black man with disabilities, the *Diary* raises questions about spectatorship and consumption of images, and thwarts the audience's suspension of disbelief. The usual codes are scrambled, refusing to permit the viewer to pretend some sort of detached, objective position of observation.[17]

Instead of having the meaning of his disability constructed by a non-disabled person, as is often the case with photographs of people with disabilities by non-disabled people,[18] Shonibare disrupts the usual unequal power relationship between the staring able-bodied person and the stared-at person with disabilities by commandeering the viewer's gaze, in part by his staging of racial otherness. While in real life, Shonibare's tilted head and ambulatory impairments might provoke surprised stares of curiosity, Shonibare as the dandy elicits dumbfounded stares of admiration. He regards the viewer, when he deigns to, with an air of decided, and even theatrical, superiority, typical of the dandy.

Historically, the disabled body and the freak have served to define the abnormal that sustains the mirage of normalcy.[19] Disability studies scholar Rosemarie Garland-Thomson describes freaks as extraordinary bodies "that challenge the status quo of human embodiment,"[20] displayed in such a way as to reinforce the viewer's sense of his or her conventional embodiment. The historical and literary figure of the dandy, a freak of sorts in its emphasis on display of the extraordinary body, inhabits and exceeds stereotypes and conventions to command shocked adulation.[21] Jules Amédée Barbey d'Aurevilley, an author who was himself a dandy, uses interesting language to address the freakishness of the dandy: for Barbey, the dandy was a monster for whom the head ruled the heart.[22] The Victorian era, as Garland-Thomson has demonstrated, is when the term "freak" came to be associated with anomalous human beings and monsters.[23] Garland-Thomson points out that the "image of the disabled body as a visual assault, a shocking spectacle to the normate eye, captures a defining aspect of disabled experience."[24] Yet while the body of the person with visible disabilities may arouse distaste or even disgust in the normate person trained by cultural conventions,[25] the dandy is a freak of aesthetic pleasure. For example, according to performance scholar Rhonda Garelick, original dandy Beau Brummell's "greatest achievement . . . lay in his ability to provoke surprise, desire, and envy, while, on his part, evincing no emotion at all,"[26] a talent amply demonstrated by Shonibare's dandy. As literary scholar Marlene Trompe notes, freak shows presented oddities that challenged common knowledge in such a way that the public were encouraged to question their authenticity:

> [T]his interrogatory practice made freak shows volatile interpretive spaces that repeatedly called the boundary between the imaginary and the real into question, and by extension challenged the authority of discourses like medical science to name and explain the significance of the human body, as well as that of mainstream culture to determine all notions of normalcy.[27]

This volatility of interpretation associated with the display of the extraordinary creates a rich ambiguity. Shonibare also strategically uses the indeterminacy of reality versus imagination in the case of the dandy and the *Diary* to challenge the authority of ideological discourses, like a sideshow barker calling the crowd to see the freakish dandy.

The dandy Victorian

In the *Diary*, the fact that the dandy is black makes him an even more freakish subcategory of dandy. While it is possible to identify actual historical black men who could have potentially walked in this dandy's footsteps, including Olaudah Equiano, Omai, and even Frederick Douglass (who visited Britain several times),[28] they would have been seen as anomalies rather than the objects of pure admiration,[29] like Shonibare's dandy. In the *Diary*, Shonibare leaves open the question of his companions' cognizance of his race, as well as his disability. Is their approval situated in the fact that he is unusual because they perceive him as an able-bodied "credit to his race"? Or are they quite accustomed to disabled black dandies? Is his isolation within the group related to his outsider status as a dandy, a status in which Shonibare has professed to be interested,[30] or because he is black? Certainly there is no hint of derision in the attitudes of the dandy's companions, whose wide-eyed observation of their friend demonstrates only admiration.

The diary

The dandy's day begins at *11.00 Hours* (fig. 9.1), when the dandy, resplendent in a thick red robe and pristine tasseled white nightcap, lies propped up in bed,

Figure 9.1 Yinka Shonibare, *Diary of a Victorian Dandy: 11.00 Hours*, 183 × 228.6 cm [72 × 90 in.], C-print, 1998. © Yinka Shonibare MBE. All Rights Reserved, DACS/ ARS, NY 2015. Courtesy James Cohan, New York / Shanghai.

appearing unwell. Landscapes by seventeenth-century Baroque artists such as Nicolas Poussin and Meindert Hobbema decorate the walls of his bedroom. Covers pushed aside, his parted robe reveals a tortuously twisted white nightgown, suggesting malaise, perhaps a queasy morning following a night of tossing and turning. Looking on is the impeccably caparisoned valet, whose livery of frock coat with gold trim and knee breeches is similar to the eighteenth-century-style costumes worn by nineteenth-century blackface dandies.[31] On the left side of the bed, a maid has raised one knee to lean solicitously over her patient, perhaps to adjust his pillows. Head tilted toward her, the dandy looks up in mild entreaty. On the opposite side, three maids attend to him, one pressing a framed object, perhaps a mirror, to her heart as her eyes linger on the dandy's face. A broad swath of sunshine illuminates the foot of the bed and the dandy himself, suggesting that it is a bit late for the dandy to continue abed. Clearly some ailment, perhaps evidence of a delightfully debauched evening (we find support for this at *03.00 Hours*; fig. 9.5), has confined him to bed until late morning.

By his next appearance, *14.00 Hours* (fig. 9.2), the dandy has to all appearances fully recovered. He holds court in a richly appointed library, the light through an unseen window softer now. Standing elegantly in a three-piece suit of lightweight

Figure 9.2 Yinka Shonibare, *Diary of a Victorian Dandy: 14.00 Hours*, 183 × 228.6 cm [72 × 90 in.], C-print, 1998. © Yinka Shonibare MBE. All Rights Reserved, DACS/ARS, NY 2015. Courtesy James Cohan, New York / Shanghai.

gray-blue fabric, the dandy, although evidently silent, seems to have just uttered some captivating witticism—which we have just missed, but that the liveried valet has captured with a quill pen—to which his manly comrades react with smiles, applause, and gesticulations of approval. Shonibare reminds the viewer of the dandy's racial difference, as well as the exploitative colonial origins of much British wealth, by placing a carved tusk on a bookshelf to the right of the dandy, a tribal artifact that stands out in the otherwise quite European décor. Eavesdropping in the doorway, uniformed maids listen eagerly, enraptured. The transition from late-morning evidently invalided patient to afternoon orator is a significant one. If we see these images as a cycle, then we know that the dandy will probably end up having another late morning, but that he will recover. Perhaps indisposition as well was a charade, another opportunity to charm, a calculated contrast to his foppish bravado.

At *17.00 Hours* (fig. 9.3), we find the dandy in a gaming room, walls adorned with portraits of horses. A heated altercation involving a billiards game occupies the gentlemen. Wearing a scarlet velvet double-breasted tailcoat with a vest of a slightly lighter shade, a frothing jabot, and plaid trousers, the dandy also sports a drop earring festooned with enormous pearls; like the carved tusk, the earring brings a note of exoticism to the otherwise staidly British scene. The prominent lamps hanging

Figure 9.3 Yinka Shonibare, *Diary of a Victorian Dandy: 17.00 Hours*, 183 × 228.6 cm [72 × 90 in.], C-print, 1998. © Yinka Shonibare MBE. All Rights Reserved, DACS/ ARS, NY 2015. Courtesy James Cohan, New York / Shanghai.

overhead, with their black and white shades, reiterate the racial difference among the men. The dandy faces down an adversary across the table; both players brandish slips of paper probably representing bets, while the valet leans in with yet more. But the dandy is unperturbed, manfully facing the challenger, as three of his comrades look on with delighted encouragement and absolute confidence. Here the tilt of the dandy's head comes across as an expression of restrained anger.

At *19.00 Hours* (fig. 9.4), we find the dandy in a fine drawing room hung with eighteenth-century ancestral (white) portraits. Accoutered in a fine black tailcoat suit accented by his pale pink velvet waistcoat and paisley silk jacquard cravat, the dandy, left hand resting lightly on a cane, basks in the delighted attention of the assembled company. As if surveying the viewer, he tips his head back and to his right, suggesting a regal, and a perhaps a touch disdainful, acknowledgment of the adulation of his companions. The other gentlemen, formally dressed like the dandy, along with corseted and crinolined ladies whose plunging necklines accent their pale décolletages, all vie for his attention. A lady in peach reaches out a white-gloved hand, tenderly touching the dandy's forearm, as another in coral pink breathlessly looks away, gloved hand over her pounding heart.

At *03.00 Hours* (fig. 9.5), the dandy reclines on a fainting couch. Close to the camera, he gazes even more directly at the viewer than in *19.00 Hours*. The

Figure 9.4 Yinka Shonibare, *Diary of a Victorian Dandy: 19.00 Hours*, 183 × 228.6 cm [72 × 90 in.], C-print, 1998. © Yinka Shonibare MBE. All Rights Reserved, DACS/ ARS, NY 2015. Courtesy James Cohan, New York / Shanghai.

The dandy Victorian 163

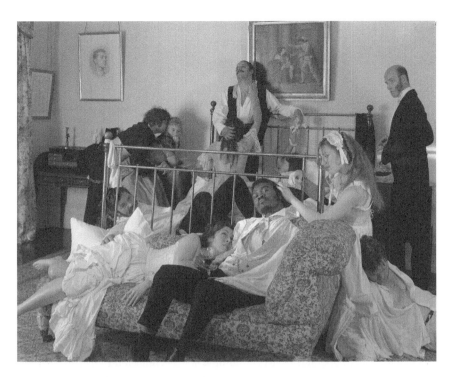

Figure 9.5 Yinka Shonibare, *Diary of a Victorian Dandy: 03.00 Hours*, 183 × 228.6 cm [72 × 90 in.], C-print, 1998. © Yinka Shonibare MBE. All Rights Reserved, DACS/ ARS, NY 2015. Courtesy James Cohan, New York / Shanghai.

musical evening has clearly been a success, and now in the wee hours the dandy experiences the veneration of the drawing room on much more intimate terms. In a different bedroom from the one in *11.00 Hours*, two of the aristocratic ladies have stripped down to their corsets and shifts, leaning on and caressing him, but he detachedly keeps one hand in his lap while holding a crystal glass of wine in the other. The tilt of his head, sideways and diagonally back into the picture, seems to invite the viewer in, at the same time that he pulls away from the lady on his right who gently caresses his hair. The position of his head and the look on his face express confidence, or perhaps arrogance, harboring no doubt that the viewer will accept his invitation. Three of his male companions cavort with other ladies, one of whom gazes distractedly at the dandy, ignoring her lover. While the dandy disregards what is going on around him, it is nevertheless a feast for the eyes of the viewer, involving sexual indiscretions of literally all sorts. The dandy has removed his jacket, but his tie is intact and his waistcoat buttoned, with his pocket watch chain swagged off to the side. He contradicts nineteenth-century stereotypical beliefs about black sexuality as primitive and uncontrolled; as the debauchery unfurls about him, he is impassive, even bored or scornful. While he is not participating, his body is clearly an object of desire. Drunk on his sexuality, his companions direct desirous looks at him, suggest that his stimulating presence is the inspiration for the carrying-on around him.

The dandy

By challenging class hierarchies, embracing idleness, and resisting cultural ideologies of manhood, the dandy represents a rejection of social convention, performed by one who rejects by conquering and mastering the very rules he breaks.[32] The dandy is an avowedly constructed identity that both bows to ideologies and at the same time demands that ideologies bow before it. Shonibare stages heavily coded scenes that appear to be stills from a movie, or perhaps a stage play. They revolve around the dandy, a figure fraught with ambivalences and tensions, and a perfect vehicle for this exploration of visibility and identity. Significantly, the title of the series states that this is a dandy's diary, and not, for example, that of a gentleman, thus indicating a specific, if somewhat amorphous, set of traits.

The concept of the dandy originates with George "Beau" Brummell, who revolutionized men's appearance in the early nineteenth century by radically simplifying clothing styles, emphasizing elegance over ostentation. Brummell took his pursuit of sartorial perfection to excess; reportedly he employed three different glove makers for each pair of gloves: one each for the palms, fingers, and thumbs.[33] These gloves may serve as a metaphor for the hybridity of the figure of the dandy, who operates between multiple social groups and identities. Brummell's social ascent, facilitated by charm and wit, intoxicatingly combined with his perfection of style, was subversive, being accomplished at a time when lines were drawn sharply between classes. The dandy in general may be seen as a figure arising from new instabilities related to society, economics, and gender.[34]

The dandy is made, self-invented, not born, but this metamorphosis must be invisible; "the dandy" is a charade, an identity adopted strategically, stage-managed to the last detail, which permits him to obtain access to social privileges not naturally his by birth.[35] The raison d'être of the dandy is to be always more refined, more chic, than anyone else, to be both adored and to escape being pinned down into particularity. His perfection, however, is intended to be purposeless; thus the dandy works particularly well as a figure to be played by someone with impaired movement. He does not do, he simply is, so standing around looking flawlessly elegant is quite appropriate.[36] If, as Davis has argued, one of the key modalities of the identification of disability is function, the dandy has in large part opted out of the potential to be evaluated on that level by emphasizing the other of Davis's modalities, appearance.[37]

Shonibare's *Diary* is in dialogue with works by eighteenth-century satirist William Hogarth, whose series, such as *The Rake's Progress* (1733), address the legibility and fluctuations of character.[38] With this reference, Shonibare's work demonstrates the complexity of the relationship of visibility to identity, and points out the fluidity of identities based on illness or disability.[39] But unlike Hogarth's dandy, Tom Rakewell, who, as Shonibare points out, "spends his father's money extravagantly, gets into debt, and ends up in a madhouse,"[40] and Brummell, who ended up living in impoverished exile in France, Shonibare's dandy flourishes: he comments, "My dandy has a wild time, has wild orgies, but he gets away with it. He challenges the notion of bourgeois morality."[41] Shonibare's dandy provides an alternate ending to the often perilous story of the hero who explores the fluidity of identity.

While dandyism is often associated with the eighteenth and early nineteenth centuries, Shonibare contextualizes his in a specifically Victorian era. The figures in the *Diary* wear clothes from between 1860 and the early 1870s, the era of the American Civil War and its immediate aftermath.[42] This situates him just after the era of the Baudelairean dandy of *The Flowers of Evil* (1857) and *The Painter of Modern Life* (1863). As queer theorist Jeremy Kaye points out, dandies influenced by Baudelaire, more than those of the eighteenth century, contest the "codifications of 'normative/pathological and homo/hetero,'"[43] and thus the historical context of Shonibare's dandy reflects the fact that Victorian dandies of the 1860s challenged more than just class. The 1860s and 1870s were also the era of the hardening of British racist ideologies during the expansion of the empire immediately preceding the so-called "scramble for Africa,"[44] which is the title of one of Shonibare's installations. The clothes also situate the dandy at the end of a period when the ideology of physical normalcy as a desirable goal emerged, from the 1840s to 1860s, according to Davis, which was instrumental in the development of the ideology of the middle class.[45] Shonibare's dandy, disavowing normalcy in several ways, performs a type of resistance to these Victorian ideologies.[46] All of these factors combine to make the specific Victorian context of Shonibare's dandy of critical importance.

Dandyism, race, and disability

The canonical dandy would be too embedded in his own social prominence to be concerned with politics and social issues,[47] but Shonibare's dandy cannot escape being embroiled in them. As a black man with disabilities, rather than the traditional able-bodied white dandy, Shonibare embeds his fictional alter ego in discourses that were the subject of controversy in the Victorian era. Shonibare's most obvious challenge to the appearance of the traditional dandy relates to race, and the dandy seems to have curated his posh wardrobe to emphasize his dark complexion. The elegant, frothing cravat he wears while playing billiards in *17.00 Hours* (fig. 9.3) sets off his chocolate skin; at *03.00 Hours* (fig. 9.5) his rich pink velvet, double-breasted waistcoat and tie bring out the glowing walnut of his face and match the pink pearliness of his nails. Everybody else, including the servants, is white; there are no black people in subservient roles here.

Dandyism has a very complex relationship to race, flourishing during a time when, in general, white prejudice framed black people as almost inherently disabled, morally and intellectually—beliefs many British abolitionists shared.[48] Advocating freedom did not go hand in hand with believing in racial equality, and the inferiority of blacks was considered a scientific fact,[49] one that supported the ideology of the dominance of the civilized colonizer over the primitive colonized.[50]

During this period, disability was pathologized as another marker of inferiority. The dandy's strategic use of style to transcend class limitations has historically also been a strategy for blacks struggling to overcome institutionalized oppression. Many Africans came to enslavement with nothing, not even clothing; they were given either rough work clothes that reinforced their status as laborers, or perhaps uniforms or livery that restated their servitude.[51] One way that freed slaves, as well as some prominent black intellectual reformers such as Frederick Douglass, sought to assert their humanity and worthiness of respect was through clothing; by dressing respectably, and even with flair, they staked a claim to their agency.[52] For black men in America, wearing fancy dress was also a form of defiance against oppression.[53] Whites at times interpreted this behavior as both a challenge to white superiority as well as a rejection of menial labor,[54] and the well-dressed black man could be met with violence, persecution, or even arrest until he could convince the authorities that his fine garments were not stolen but belonged to him.[55] Whites responded to well-dressed black men with atrocious and cruelly stereotyping satires, implying that no clothing could hide what they considered the inherent inferiority of blacks. These satires included portrayals of blacks as clumsy, uncoordinated, and intellectually impaired, as evidenced by the characters' misunderstandings and evident stupidity.

Such stereotypes—of blacks dressed ostentatiously and in poor taste, but thinking they represented the height of style—became a staple of blackface minstrelsy. Significantly, blackface minstrelsy was in part popularized in the United States by P. T. Barnum, as a form of sideshow entertainment in company with his oddities.[56] This association of the blackface minstrel show with the sideshow, best known for its displays of human oddities, further demonstrates nineteenth-century associations of blackness with disability. The black dandy was one of the main subjects of minstrel satire in Britain.[57] In minstrelsy, the dandified black man was portrayed by white performers in blackface as a buffoon, personified by characters such as Zip Coon, Dandy Jim of Caroline, and Long Tail Blue,[58] performances which policed black masculinity and made ridiculous one avenue to dignity.[59] Shonibare's dandy is black and clearly nobody's fool.

Blackface minstrelsy was at least as popular in Britain as in the United States, and persisted much later into the twentieth century than in the States. As late as 1978, a BBC variety show called *The Black and White Minstrel Show* continued the racist performances of blackface minstrelsy, and Culture Club's 1984 video for "Do You Really Want to Hurt Me?" included a "jury" of black performers in blackface. British minstrelsy, like that of the United States, was based on white impersonation of blacks. Slavery had not flourished on British soil, so British minstrelsy relied almost entirely on American minstrels' misrepresentation and stereotyping of southern black plantation life.[60] British blackface minstrels believed themselves to have taken minstrelsy to its highest levels,[61] eschewing what they perceived to be the lowbrow vulgarity of American minstrelsy, with its coarse humor and rough language. Nonetheless, British minstrel performers continued to create greatly exaggerated and stereotyped characterizations that both reflected and shaped racist attitudes.[62] This was especially true because British minstrelsy appealed to a much broader audience than American minstrelsy; in the United States, blackface minstrelsy audiences tended to be working-class white men, but in Britain, minstrelsy was popular with both genders and all classes.[63] Few actual African Americans performed in British minstrel shows, and when they did, the audience often preferred disguised whites.[64] Furthermore, because the black population in Britain, never large (around ten thousand during the late eighteenth century), dwindled throughout the nineteenth century,[65] for most Britons, their only knowledge of black people came from blackface minstrelsy.[66] Thus both the white aristocrats and the servants seen in Shonibare's *Diary* would have been more familiar with demeaning caricatures of black people seen in minstrel shows than with actual black people. While early British blackface minstrelsy included anti-slavery sentiments and cannot be characterized as uniformly racist,[67] and while Britain had led the west in the abolitionist movement in the 1830s, by the 1860s, racism was rampant, supported by "science" that confirmed white beliefs about black inferiority.[68] Taught to perceive blacks as inferior as the British Empire expanded, Britons defined themselves as white in opposition to the caricatures of blackface minstrelsy.[69] Minstrelsy's lampooning of southern American black culture went hand in hand with Britain's developing imperialism.[70]

Most white Victorian Britons would have been too influenced by the stereotype of the black minstrel show dandy to respond to Shonibare's dandy as positively they do in the *Diary*. British blackface dandies often wore costumes based on eighteenth-century British court dress, such as knee breeches, buckled shoes, and powdered wigs, similar to the costume worn by the valet, rather than the dandy, in the *Diary*.[71] The British blackface dandy, as in the United States, was portrayed as outrageously flamboyant in dress, with ridiculously exaggerated manners and flowery but grammatically incorrect speech, often deployed in pursuit of a blackface belle, usually also performed by a white man, emphasizing the dandy's sexuality and at the same time rendering it deviant.[72] Minstrel shows also lampooned the black dandy's pursuit of white women, underscoring fears of interracial sex, mixed-race offspring, and rape, as well as operating on the assumption that black men would prefer white women.[73] It was not until the late nineteenth and early twentieth centuries that this stereotype began to loosen, when American black Vaudeville performer George Walker reclaimed the dignity of the black dandy.[74] This background of racism, blackface minstrelsy, and the black dandy makes the historical setting chosen by Shonibare even more significant.

The dandy was considered so charming that everything was given to him, thus one of the canonical dandy's most important traits is his idleness.[75] This trait becomes more complicated when the dandy is black, and is further problematized by Shonibare's own physical impairment. While a white dandy's freedom from labor may seem justified by his exquisitely articulated taste, a black dandy may be vexed by stereotypes about the laziness of black workers.[76] Among the most prominent stereotypes promulgated by British blackface minstrelsy were the docility, hedonism, and idleness of black people, in contrast to the way Victorian Britons identified themselves—as industrious and hard-working.[77] Yet the dandy's purposelessness is part of his repertoire. Shonibare's impaired mobility therefore suits the role of the purposeless dandy.

Shonibare's dandy triumphs, attaining the adulation for which every dandy strives while appearing not to. He has no need to seek rights or even respect; he has them. Shonibare's dandy's blackness appears not as a sign of inequality, but as added inspiration for adoration. The viewer's pleasure comes at first from his charming appeal, and then perhaps second from the apparent absence of racism. And yet, however effective his conquering of society may be, histories of racism whisper questions about how he has accomplished this: Is the adulation due to his having overcome great adversity, or is it simply because he is so fabulous? Is he just a decadent wastrel?

Victorian attitudes toward disability

Victorian attitudes toward disability also relate to the specific chronological setting of the *Diary*. During the mid-nineteenth century, Victorian literature embraced representations of disability, reflecting ways that standards of manliness and masculinity shifted to industrious, hard-working, and thus strong and active during the Industrial Revolution.[78] Literary protagonists followed suit; a corollary to their newly emphasized masculine strength was that they were less emotional, emotions being perceived as feminine, and also less talkative. The hero's friend, an invalid or disabled man, provided the affect and speech suppressed in the muscular hero, and many novels explored the trope of such friendships, demonstrating Victorians' fascination with disability.[79] While the figure of the dandy-invalid did not appear until the end of the nineteenth century,[80] the popularity of the trope of the invalid friend nonetheless points to an awareness of male disability during the historical era of the *Diary*. Part of this awareness included the belief that visible disability was particularly repellent and thus an additional burden for the disabled man, who was thought to suffer as much from the revulsion of others as from the illness or disability itself.[81] Victorians associated sickness and disability with suffering and sympathy, making the disabled body a locus of feeling.[82] An example of this belief is reflected in the idea that English Romantic poet Lord Byron's sensitive and poetic nature was a result of his being born with a club foot.[83] This attitude reflected Victorian sympathy toward disability, particularly when the disability was the result of fate and not, for example, some reckless or careless behavior on the part of the individual, in contrast to eighteenth-century beliefs that disability and deformity were either comical or villainous.[84] Furthermore, Victorians did not perceive disability per se as stigmatizing, although certainly deserving of sympathy or charity, as we do today.[85]

The literary invalid or disabled man was in general described as smaller and weaker than his hardy counterpart, who was portrayed more uniformly as being tall, with broad shoulders and a deep chest.[86] The robust protagonist was also frequently characterized as being fair-skinned and blond, while the disabled man more often had a darker complexion and dark hair.[87] Shonibare's dandy, then, flirts with these Victorian ideas about masculinity and disability. His dandy is tall and strong-looking, with the requisite broad shoulders and deep chest of the literary hero, with a disability that does not mar his vitality by being visible. Shonibare's photographs bring together or even merge (in one body) physical characteristics that were believed to indicate or be embodied by opposite kinds or statuses of men.

Race, disability, and art history

Traditionally in art historical representations, both black people and people with disabilities have tended to be either marginalized or presented for perusal as fascinatingly other.[88] In terms of race, as Shonibare points out, ". . . if you see a painting from that period, the black face is not going to be the guy in front, it is going to be the servant or the slave."[89] A dandified black servant reflected the stylishness of his or her masters, while also often providing a "primitive" contrast to the "highly evolved" white aristocrats. Such individuals, whose lavish dress and apparent freedom from heavy labor were indicative of their masters' great prosperity, were called prestige or luxury slaves.[90] Often enslaved as young boys and forced into foppery, they were both elevated by their masters and made silly or pretentious, and were not infrequently the targets of satire and caricature.[91] Exceptions exist, such as Hogarth's Scene 4, *La Toilette*, from *Marriage à la Mode* (1743) which depicts a finely liveried black servant whose moral sensibility reflects negatively on the dissipated whites surrounding him.

In addition to being marginalized in representations, black people were (and are) also marginalized by art history. Art historian David Dabydeen remarks,

> I remember, in the early 1980s, reading practically everything ever written on William Hogarth and not coming cross any acknowledgment of his black figures, never mind their roles in his complex narratives. . . . The irony is that whilst actual black bodies were (as slaves) lucrative, there was no corresponding value attached to their images, hence they were overlooked. Nor was there any recognition that many of the great houses in Britain were stocked with art purchased from the revenues of slavery.[92]

The setting of Shonibare's *Diary* in a stately home decorated with Persian rugs and a carved tusk calls attention to such exploitative colonial sources of wealth. Furthermore, Dabydeen, writing in 2005, noted that it was not until the 1970s that black history started to be comprehensively addressed in British historiography, and that furthermore art galleries' and museums' acknowledgment of the importance of images of black people and historical artifacts associated with black culture occurred even later.[93] Shonibare, with his adored black dandy, who is not even faintly the object of ridicule, is upending an entire tradition of the portrayal of blacks in British art, as well as demanding an art historical reconsideration of their appearance in such images.

In terms of representations of disability in art, Siebers has argued that modern art's interest in the asymmetrical, imperfect, and abstract has close ties to visible disability. Furthermore, he points out that while when presented as abstraction, such images are hailed as experimental and avant-garde, that more naturalistic or realistic depictions of disability are seen as symptoms that art itself is diseased, as in his analysis of Marc Quinn's *Allison Lapper Pregnant* (2002).[94]

Passing

While Shonibare's dark skin would prohibit his easily passing for white, the *Diary* portrays a black man who enters a specifically white world quite successfully. Because dandies use dress and appearance to transcend their original social status, they could be thought of as passing, a term most strongly associated with racial passing in America during the eras of slavery and Jim Crow, in which light-skinned individuals of mixed racial ancestry, who were legally considered black but appeared white, assumed new identities, whether occasionally or permanently, in order to obtain rights or privileges otherwise unavailable to them. Passing implies a cutting off from one's native identity and very often family of origin, a demanding price to pay. Novelist and cultural critic Touré writes,

> ... once they cross the line, they're fugitives hiding in plain sight, on the lam from themselves and their histories, cut off from their families, unchained from racism but chained to a secret whose revelation would bring an end to a life built on lies and a stolen place in the dominant culture ... they've got Huck Finn's independence, an identity in turmoil, a secret that could destroy their world, a refusal to be defined by others and a vantage on race that very few ever get to have.[95]

Indeed, as literary scholar Elaine Ginsberg points out, "Passing is about identities: their creation or imposition, their adoption or rejection, their accompanying rewards or penalties."[96] In passing, the creation of a new identity requires the abandoning or at least suppression of another.

The flip side of the issue of the visibility of identity that is at stake in passing is that at times one's primary identification of identity may not be visible. Gender studies scholar Lisa Walker notes that "[t]he impulse to privilege the visible often arises out of the need to reclaim signifiers of difference which dominant ideologies have used to define minority identities negatively."[97] For example, claiming identification based on skin color or visible disability allows a group to assert its identity. Yet this strategy problematically may also make invisible members of that group for whom the signifier of difference is not visible, or for whom signs of another identity are visible.[98] Critical theorist Margery Garber refers to such situations as category crises,[99] in which ways that appearance and behavior relate to identity fail to add up.[100] Thus dandyism may be a strategic use of the category crisis, in its facilitation of crossing class barriers, and both following and breaking rules. The dandy has the skills to exploit the places where distinctions between identities break down, and the *Diary* emphasizes this in the variety of stages on which the dandy performs: as invalid, as orator, as gambling gamesman, as formally clad heartthrob, and as abstinent fomenter of desire. The dandy is at home in the space between identifiable identities. And pleasurable as it looks in Shonibare's work, this is not a game but a form of resistance.[101]

Passing also plays a role in disability theory, some of which concerns the visibility of disability. Many disabilities and impairments, like Shonibare's, are not immediately evident visually, requiring continuous negotiation of the threshold of passing or coming out, a constant reassessment of situations in terms of whether or not the announcement of disability is appropriate or useful. To be disabled, and yet pass as abled, may be useful but also create, as literary scholar Ellen Samuels puts it, "a profound sense of misrecognition and internal dissonance."[102] Ginsberg notes that "passing forces reconsideration of the cultural logic that the physical body is the site of identic intelligibility,"[103] which is at the heart of what the *Diary* explores: the undecidability signified by the multiply passing dandy resists any sound identification. In this economy of identity, passing is perceived as assimilationist with dominant ideologies, as conservative, as compliant.[104] Problems arise when someone with a nonvisible disability is misperceived as lazy, deceitful, or entitled, such as being forced to produce proof or documentation, or even experiencing the harassment of disbelieving strangers.[105] Yet Samuels demonstrates that "passing can become a subversive practice . . . the passing subject may be read not as an assimilationist victim but as a defiant figure who, by crossing the borders of identities, reveals their instability."[106] This seems to be the liminal space Shonibare's dandy occupies.

Photography in particular has a capacity to facilitate the passing of disability. Disability studies scholar Mark Jeffreys writes of his complex feelings about a photograph taken on his brother's wedding day: he and his father, both living with brittle bone disease, stood precariously, when a fall could be disastrous: "My own brittle bones were at that time supporting me fairly well, so I stand in front with a smug look on my face, perhaps because I knew that I could pass." His brother, "Peter, born with spina bifida, stands so that his partial paralysis looks more like a casual, hipster's slouch."[107] The groom, who was born without legs, usually used a wheelchair, but wore prosthetic legs for the occasion, balancing carefully. Jeffreys says, "We understood that if our disabilities were framed, our disabilities would frame us, and we wanted to exclude them so we wouldn't vanish behind them."[108] And yet to pass as able-bodied, to disavow a body with limitations, may be a form of complicity with society's biases. Jeffreys is intently aware of the spectacle that disability may present, as well as of the complexities of manipulating that spectacle.

Clearly Shonibare's dandy is a spectacle, accepting the rapturous looks cast his way by his companions as his natural due. These images are engineered to be seen, gazed at, stared at, for a sustained period of time. If as Garland-Thomson says, "Disability operates visually by juxtaposing the singular (therefore strange) mark of impairment in a surrounding context of the expected,"[109] here, paradoxically, not impairment but multiple singularities startle the eye with a shock of difference: the dandy's exquisite perfection and the failure of his racial difference to create the usual tensions and hierarchies. Shonibare has expertly co-opted the shock of appreciation the dandy desired from his audience. Most important of all,

Shonibare has really not hidden evidence of disability, but rather failed to draw attention to it.

Photographically, disability theorist David Hevey observes, disabled people are represented "almost exclusively as symbols of 'otherness,' placed within equations which have no engagement to them and which take their non-integration as a natural by-product of their impairment."[110] Faced with this long tradition of representation by others, what are the options for a person with disabilities who wishes to represent him or herself?[111] As Garland-Thomson has pointed out, "With the actual disabled body absent, photography stylizes staring, exaggerating and fixing the conventions of display and eliminating the possibility for interaction or spontaneity between viewer and viewed."[112] Thus photography liberates the viewer to stare at will without repercussion.[113] The dandy is a professional stylist of staring who, as we see in the *Diary*, tends to eliminate interaction by his sheer magnificence. Knowing that the *Diary* promotes long staring that is free from worry about bad manners, Shonibare deliberately plays with issues of the gaze, the stare, and disability, and when society does and does not deem sustained looking acceptable. Garland-Thomson argues that human beings are in fact somewhat helpless when it comes to staring: "Oddness or singularity is both fascinating and troubling," she writes, and the traditional white dandy is already a singular, if not necessarily odd, figure.[114] We are hard-wired to stare at unfamiliar sights, and certainly a black Victorian dandy qualifies.

Staring, Garland-Thomson argues, is a way of taming the world, of processing the unfamiliar. We are threatened by the new and unfamiliar, which causes the neurotransmitter dopamine to flow; through the stare, we attempt to reconcile the unknown with the familiar.[115] We can't help the initial stare when something unknown captures our eyes; all we can do is regain control of the stare and turn away, following the rules of polite society that prohibit staring. But here, we may feast our eyes on Shonibare's fine fellow, and in fact, as good upstanding viewers of art, we must. Yet the viewer's stare, the devouring look that Shonibare encourages by saturating his images with beauty and luxury, fails, at least initially, to perceive the aspects of his appearance that would in the real world undoubtedly attract our attention because of their physical anomalousness.

Constructed identities

As gender studies scholar Anne Fausto-Sterling argues, the body is a "somatic fact created by cultural effect."[116] Elaborating, gender studies scholar Marlene Tromp explains that

> [t]he body—whether normative or not—is structured by the cultural context. This does not mean that the "body" is simply discursive, that there is no body or potential bodily difference to comprehend or figure or that these constructs are not multiple and slippery. Rather, it suggests that the body and its characteristics only come to mean something within a particular social and conceptual system and that the body is, in fact, determined by context.[117]

The markers designated to demarcate identity are differences more cultural than biological. Differences exist, but their meaning and hierarchization are created culturally. The dandy is a figure who constructs his own identity and uses it to ascertain that he is forever in control of the setting in which it will be perceived. Shonibare, posing as the dandy, a human work of art, a spectacle both inside the picture as the black dandy and in our world as a man with disabilities, asks us to look at him, even to stare at him. It is worth noting that the *Diary* was originally shown in poster form in the London Underground, where commuters often have nothing at all to do while waiting for trains except peruse the ads around them; furthermore, and ironically, the London Underground is not known for its accessibility, so these viewers were more than likely not disabled. The *Diary* explores the dandy as the object of the gaze, or even of gawking[118] stares. As art historian W.J.T. Mitchell has pointed out, a work of art is an object that asks us to look at it.[119] The adoring gazes of the figures accompanying him in the *Diary* also encourage us to engage in sustained looking. Shonibare, as the dandy, a human work of art, a spectacle both inside the picture as the black dandy and in our world as a man with disabilities, asks us to look at him, even to stare at him. At the same time, he refuses the stare which, for Garland-Thomson, "is the gesture that creates disability as an oppressive social relationship."[120]

Shonibare's *Diary of a Victorian Dandy* is less a reimagining of himself as able-bodied, or as upper class and passing for white, than it is an exploration of visibility and identity. Shonibare's dandy doesn't pass for white, but the staging of the *Diary* results in a setting "in which race doesn't carry the usual connotations or fall into stereotypical hierarchies."[121] Shonibare, with dandyish charm, fearlessly shows us that our anxieties about categories of identity are historical and entrenched; requests, sternly but politely, that we attend to this history and then with great generosity, welcomes us into his world. His exploration of dandified passing is not a reinvention of a self that denies another aspect of identity, but instead one that powerfully contests the containments of identity that so often structure how we think about each other.

Notes

1. Dandies in literature and history are predominantly male; scholarship addressing dandyism and gender includes Miranda Gill, "The Myth of the Female Dandy," *French Studies* LXI, no. 2 (2007): 167–181; Rhonda K. Garelick, *Rising Star: Dandyism, Gender, and Performance in the Fin de Siècle* (Princeton, NJ: Princeton University Press, 1998).
2. Barbara J. Black, "The Pleasure of Your Company in Late-Victorian Clubland," *Nineteenth-Century Contexts* 32, no. 4 (Dec. 2010): 283.
3. Anna Marie Peña, "A Terrible Beauty: Politics, Sex, and the Decline of Empires," *C Magazine* 114 (Summer 2012): 19.
4. Jane Wilkinson, "Prospero's Magic or Prospero's Monsters? Disabling Empire in David Dabydeen and Yinka Shonibare," *Textus* XXIII (2010): 498.
5. *The Swing, after Fragonard*, 2001.
6. For example: *How to Blow Up Two Heads at Once (Ladies)*, 2006; *Lady on Unicycle*, 2005; *Gallantry and Criminal Conversation*, 2002.

7 Jaap Guldemond and Gabriele Mackert, "To Entertain and Provoke: Western Influences in the Work of Yinka Shonibare," in *Yinka Shonibare: Double Dutch*, ed. Guldemond and Mackert (Rotterdam: NAi Publishers, 2004), 41.
8 Guldemond and Mackert, "To Entertain and Provoke," 41.
9 Lennard J. Davis, "Nude Venuses, Medusa's Body, and Phantom Limbs: Disability and Visuality," in *The Body and Physical Difference*, ed. David Mitchell and Sharon L. Snyder (University of Michigan Press, 1997), 63.
10 bell hooks, *Black Looks: Race and Representation* (South End Press: Boston, 1992), 133.
11 Cited in Anthony Downey, "Setting the Stage: Yinka Shonibare MBE in Conversation with Anthony Downey," in *Yinka Shonibare MBE*, ed. Rachel Kent (New York and London: Prestel, 2014), 48.
12 Monica Miller, *Slaves to Fashion: Black Dandyism and the Styling of Black Diasporic Identity* (Durham and London: Duke University Press, 2009), 9.
13 Ellen Samuels, "My Body, My Closet: Invisible Disability and the Limits of Coming-Out Discourse," *GLQ: A Journal of Lesbian and Gay Studies* 9, no. 1–2 (2003): 238. Following Samuels, I use "nonvisible" in relation to disability to refer to unmarked identity rather than marginalized or invisible identity.
14 Deborah Sontag, "Headless Bodies from a Bottomless Imagination," *The New York Times*, accessed June 17, 2009.
15 Janice Cheddie, "A Note: Yinka Shonibare: Dress Tells the Woman's Story," *Fashion Theory* 4, no. 3 (2000): 352.
16 Samuels, "My Body, My Closet," 236.
17 These ideas about spectatorship in relation to Shonibare are inspired by Lisa Bloom, "Introducing *With Other Eyes: Looking at Race and Gender in Visual Culture*," in *With Other Eyes: Looking at Race and Gender in Visual Culture*, ed. Bloom (Minneapolis: University of Minnesota Press, 1999), 4.
18 David Hevey, "The Enfreakment of Photography," in *The Disability Studies Reader*, ed. Lennard J. Davis (New York and London: 1997), 345.
19 Garland-Thomson, "Seeing the Disabled: Visual Rhetorics of Disability in Popular Photography," in *The New Disability History: American Perspectives*, ed. Paul K. Longmore and Lauri Umansky (New York: New York University Press, 2001), 348.
20 Garland-Thomson, "Staring at the Other," *Disability Studies Quarterly* 25, no. 4 (Fall 2005), http://dsq-sds.org/article/view/610/787
21 Rhonda K. Garelick, "The Layered Look: Coco Chanel and Contagious Celebrity," in *Dandies: Fashion and Finesse in Art and Culture*, ed. Susan Fillin-Yeh (New York: NYU Press, 2001), 36.
22 "Un de ces monstres chez qui la tete est au-dessus du Coeur," Gill, 176.
23 Garland-Thomson, *Freakery: Cultural Spectacles of the Extraordinary Body* (New York: New York University Press, 1996), 4.
24 Garland-Thomson, *Extraordinary Bodies*, 25; see also Siebers, *Disability Aesthetics* (Minneapolis: University of Michigan Press, 2010), 1; Lennard J. Davis, *Enforcing Normalcy: Disability, Deafness, and the Body* (New York: Verso, 1995), 12.
25 Davis, *Enforcing Normalcy*, 12.
26 Garelick, "The Layered Look," 36.
27 Marlene Trompe, "Introduction: Toward Situating the Victorian Freak," in *Victorian Freaks: The Social Context of Freakery in Britain*, ed. Trompe (Columbus: The Ohio State University Press, 2008), 8.
28 Robert Nowatzki, *Representing African Americans in Transatlantic Abolitionism and Blackface* (Baton Rouge: Louisiana State University Press, 2010), 55.
29 Rachel Kent, "Time and Transformation in the Art of Yinka Shonibare," in *Yinka Shonibare MBE*, 17.
30 Downey, "Setting the Stage," 48.
31 Michael Pickering, *Blackface Minstrelsy in Britain* (London: Ashgate, 2008), 21, describes the costumes worn by the Coloured Opera Troupe in this way. They were a group of white British performers who wore blackface.

32 Nigel Lezama, "The Nineteenth-Century Dandy's Heroic Renunciation through Fashion," *Critical Studies in Fashion and Beauty* 3, nos. 1 and 2 (2012): 90.
33 Garelick, "The Layered Look," 36.
34 Lezama, "The Nineteenth-Century Dandy's Heroic Renunciation," 88.
35 Miller, *Slaves to Fashion*, 9. As the recent events surrounding Rachel Dolezal demonstrate, the adoption of race is much more complicated.
36 See Carter Ratcliff, "Dandyism and Abstraction in a Universe Defined by Newton," in Fillin-Yeh, 101–102, quoting Thomas Carlyle: "the dandy's wish to be no more than 'a visual object, or a thing that will reflect rays of light. Your silver or your gold . . . he solicits not; simply the glance of your eyes . . . [D]o but look at him, and he is contented." Citing Carlyle, *Sartor Resartus: The Life and Opinions of Herr Teufelsdroch*, ed. Kerry McSweeney and Peter Sabor (1836; Oxford: Oxford University Press, 1987), 207, 212–215.
37 Davis, *Enforcing Normalcy*, 11.
38 Miller, *Slaves to Fashion*, 69.
39 Karen Bourrier, *The Measure of Manliness: Disability and Masculinity in the Mid-Victorian Novel* (Detroit: Michigan University Press, 2015), 17.
40 Clive Kellner, "Interview with Yinka Shonibare," in *Yinka Shonibare* (Johannesburg: Camouflage/Coartnews Publishing, 2001), 9, cited in Kent, 9.
41 Kellner, "Interview with Yinka Shonibare," 9, cited in Kent, 16.
42 See John Peacock, *Men's Fashion: The Complete Sourcebook* (London, Thames and Hudson: 1996), 86–87.
43 Jeremy Kaye, "Twenty-First-Century Victorian Dandy: What Metrosexuality and the Heterosexual Matrix Reveal about Victorian Men," *The Journal of Popular Culture* 42, no. 1 (2009): 121.
44 Pickering, *Blackface Minstrelsy*, 113–114; Nowatzki, *Representing African Americans*, 2.
45 Davis, *Enforcing Normalcy*, 130.
46 Davis, "Constructing Normalcy," in *The Disability Studies Reader*, ed. Davis (New York: Routledge, 2013), 10, 11.
47 Kaye, "Twenty-First-Century Victorian Dandy," 120.
48 Nowatzki, *Representing African Americans*, 11.
49 Nowatzki, *Representing African Americans*, 65.
50 Pickering, *Blackface Minstrelsy*, 124.
51 Miller, *Slaves to Fashion*, 66, 87, 91.
52 See Miller, *Slaves to Fashion*, Chapter 2: Crimes of Fashion, 77–136.
53 Barbara L. Webb, "The Black Dandyism of George Walker: A Case Study in Genealogical Method," *The Drama Review* 45, no. 4 (Winter 2001): 12.
54 Webb, "The Black Dandyism of George Walker," 18; Elle Reynolds Weatherup, "Understanding Dandyism in Three Acts: A Comparison of the Revolutionary Performances of Beau Brummell, George Walker, and Zoot Suit Culture" (PhD Dissertation, University of California-San Diego, 2011), 124.
55 Webb, "The Black Dandyism of George Walker," 12, 16.
56 Weatherup, "Understanding Dandyism in Three Acts," 76; Pickering, *Blackface Minstrelsy*, 61.
57 Pickering, *Blackface Minstrelsy*, 20.
58 Webb, "The Black Dandyism of George Walker," 9.
59 Webb, "The Black Dandyism of George Walker," 11.
60 Nowatzki, *Representing African Americans*, 44.
61 Nowatzki, *Representing African Americans*, 63.
62 Pickering, *Blackface Minstrelsy*, 2–3; Nowatzki, 63–64.
63 Pickering, *Blackface Minstrelsy*, 3–4, 23.
64 Nowatzki, *Representing African Americans*, 73.
65 Pickering, *Blackface Minstrelsy*, 75, 123.
66 Pickering, *Blackface Minstrelsy*, 75.

67 Nowatski, *Representing African Americans*, 7.
68 Nowatzki, *Representing African Americans*, 65.
69 Pickering, *Blackface Minstrelsy*, 110–111.
70 Pickering, *Blackface Minstrelsy*, 114.
71 Pickering, *Blackface Minstrelsy*, 21.
72 Pickering, *Blackface Minstrelsy*, 134.
73 Nowatzki, *Representing African Americans*, 33.
74 Webb, "The Black Dandyism of George Walker," 15.
75 Weatherup, "Understanding Dandyism in Three Acts," 11.
76 Elisa F. Glick, "Harlem's Queer Dandy: African-American Modernism and the Artifice of Blackness," *Modern Fiction Studies* 49, no. 3 (Fall 2003): 420.
77 Nowatzki, *Representing African Americans*, 142; Pickering, *Blackface Minstrelsy*, 113–114.
78 Bourrier, *The Measure of Manliness*, 2.
79 Bourrier, *The Measure of Manliness*, 2–3. Bourrier's book explores the narrative pairing of disability and strength in works including Charlotte Yonge's *The Heir of Redclyffe* (1853), Dinah Mulock Craik's *John Halifax, Gentleman* (1856), Charles Kingsley's *Westward Ho!* (1855), and *Two Years Ago* (1857), Thomas Hughes, Henry James's *The Portrait of a Lady* (1881), and George Eliot's *The Mill on the Floss* (1860).
80 Bourrier, *The Measure of Manliness*, 23.
81 Bourrier, *The Measure of Manliness*, 4.
82 Bourrier, *The Measure of Manliness*, 3.
83 Bourrier, *The Measure of Manliness*, 5.
84 Bourrier, *The Measure of Manliness*, 10, 14.
85 Bourrier, *The Measure of Manliness*, 16.
86 Bourrier, *The Measure of Manliness*, 8.
87 Bourrier, *The Measure of Manliness*, 7.
88 Black Victorians were also underrepresented in photography. Recent exhibitions curated by Autograph ABP in London entitled "Black Chronicles I" and "Black Chronicles II" have explored the photographs that do exist.
89 Guldemond and Mackert, "To Entertain and Provoke," 38.
90 Miller, *Slaves to Fashion*, 39; 48–55, 278–280.
91 Miller, *Slaves to Fashion*, 49.
92 David Dabydeen, foreword to *Black Victorians: Black People in British Art*, ed. Jan Marsh (London; Ashgate, 2005), 9.
93 Dabydeen, foreword to *Black Victorians*, 9.
94 Siebers, *Disability Aesthetics*, 42.
95 Touré, "Do Not Pass," *The New York Times Book Review*, February 21, 2010, 23.
96 Elaine Ginsberg, introduction to *Passing and the Fictions of Identity*, ed. Ginsberg (Durham: Duke University Press, 1996), 2.
97 Lisa Walker, *Looking Like What You Are: Sexual Style, Race, and Lesbian Identity* (New York: New York University Press, 2001), 209–210, cited in Samuels, "My Body, My Closet," 244.
98 Walker, *Looking Like What You Are*, 209–210.
99 Margery Garber, *Vested Interests; Cross-Dressing and Cultural Anxiety* (New York and London: Routledge, 1992), 16, cited in Samuels, "My Body, My Closet," 244.
100 Samuels, "My Body, My Closet," 244, citing Ginsberg, *Passing*, 8 who is citing Garber, *Vested Interests*, 16–17.
101 Samuels, "My Body, My Closet," discusses occupying these in-between states, 250.
102 Samuels, "My Body, My Closet," 239.
103 Ginsburg, *Passing*, 4, cited in Samuels.
104 Samuels, "My Body, My Closet," 247.
105 Samuels, "My Body, My Closet," 247.

106 Samuels, "My Body, My Closet," 243.
107 Mark Jeffreys, "The Visible Cripple (Scars and Other Disfiguring Displays Included)," in *Disability Studies: Enabling the Humanities*, ed. Sharon L. Snyder, Brenda Jo Brueggemann, and Rosemarie Garland-Thomson (New York: Modern Language Association, 2002), 37.
108 Jeffreys, "The Visible Cripple," 37.
109 Garland-Thomson, "The Politics of Staring: Visual Rhetorics of Disability in Popular Photography," in *Disability Studies: Enabling the Humanities*, ed. Sharon L. Snyder, Brenda Jo Brueggeman, and Rosemarie Garland-Thomson (New York: Modern Language Association, 2002), 59.
110 Hevey, *The Enfreakment of Photography*, 333.
111 Brenda Brueggeman comments, "That we don't know how to represent ourselves is the fifth problem handed to us by disability. Faced with the incomplete and now obviously instable face of disability, we're not sure what to draw in there . . . what we say and do and believe about disability suddenly begins to be what we say and do and believe about ourselves. These representations are getting sticky—tricky too." in "Interlude I: On (Almost) Passing," *The Disability Studies Reader*, ed. Lennard J. Davis (New York: Routledge, 2006), 320.
112 Garland-Thomson, "Politics," 59.
113 Garland-Thomson, "Politics," 59.
114 Miller, *Slaves to Fashion*, 69.
115 Garland-Thomson, "*Staring*," 18.
116 Anne Fausto-Sterling, *Sexing the Body: Gender Politics and the Construction of Sexuality* (New York: Basic Books, 2000), 21.
117 Marlene Trompe and Karyn Valerius, "Toward Situating the Victorian Freak," *Victorian Freaks*, ed. Trompe, 3.
118 Garland-Thomson, "Politics," 57.
119 Garland-Thomson, *Staring: How We Look* (Oxford: Oxford University Press, 2009), 7, referring to WJT Mitchell (2005).
120 Rosemarie Garland-Thomson, *Extraordinary Bodies: Figuring Physical Disability in American Culture and Literature* (New York: Columbia University Press, 1997), 26. See also Davis on the power of this look, *Enforcing Normalcy*, 12.
121 Ann Millett-Gallant, personal communication.

10 Crafting disabled sexuality
The visual language of Nomy Lamm's "Wall of Fire"

Shayda Kafai

Whether in sociocultural or medicalized contexts, disabled individuals have been profoundly desexualized. This violent erasure of sexuality creates an absence that is in need of radical visibility and politicized voice. Disability studies as a discipline has identified that the medical model of disability is what silences disabled individuals, rendering them a sexual minority.[1] While the literature most certainly continues to challenge this regressive myth,[2] this chapter explores how performance art in particular serves as a productive location for exploring sexual empowerment and crafting sexual culture for the disability community. In particular, I will ground my discussion in the work of San Francisco–based performance artist Nomy Lamm, a self-defined "bad ass, fat ass, Jew dyke amputee . . . feminist, dancer, performance artist, writer."[3] By foregrounding her body and her sexuality in her art-making, Nomy honors her sexuality and crafts alternatives to the desexualization so frequently ascribed to disabled individuals.[4] Nomy's performance art enters here, offering an alternative to the violent and systematic ways the identities and bodies of disabled individuals are made sexually invisible. Her art-making praxis is, in part, based on the political, radical act of sexual visibility.

Nomy's 2008 performance "Wall of Fire" serves dually as a piece of art and activism, as it offers a bold and erotic language that facilitates discussions of sexuality in the disability community. Not only does Nomy rewrite the disabled body as sexual and politicized, but she also expands the discussion of sexual agency to the fat body.[5] Nomy's "Wall of Fire" provocatively re-inscribes Western culture's ableist and sizeist imperatives that restrict disabled sexuality.

Before beginning to uncover the themes of eroticism and sexuality that are critical to Nomy's performance art, it is vital to first define performance art and disability performance art as disciplines.[6] In her expansive overview of performance art entitled *Performance Live Art Since 1960*, art historian RoseLee Goldberg locates the trajectory of performance art in a desire to challenge and politicize the everyday.[7] For Goldberg, such performances function as "a means of articulating broader cultural spasms from shifts in political or economic strata."[8] In this context, then, performance art possesses a political tenor and serves as a fertile location for the exploration of identity-centric art. Nomy's "Wall of Fire" creates art that explores the interconnections between her identities as a fat, amputee woman. Akin to Goldberg's assessment that performance art fosters ways to challenge and shift political and cultural norms, Nomy seeks to expand the ways we view femininity, disability, and sexuality. "Wall of Fire" becomes a performance that urges we shift and complicate readings of corporality.

Central to performance art is the live performance, though this definition does not consider or make way for performances that are recorded and replayed.[9] Beyond this limited definition, however, there is no one, simple way to define performance art. Goldberg identifies the disciplinary and artistic limits of performance art by arguing that, "[u]nlike the theatre, the performer *is* the artist, seldom a character like an actor, and the content rarely follows a traditional plot or narrative. The performance might be a series of intimate gestures or large-scale visual theatre, lasting from a few minutes to many hours."[10] Although this definition is porous, Goldberg's framing of performance art does speak to its integral properties of raising political and cultural awareness as it strives to bring into focus the stigmas, stereotypes, and oppressions that regulate and discipline individuals who have, because of their identities, been restricted to the margins.

Grounded within disability culture,[11] a unique blending of the disability rights movement and disability arts production,[12] disability performance art seeks to rewrite the political, sociocultural, and medical mandates of ableism. Akin to racism, sexism, classism, and heterosexism, ableism refers to the institutionalized forms of oppression that are exercised against people with disabilities. Perpetuated by intolerance for difference, ableism argues that there is a normative corporeal, mental, and emotional standard against which all variations are judged. We can witness disability culture's use of performance art as a way to challenge ableism in David Mitchell and Sharon Snyder's 1995 documentary *Vital Signs*.[13] For Mitchell and Snyder, disability performance art sculpts disability identity in contrast to an ableist construction that mistakenly portrays the disabled individual as a defective and passive societal burden.[14] Unlike other forms of art or activism, disability scholar and performance artist Petra Kuppers determines that performance art serves as a "laboratory"—a fertile, transformative location of growth. She emphasizes that, "[i]n the laboratory of the performance situation, these knowledges can be re-examined, and questioned again and again."[15] For Kuppers, performance art allows audience members to access new perspectives in ways more complex and dynamic than simply using language.[16] In this landscape, disabled performance artists can replace the connotations associated with disability with narratives that are politically conscious and transformative.[17]

Serving as a performative extension of disability culture's goal of challenging regressive, ableist stereotypes, disability performance art allows artists to create inclusive and political depictions of disability that reflect their own lived experiences.[18] Herein lies one of the most fruitful results of disability performance art: it creates a rebellious climate that elevates the performance of disability as an identity to the realm of protest, to where the body can "cause commotion"[19] and rewrite stigma. As a performance artist and activist, Nomy, through her art, rewrites ableist representations of disabled identity and corporeality as desexualized. By politicizing her intersectional identities, "Wall of Fire" creates a sexualized context that is at once protest and seduction. I must note here that I have chosen to refer to this institutionalized removal of sexuality as desexuality as opposed to asexuality. This revision is strategic. Rather than generalizing that all disabled individuals are asexual, that they have no sexual desire, the term "desexual" suggests that disabled individuals are assumed to be childlike and devoid of sexuality.[20] While certainly some disabled individuals may identify as asexual, I am more concerned here with the rampant process of desexualizing disabled individuals that occurs in Western culture.

Nomy's art-making has many political and activist roots. Most prominently, she is an artist and active member of the performance project Sins Invalid. Based in the San Francisco Bay Area, Sins Invalid supports the performance art of disabled artists of color who identify as queer and/or gender-variant.[21] The first time I saw Nomy perform, she was singing and playing her accordion at the 2013 Crip Soirée and Speakeasy, an event hosted by Sins Invalid in Oakland, California. Grounded in Sins Invalid's creative, politicized context, her performative work bases itself on body image, as informed by the Fat Liberation movement. The Fat Liberation Movement, also referred to as the Fat Pride Movement, follows a trajectory similar to the Women's Liberation Movement. In their exploration of fat studies, fat activist and attorney Sondra Solovay and women's studies professor Esther Rothblum point to the 1969 founding of the National Association to Advance Fat Acceptance as a moment when stereotypes of fatness and fat people began to be challenged.[22] Nomy's performance art serves as a critical extension of this history.

Just as Nomy makes work informed by numerous activist and social justice movements, she also engages in multiple art genres. Influenced by the Riot Grrrl production of self-made zines, Nomy began her popular electronic zine *I'm So Fucking Beautiful* in the 1990s. As a grassroots youth culture that sought to rewrite stereotypes associated with girlhood and femininity, the Riot Grrrl movement provided Nomy with the framework she needed to view her body and her identities as political.[23] By reflecting on her own body image narratives, she was empowered to critique Western culture's perpetuation of sizeism, discrimination based on an individual's size, urging that we reclaim the word "fat" as a politicized identity. Because of her writings, Nomy received *Ms.* magazine's Woman of the Year award in 1997. Since then, she has explored the intersections of language, identity, politics, and performance by touring in 1999 with *Sister Spit*, a feminist spoken word collective based in San Francisco. Nomy is also engaged in music-making and has two self-released albums; the first was her 1999 punk rock album *Anthem*, released on Talent Show, and the second, *Effigy*, released on Yoyo Recordings in 2002, is an album of electronica. While these genres are distinct, Nomy's "Wall of Fire" is a performance in which both her activist politics and her ability to traverse genres coalesce. With intimacy, song, and movement, Nomy communicates politically with her audience.

In her 2008 performance of "Wall of Fire," as the stage lights turn on, we first hear Nomy breathe in deeply before she begins singing.[24] Immediately, in this darkened space, we are grounded in the sounds of her body, in the larynx and the pause—the moments when sound ceases. She stands by a table, her left arm resting on the reverb machine while her right hand holds the microphone close to her mouth. Initially, Nomy does not reveal her disability to the audience. She sits

Crafting disabled sexuality 181

on stage wearing a form-fitting red negligée. Adorned in tight red fabric and lace, with sheer red fabric over her breasts and sleeves pushed down past her shoulders, Nomy's dress communicates lust. She wears red-and-white striped knee-high socks, and her hair, except for a few curly wisps, is pulled back. Her body glows in the dimness of the light. Nomy begins to sing: "Stroke-one-two-three / Breathe-one-two-three / Stroke-one-two-three / Breathe-one-two-three."[25] These lines escape her lips slowly and meditatively.

Just as I listen, drawn to her voice, her dress lures my eyes. She has chosen to wear a color that cannot be ignored, a decision connected to her Fat Liberation politics. Here, I am reminded of the connections between fat activism and fashion that fat activist and fatshionista Lesley Kinzel explores in her book *Two Whole Cakes: How to Stop Dieting and Learn to Love Your Body*. Kinzel argues that "[c]lothing is language, for better or worse. Each garment carries an encoded meaning, woven directly into the fabric between the warp and weft."[26] To position clothing as language, as verb, is a powerful gesture. When one considers the relationships a sizeist culture creates between clothing and fat bodies, one can identify how particularly valuable this renaming is for Kinzel and, by extension, for Nomy. In mainstream malls and stores, plus-size clothing options are often either very limited, or if they do exist, they are matronly, dull in color, or not form-fitting. Kinzel uses fashion to rebel against sizeist language, naming "fatshion" a new kind of activism: "Fatshion—fat + fashion—is a means of increasing visibility."[27] Fatshion, according to Kinzel, intervenes in a cultural discourse that reinforces the fat body as lazy, unhealthy, and unattractive,[28] and visually challenges a stigma that demands fat bodies stay hidden and out of sight. By refusing to wear dull, baggy clothing, and by instead choosing to wear a red sundress, Nomy pushes back against the sizeist principle that certain bodies do not deserve to be acknowledged or viewed as sexual and desirable.[29] In this way, Nomy sets a constructive tone in the first thirty seconds of her performance by creating a radical narrative of fat visibility.

While her performance begins visually in its allusion to fat activism and visibility, Nomy strategically continues to keep her disability invisible. Once she begins to play her first stanza on a loop on the reverb machine, she repeats and layers on the words "stroke" and "breathe." As she says these words, she faces the audience, gazing downward. Nomy's dress, the velvet offering of these words, and the dimmed light create intimacy. She signals to me, as the viewer, that I am entering into an erotic space. Nomy continues singing as the lights on stage rise to their full brightness. As she fluidly takes her seat, the slit of her dress rises to the top of her left thigh. Nomy further exposes her thigh by slowly and intentionally lifting her skirt, an act that urges us to focus on her left leg. With the abrupt change in light, in the way it reflects off of her left thigh but not her right, we can see that Nomy wears a prosthetic leg. She puts down the microphone and seductively lifts her dress to the top of her thigh as the loop plays in the background. Nomy leans back out of her prosthesis, holding the leg in front of her body, almost as if she is presenting it to the audience as an offering. As the recording of her voice continues, Nomy lifts her leg, strokes it, and begins using it as a drum (fig. 10.1). The slaps are rhythmic and deliberate. Her body is still as she looks stoically over the audience.

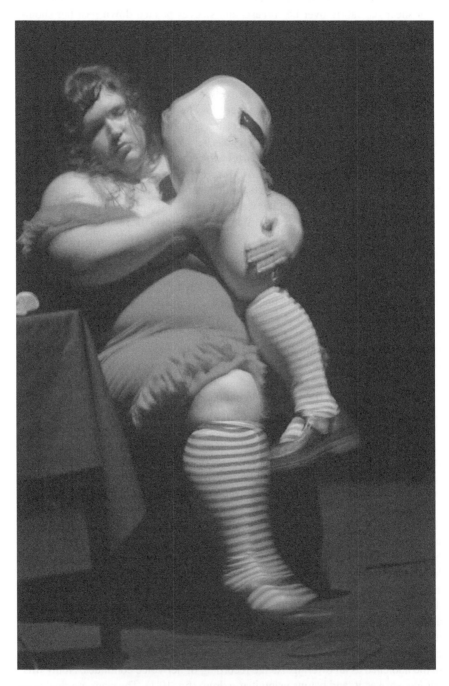

Figure 10.1 Nomy Lamm performing "Wall of Fire" in Sins Invalid 2008 show. Photograph by Richard Downing © 2008. Courtesy of Sins Invalid.

Once she uses her leg, her prosthesis, as an instrument, she places it on the floor and reaches over to the microphone. Although Nomy has made herself quite visible in her red dress, the removal of her prosthesis serves as a generative moment. Her body asks that we as viewers expand our understanding of what the sexual and erotic disabled woman looks like.

To sculpt a narrative of eroticism in "Wall of Fire" is a political act for Nomy. As a fat, crip woman, her art is invested in creating a sexual culture that makes space for and honors the sexuality of what an ableist culture renders invisible and nonexistent. The term "crip" reclaims the derogatory term "cripple" and serves as an identity that is adopted by disabled individuals and allies alike. Crip is a fluid term inclusive of all disabilities; a person who identifies as crip often also acknowledges the interconnections between disability culture, politics, and activism.[30] When I asked Nomy about the importance of performing eroticism and sexuality as a crip woman, she observed that "sexuality is magic, it is a way that we weave ourselves into the world from the inside out, and people with disabilities have to work hard to claim our sexualities, so that what we are bringing into the world is powerful [and] concentrated."[31] Her dress, the removal of her prosthesis, and the repetitive, velvet loop of her voice forge a radical sexual culture that is inclusive of all bodies. This is the importance of her concentrated weaving: the visibility of her performance and its eroticism reminds audiences of the dangers of invisibility that arise when disabled individuals are viewed as desexualized, passive, infantile, and dependent.

Feminist philosopher Margrit Shildrick argues that one reason why our framing of sexuality is so limited is because we, as Westerners living in an ableist culture, cannot even begin to fathom the disabled person as sexual, because sex is an act correlated with adult independence. For Shildrick, this disabled sexual body "exceed[s] the limits of what is thinkable."[32] A central aspect of the medical model of disability is the belief that because a disabled individual is read as passive and limited, the individual is then not capable of having a sexual identity.[33] The lack of sex education, specifically within the disability community, and the hyper-visibility of disabled individuals in hospitals, doctors' offices, and nursing care facilities all compound the process of desexualization. Disability scholar Tobin Siebers argues that these medicalized locations limit access to privacy and instead place the disabled body in a regulated state of observation and control: "This medical zone of publicness replaces for people with disabilities everything formally considered private."[34] In this place, there is no room for bodily exploration, for the independent decision-making and self-determination that are so connected to sexuality and sex.[35]

Nomy's "Wall of Fire" pulls on the threads of these falsehoods. Within the first minute of her performance, we as audience members are taken on a journey of revision. Her body, the entirety of which challenges the ableist notions of what it means to be whole, creates an erotic landscape that seductively troubles the narrative of desexualization. The beginning of her performance calls our attention to the falsity and constructed nature of the myth of desexualized, disabled bodies, and this is truly radical—watching as a disabled woman, I, too, am given voice.

Here, Nomy begins to draw alliances with the principles of sexual agency. Queer theory and disability studies scholar Abby Wilkerson argues that positioning a disabled individual as desexualized is oppressive and requires political intervention. As a way to demonstrate the political value of sexuality, Wilkerson defines sexual agency

> not simply as the capacity to choose, engage in, or refuse sex acts, but as a more profound good that is in many ways socially based, involving not only a sense of oneself as a sexual being but also a larger social dimension in which others recognize and respect one's identity.[36]

To exercise sexual agency means to be grounded in oneself, to be aware of one's body as sexual, and to practice the right of being a desiring individual. Wilkerson extends this argument by urging that sexuality must be taken up as an important political issue within disability studies and rights movements alike.[37]

As the performance continues, with the first stanza looping in the background, Nomy begins to sing: "Magic breathes, and magic comes / I believe in magic theorems / Take me to your inner sanctum / I'm going to watch you come / I'm going to watch you come."[38] The music is sultry. The bass strums repetitively, like heartbeats. As she sings the first two lines, a smile forms on her lips when she says the word "come." As a play on the words—come and cum—the eroticism of her performance and her lyrics is unmistakable. This is a temptation song, a desire song. While sitting on the box on stage, her right leg keeps time as her body flirts by swaying, by adding movement to the beat. Her hand rests over her belly, under her rising chest. At one point in the performance, while the music and lyrics loop, Nomy begins to delicately pull up the microphone's cord, folding it and encircling it in her hands (fig. 10.2). Here, she reminds us of touch, enticing us with the provocation of fingers. She seduces us with these movements. Akin to Wilkerson's call for embodying sexual agency, Nomy unites sexuality and disability in her performance art, urging that both can and need to be in conversation with one another. They should engage together in one body, on one stage.

During our interview, I asked Nomy to talk about the performance of sexuality in "Wall of Fire," the politics of sexual agency, and her prosthetic leg. She told me the following:

> For me being able to claim my own sexuality has meant walking into the fire in a way. There is stuff that is really scary . . . to claim my own desire has been quite a process. Performance has been a ritual that I have used in my life to bring things into reality. . . . My leg in most of my relationships is phallic because I can fuck people with it. There is something so intensely healthy about reclaiming pleasure with the parts of the body that have been medicalized.[39]

In her identification of performance as a ritualistic space in which she forms reality, Nomy draws parallels back to Kuppers's framing of the performance as a

Figure 10.2 Nomy Lamm performing "Wall of Fire" in Sins Invalid 2008 show. Photograph by Richard Downing © 2008. Courtesy of Sins Invalid.

location where knowledges are re-examined. In this case, Nomy is able to re-examine ableism's forceful desexualization of her body by entering the fire, a place of tension that she must journey through in order to change the knowledges crafted about disability and sexuality. By performing her sexual reclamation in such a vocal and visible way, Nomy undoes oppression and confronts the silencing effects of shame. In the context of sexuality and disability, shame is most certainly a violent part of ableism that censors individuals, distancing them and removing them from their bodies.[40] Here, sexual shame becomes an assertive force. By using performance as a ritualistic tool, Nomy rewrites the painful and isolating connotations that have been socially, medically, and ideologically connected with her body and her sexuality. When speaking about her amputated leg, for example, she refers to it as a phallus. Used to penetrate her partners during sex, the leg is actively sexual; it fucks. As opposed to remaining in a culture that devalues her desire, Nomy takes the risk of walking into the metaphoric fire, reclaiming her sexuality. This path through fire references the ways that sexual shaming is reductive and totalizing in the ways it burns. If one allows it, fire can eradicate sexuality and reduce it to the unthinkable. As her performance demonstrates, however, fire is a dichotomous entity. In its proliferations, it also liberates and cleanses.

"Wall of Fire" exemplifies performance art's capacity for shifting and bending ideologies and ableist regulations about sexuality. Performance is where Nomy reclaims her body, identity, and sexuality. It is a place that offers her a journey into a self-crafted, self-fought-for reality where sexual agency is not just possible for the disabled individual, but is a necessity. Because she must walk into the fire to claim her sexuality, Nomy's performance reminds us of the immense work that still needs to take place to undo the desexualization that is so aggressively projected onto individuals within the disability community. Her third stanza alludes to this: "Now I can't run and there's nowhere to hide / I gotta get back inside / The wall of fire it's so intimidating / But I gotta get mine and I'm not waiting."[41] Despite the sociocultural and medical intimidation that positions the disabled body as abject, passive, defective, and unworthy of love, Nomy pushes through these stereotypes. While the urge to "get back inside" references the shame that encapsulates sexuality for disabled individuals, Nomy combats this when she embraces her sexuality in "Wall of Fire" with visibility and movement: the shimmy, the grace of the exposed shoulders, the stroke, the arched back, and the smile. These characteristics of eroticism are not specific to Nomy or to disability culture. Rather, her engagement in these common tropes of sexuality makes her performance of sexuality familiar. In this politicized space of performance, Nomy proclaims the fat, crip woman as a desiring being. Her sexual culture is non-medicalized, and the removal of her prosthesis speaks to this undoing. As she strips her body of the medical, Nomy removes the medicalization and invisibility traditionally attributed to disabled individuals who seek to express their sexuality. She names her entry into this culture when she sings, "Oooh, I'm going to move into you."[42]

Central to the creation of Nomy's sexual culture is the re-inscription and complication of the ableist concept of corporeal wholeness. In her eroticized bodyscape, coming out of her prosthesis is sexual as it invites looking. By claiming the visibility of her crip body, Nomy speaks against a discourse begun in the nineteenth century during the American Civil War that roots prosthetics in hyper-medicalization, rehabilitation, and passing.[43] After treating injured soldiers, physician Oliver Wendell Holmes argued that the disabled body was a "damaged" body, and thus was not an effective reflection of the ideal citizen for a post–Civil War America. Holmes focused his research and solution on a prosthesis formed by American inventor and amputee B. Frank Palmer. Distinct from the traditional peg leg, the Palmer leg was built with the intent of looking like a natural leg. Holmes viewed the peg leg, an obvious marker of disability and absence, as grotesque; it was a signifier that shattered the illusion of corporeal wholeness.[44] In a contemporary exploration of prosthetics, art historian and cultural studies scholar Marquard Smith similarly argues that the goal of the prosthesis should be to "turn the *dis*abled into the *able*-bodied ... [and] to conceal missing body parts."[45] What is most toxic about this explanation is that it continues the nineteenth-century framing of the disabled body as incomplete, damaged, and in need of fixing.

Nomy shatters this prosthetic rhetoric—the constructed necessity of wholeness and nondisability, and the unwhole body's ableist construction as offensive and abject—with the embrace of her sexual agency. She challenges the belief that a "natural" and aesthetically pleasing body must be whole or must pass as whole. With the visible sharing of her crip, amputee body within the first 50 seconds of

"Wall of Fire," Nomy's removal of her prosthetic leg becomes a political gesture. Rather than remaining within a medicalized framing of her body, she creates her own narrative, a literal and figurative disconnection from medicine. In refusing to hide her disability, Nomy boldly challenges Holmes's assertion that to not wear a visually precise replica of a leg and instead to reveal its absence is grotesque and intolerable. She materializes this belief and burns it, revealing something transformed in its wake. The body need not be whole, need not replicate a nondisabled frame. The body can simply be.

Halfway through her performance, Nomy stands fluidly, chest first. She sways from one side to another as a smile curls its way over her mouth. Slowly the light on stage dims so that only one light spotlights her standing body, as her prosthetic leg rests off to the side. She sings, "We're so afraid of getting burned / But if we become the fire then we won't get hurt." The third time she repeats this line, she holds her amputated leg and raises it parallel to the stage. Nomy stands, haloed in light, balanced on one leg. As she slowly releases her leg, she sits down and continues, "This is my dream, yeah this is my desire / Oh the wall of fire."[46] It is here that we are made aware of "Wall of Fire"'s use of the shadow. Adding a second dimension to Nomy's performance, when the camera pulls back, we see her shadow, projected largely on the stage wall (fig. 10.3).

This projection of Nomy, her singing, sensual, dancing body, is what emerges when, as her lyrics say, she *becomes* the fire. The role of the shadow here is profound. First, it creates another level of intimacy on stage. We are able to bear

Figure 10.3 Nomy Lamm performing "Wall of Fire" in Sins Invalid 2008 show. Photograph by Richard Downing © 2008. Courtesy of Sins Invalid.

witness to the way the light casts her shadow's reflection against the back of the stage, the outline of the body that often appears in moments of intimacy when the lights are drawn. Continuing the language of intimacy, the shadow's eroticism also renders Nomy's body visible. Projected behind her, her shadow, the parameters of her body, appears almost larger than life. The shadow of her fat, crip body curves and dances on the wall. In this intimate place, her sexuality is distinct from ableist and sizeist framings that position her sexuality as undesirable and unthinkable. In the outline projected on the wall, the blending of shadow and light, she is sensual and present. She is here.

Once the music and lyrics stop looping, Nomy places the microphone back on its stand. Jarringly, the music shifts from a seductive heartbeat to a playful piano reminiscent of 1920s burlesque music. The audience immediately reacts to the playfulness of the music by clapping, cheering, and whistling; as I watch, I cheer, I smile. Working from this collective energy, Nomy flirtatiously takes her suction liner sock, material that creates suction between the remaining limb and the prosthetic, and begins to put it back over her upper thigh. Her shoulders begin to shift as she smiles coyly at the audience. She picks up her prosthetic leg from the floor and stands up in front of it. The contrast of her dress, its redness against the pale skin of her leg, is stark. After stepping into her leg, the audience begins to clap. Nomy raises her arms and her left leg before twirling off stage. She becomes a smile, a moving blur of body and red.

For Nomy, it is political to publically develop a sexual culture that honors and makes space for disabled individuals. What is most radical in her art-making praxis is the way she defines her sexual agency as a genderqueer, fat, crip woman despite the regressive frameworks of ableism and sizeism. With her arrival on stage, Nomy stakes claim to her right to be seen as an erotic, sexual being. Similar to Wilkerson's call for politicizing disabled sexuality, Nomy fiercely undoes ableism's demand that her sexuality remain invisible and unthinkable. In this way, "Wall of Fire" is a manifestation of change. When discussing this process, Nomy shared that "there's a revolutionary, world-altering element to our claiming of beauty and pleasure . . . my sexuality has been fought for."[47] Indeed, journeying through the wall of fire indicates battle, rejuvenation, and rebirth. As audience members, we are invited to leave behind our stereotypes in the fire and exit the space of performance with a fierce claiming of our own bodies. Nomy offers us a roadmap for how we too may fight for our sexualities, reminding us that if we choose to, we can access and embrace our eroticism. We no longer have to be medicalized. We can be desiring bodies.

Notes

1 The 1990s landmark research conducted by disability scholars Tom Shakespeare, Kath Gillespie-Sells, and Dominic Davies explored the institutions that render sexuality for disabled individuals as improbable. Their interviews and analyses were published in the book *The Sexual Politics of Disability: Untold Desires* (London: Cassell, 1996). This critical text urges that sex and sexuality be viewed as rights for all human beings, and not privileges of the nondisabled.

2 Disability scholars who explore the intersections of sex, sexuality, and disability include Eli Clare, *Exile and Pride: Disability, Queerness, and Liberation* (Cambridge: South End Press, 1999); Barbara Waxman Fiduccia, "Current Issues in Sexuality and the Disability Movement," *Sexuality and Disability* 18, no. 3 (2000): 167–174; Victoria Kannen, "Identity Treason: Race, Disability, Queerness and the Ethics of (Post) Identity Practices," *Culture, Theory, and Critique* 49, no. 2 (2008): 149–163; Robert McRuer, *Crip Theory: Cultural Signs of Queerness and Disability* (New York: New York University Press, 2006); Ellen Samuels, "My Body, My Closet: Invisible Disability and the Limits of the Coming-Out Discourse," *GLQ: A Journal of Lesbian and Gay Studies* 9, no. 1–2 (2003): 233–255; Carrie Sandahl, "Queering the Crip or Cripping the Queer: Intersections of Queer and Crip Identities in Solo Autobiographical Performance," *A Journal of Lesbian and Gay Studies* 9, no. 1–2 (2003): 25–56; Mark Sherry, "Overlaps and Contradictions Between Queer Theory and Disability Studies," *Disability & Society* 19, no. 7 (2004): 769–783; Abby L. Wilkerson, "Disability, Sex Radicalism, and Political Agency," *NWSA Journal* 14, no. 3 (2002): 33–57.
3 Nolose.org accessed December 1, 2013.
4 Rather than refer to Nomy by her last name, a traditional act reserved for authors and artists, I have chosen to use her first name as a way to reinforce Nomy's identities and stress that she is more than an object of study.
5 I use the word "fat" here as a political term as opposed to a derogatory one, a reframing used in fat studies and the Fat Liberation movement.
6 With a unique history of its own informed by New York University and Northwestern University, performance art includes diverse genres including theatre, acting, and performances of the mundane and ordinary.
7 RoseLee Goldberg, *Performance Live Art Since 1960* (New York: Harry N. Abrams Publishers, 1998), 39.
8 Goldberg, *Performance Live Art Since 1960*, 39.
9 Laurie Carlos, introduction to RoseLee Goldberg, *Performance Live Art Since 1960* (New York: Harry N. Abrams Publishers, 1998), 12.
10 RoseLee Goldberg, "Performance Art from Futurism to the Present," in *The Twentieth Century Performance Reader*, ed. Teresa Brayshaw and Noel Witts (New York: Routledge, 2013), 214.
11 For historical information about disability culture, see Colin Barnes, "Effective Change: Disability, Art, and Culture?" presented at Finding the Spotlight Conference, Liverpool Institute for the Performing Arts, May 28–31, 2003; Colin Barnes and Geof Mercer, "Disability Culture: Assimilation or Inclusion?" in *Handbook of Disability Studies*, ed. Gary L. Albrecht, Katherine D. Seelman, and Michael Bury (Thousand Oaks: Sage, 2001), 515–535; Petra Kuppers, *Disability Culture and Community Performance: Find a Strange and Twisted Shape* (New York: Palgrave Macmillan, 2011).
12 Barnes, "Effecting Change: Disability, Art, and Culture?" 13.
13 While *Vital Signs* was a critical origin point for disability performance art, it does not capture all the faces of the disability community. Directed by David Mitchell and Sharon Snyder in 1995, disabled artists of color are discursively erased from the documentary.
14 Simi Linton, *Claiming Disability: Knowledge and Identity* (New York: New York University Press, 1998), 11.
15 Petra Kuppers, *Disability and Contemporary Performance: Bodies on the Edge* (Routledge: New York, 2004), 3.
16 Kuppers, *Disability and Contemporary Performance*, 2.
17 Susan Crutchfield and Marcy Epstein, introduction to *Points of Contact: Disability, Art, and Culture*, ed. Crutchfield and Epstein (Ann Arbor: University of Michigan Press, 2009), 18.
18 Crutchfield and Epstein, *Points of Contact: Disability, Art, and Culture*, 18.

19 Carrie Sandahl and Philip Auslander, introduction to *Bodies in Commotion: Disability and Performance*, ed. Sandahl and Auslander (Ann Arbor: University of Michigan Press, 2005), 2.
20 See Eunjung Kim, "Asexuality in Disability Narratives," *Sexualities* 14 (2011): 479–493.
21 Co-founded by Leroy F. Moore Jr., Patty Berne, Todd Herman, and Amanda Coslor, Sins Invalid is a performance project that functions under a disability justice framework, one that explores and challenges the ableist paradigms of corporality and identity through political art-making.
22 Esther Rothblum and Sondra Solovay, introduction to *The Fat Studies Reader*, ed. Rothblum and Solovay (New York: New York University Press, 2009), 4.
23 Mary Celeste Kearney, "The Missing Links," in *Sexing the Groove*, ed. Sheila Whiteley (New York: Routledge, 1997), 210.
24 I saw this original, 2008 version of "Wall of Fire" online at the Sins Invalid website, www.sinsinvalid.org. While most definitions of performance art argue that it is something that is witnessed live, much can be said about the accessibility of viewing a pre-recorded performance or holding viewing parties. While some can argue that the emotional resonance is different, we should not forget the evocative process in the act of viewing a performance piece. I, for example, powerfully felt and experienced Nomy's performance even though I sat by myself, at my desk.
25 Nomy Lamm, "Wall of Fire" (2008, Oakland, Sins Invalid), performance.
26 Lesley Kinzel, "Standing Out Is Okay: An Excerpt from *Two Whole Cakes*," *Bitch Magazine* 54 (2012): 46.
27 Kinzel, "Standing Out is Okay," 49.
28 Amy E. Farrell, *Fat Shame: Stigma and the Fat Body in American Culture* (New York: New York University Press, 2011), 6.
29 Samantha Murray, "Locating Aesthetics: Sexing the Fat Woman," *Social Semiotics* 14 (2004): 239.
30 Sandahl, "Queering the Crip or Cripping the Queer?" 25.
31 Nomy Lamm, e-mail message to author, January 31, 2015.
32 Margrit Shildrick, "Contested Pleasures: The Sociopolitical Economy of Disability and Sexuality," *Sexuality Research and Social Policy* 4 (2007): 53.
33 Tobin Siebers, *Disability Theory* (Ann Arbor: University of Michigan Press, 2008), 142.
34 Siebers, *Disability Theory*, 147.
35 Shakespeare, Gillespie-Sells, and Davies, *The Sexual Politics of Disability: Untold Desires*; Tobin Siebers, *Disability Theory* (Ann Arbor: University of Michigan Press, 2008); Wilkerson, "Disability, Sex Radicalism, and Political Agency."
36 Wilkerson, "Disability, Sex Radicalism, and Political Agency," 195.
37 Wilkerson, "Disability, Sex Radicalism, and Political Agency," 195.
38 Lamm, "Wall of Fire," performance.
39 Lamm, Skype interview with the author, April 4, 2014.
40 Wilkerson, "Disability, Sex Radicalism, and Political Agency," 207.
41 Lamm,"Wall of Fire," performance.
42 Lamm, "Wall of Fire," performance.
43 Lisa Herschbach, "Prosthetic Reconstructions: Making the Industry, Remaking the Body, Modeling the Nation," *History Workshop Journal* 44 (1997): 22–57; Sarah S. Jain, "The Prosthetic Imagination: Enabling and Disabling the Prosthesis Trope," *Science, Technology, & Human Values* 24, no. 1 (1999): 31–54; Steven L. Kruzman, "Presence and Prosthesis: A Response to Nelson and Wright," *Cultural Anthropology* 16, no. 3 (2001): 374–387.
44 David D. Yuan, "Disfigurement and Reconstruction in Oliver Holmes's 'The Human Wheel, Its Spokes and Felloes,'" in *The Body and Physical Difference: Discourses of Disability*, ed. David T. Mitchell and Sharon L. Snyder (Ann Arbor: The University of Michigan Press, 1997), 72, 80.

45 Marquard Smith, "The Vulnerable Articulate: James Gillingham, Aimee Mullins, and Matthew Barney," in *The Prosthetic Impulse: From a Posthuman Present to a Biocultural Future*, ed. Marquard Smith and Joanne Morra (Columbia: Massachusetts Institute of Technology, 2006), 50.
46 Lamm, "Wall of Fire" (2008, Oakland, Sins Invalid), performance.
47 Nomy Lamm, e-mail message to author, January 31, 2015.

Index

Abberley, Paul 77n8
ableism 2, 9, 178, 179, 183, 185, 186, 188, 190n21
activism 77, 115, 116, 146, 156, 178, 179, 180, 181, 183
ADA (Americans with Disabilities Act) 1, 10n3
Adams, Rachel 20
Adelson, Betty M. 79n30
Allred, Jeff 97n41
Alva, Walter 58n13, 59n23
ambiguity 67, 78n10, 147, 152, 153, 156, 158; Krieger's theory of 29, 30, 31, 34, 42
amputation 76; amputee 120, 121, 122, 128n15, 132, 134, 136, 138, 152, 153, 178, 185, 186, 187
Anglade, Guy 118n40
animal-self 49, 50, 54, 55
anthropomorphism 134, 138
Appel, Mary Jane 97n30
Appen, Ralf von 41
Arbus, Diane 6, 13, 17, 18–23, 27n8, 27n18
archaeology 59, 60, 68, 69, 70, 72, 73, 75, 76, 77n5, 78, 80n35, 81n49, 81n54
art brut 5
art history (definition) 3
Asplan, Michael J. 78n11, 78n17
attitude, biased 7, 29, 30, 31, 37, 39, 40–1, 42, 167, 168
Auslander, Philip 190n19
Aztec 20, 21, 62, 67, 68, 77n5, 79n21, 79n27

Baldwin, Robert 10n9
Balzer, Marjorie Mandelstam 58n2
Barbey d'Aurevilley, Jules Amédée 158
Barnes, Colin 39, 117n4, 198nn11–12

Barnum, P.T. 166
Barrett, David 34
Bartana, Yael 8, 119, 122, 124, 125, 126, 127, 130, 131; *Degenerate Art Lives* 8, 119, 122–7
Bataille, Georges 136
Baudelaire, Charles 165
Beat movement 105
beauty 25, 130n38, 138, 140, 141, 146, 150, 154, 172, 188; convulsive beauty 133, 138, 154
Beckmann, Max 121, 128n12
Beech, Dave 43n14
Bellmer, Hans 8, 132, 133, 136, 139, 140, 141, 147, 149, 150, 152, 153
Bendersky, Gordon 73, 75, 78n18, 81nn57–9
Bergius, Hanne 128n5, 128n10
Berne, Patty 190n21
Berrelleza, Juan Alberto Román 77n5
Biklen, Douglas 100, 104
Bilu, Yoram 131n48
binary opposition 5, 77n9, 100, 104, 105, 108, 113, 117n5
Black, Barbara J. 173n2
blackface 157, 160, 166–7, 174n31
blindness 1, 3, 7, 10n9, 54, 55, 57, 77n6, 93, 115; *see also* cataracts
Bloom, Lisa 174n17
body: war-disabled 121, 127, 129n27; parts of: big toe 132, 140, 141, 142, 146, 154; feet 21, 33, 70, 78, 87, 98, 132, 141, 146; fingers 140; hands 19, 23, 24, 50, 55, 70, 87, 88, 97, 102, 117, 122, 132, 141, 142, 146, 152, 157, 184; heels 146
Bogdan, Robert 6, 27nn14–17, 83, 96nn4–5, 96n17, 100, 104
Boiffard, Jacques-André 8, 132, 142

Bois, Yves-Alain 154n22
Bologna, Giovanni *see* Giovanni Bologna
bondage 139, 140
Bourke-White, Margaret 82–6, 89–90, 93, 95; *You Have Seen Their Faces* 82, 89–90, 93, 95
Bourrier, Karen 175n39, 176nn78–87
Braniff, Máire 131n52
Brannan, Beverly 97n30
Brisenden, Simon 59n18
Brooke, Iris 11n18
Brueggeman, Brenda 177n11
Brummell, George "Beau," 158, 164, 165
Brunner, José 130nn46–7, 131nn49–51
Buchloh, Benjamin 154n22
Bufano, Lisa 8, 132, 134, 136, 138, 140, 142, 152, 153
Burkhart, Louise M. 68, 77n6
Byron, Lord George Gordon 168

Cachia, Amanda 118n33, 132–54
Caldwell, Erskine 89; *You Seen Their Faces* 82–98
Callahan, Harry 26
Callahan, Sean 95n2
Campbell, Joseph 58n2
Capa, Cornell 8, 105, 107–10, 113, 118n27
Carey, Allison C. 6, 87, 96n9, 98n51
Carlos, Laurie 189n9
Carlyle, Thomas 175n36
Carroll, Lewis 26n5
Cashell, Kieran 30, 41, 44n25
Castillo, Bernal Díaz del 79n25, 79n27
castration 133, 142, 147, 153; castrating woman 134
cataracts 47, 55; *see also* blindness
cerebral palsy 100, 102, 104, 113, Cerebral Palsy Institute 103; National Foundation for Cerebral Palsy/United Cerebral Palsy 116
Chaney, Lon 117n9
Chapman, Jake and Dinos 6, 29, 31, 33, 34, 37
Charles I (King of England) 5
Cheddie, Janice 157
cheetah 146
Cheng, Sandra 10n9
children/childhood 5, 6, 12, 13–15, 17, 20, 21, 25, 26n5, 50, 67, 86, 87, 90, 93, 100, 102, 103, 104, 105, 107, 108, 109, 110, 113, 116, 138

Civil Rights movement 3, 99, 116
Civil War, American 82, 165, 186
Clare, Eli 189n2
Clark, T.J. 11nn19–20
Close, Chuck 5
Coe, Michael D. 77n2
Conzelmann, Otto 128nn2–3
Cooper, Dr. William 102–3
Corker, Mairian 100
Cortés, Hernán 20, 67, 79nn27–8
Coslor, Amanda 190n21
cottage plan 83
cranium bifida 70
crip 2, 10, 180, 183, 186, 188
cripple 3, 4, 8, 102, 104, 119–22, 125–7, 128n4, 138
crochet 21, 140
Crutchfield, Susan 189nn17–18
Curtis, James 89, 97n30

Dada 6, 8, 120, 122, 126, 130n38
Dali, Salvador 133, 134
dandy viii, xiv, 9, 155–73
D'Anglure, Bernard Saladin 58n2
David, Jacques-Louis; *Bonaparte franchissant le Grand Saint Bernard* 36–7
Davidson, Bruce 8, 110–14
Davies, Dominic 188n1, 190n35
Davis, Lennard J. 1, 2, 156, 164, 165, 174nn24–5, 175n46, 177n20
Davis, Myron H. 107
Davis, Whitney 80n41
deformation 5, 27, 67, 76, 104, 139, 142
De Fren, Allison 149, 150, 154n10, 154n12, 154n23
degenerate art 8, 119, 122, 124, 125, 127, 129n30, 130n38
Derrida, Jacques 100
desexualization 178, 179, 180, 183, 184, 185, 186
developmental disabilities 6, 7, 12, 13, 17, 18, 20–3, 37–42, 82, 83, 84, 86, 87, 104, 116; and the National Association for Retarded Citizens 116; and the President's Panel on Mental Retardation of 1963, 116; and the President's Committee on Mental Retardation of 1966, 86, 96, 116; retardation used in reference to 20, 21–2, 27n19, 86, 105, 108, 118
deviancy 20, 61, 133, 142, 167
Díaz del Castillo 67, 68, 79

Diehl, Richard A. 78n13
difference (from norm) 4, 5, 8, 20, 40, 47, 49, 55, 57, 58n3, 60, 67, 87, 99, 102, 104, 105, 107, 108, 110, 111, 113, 114, 115, 118n38, 134, 138, 140, 150, 156, 161, 162, 170, 171, 172, 173, 179
Dijan, Sandrine Brenner 130n47
disability, disability aesthetic in the work of Tobin Siebers 5, 118, 132, 169–70; disability art 3, 30, 132, 133, 141, 153, 179, 189n13; disability culture 2, 179, 183, 186; disability fashion 142, disability studies 1–9, 10n2, 21–2, 30–1, 39, 43, 57, 60, 61, 76, 82, 83, 99, 100, 112–13, 118n38, 119, 128n1, 132, 158, 171, 177n11, 178, 184; disability, models of, medical model 1, 2, 3, 6, 7, 50, 60, 61, 71, 76, 77nn7–8, 79, 93, 99, 178, 183; social model 1, 2, 6, 60, 77nn8–9, 99, 100, 128n1, 183; visibility or invisibility of 83, 89, 93, 155, 158, 168, 170, 171–2, 174n13, 180, 181, 186, 187
discrimination 1, 39, 83, 87, 90, 100, 116, 127, 128n4, 129n28, 180
Dix, Otto 8, 119–31; *The Cripples* (1920) 8, 119, 120, 121, 122, 126, 127, 129; *Prague Street* (1920) 120, 127, 129; *The Skat Players* (1920) 120, 127, 128, 129
doll 132, 133, 147, 149, 150, 153; *see also* mannequin; poupée
Dombeck, Mark 27n21
Donnan, Christopher 58nn13–15, 59n16, 59n24, 59n38
Douglass, Frederick 159, 166
Down, J. Langdon 20
Downey, Anthony 174n11, 174n30
Down syndrome 20, 21
Doyle, James A. 78n14
Dracula 117n9
dream interpretation 132
Drinkwater, Chris 103
Dubuffet, Jean 5
Durán, Diego 67, 79n27, 79n29
Dutch wax cloth 156
dwarfism 4, 5, 7, 10n11, 50, 60–70, 73, 75, 77n4, 78–80, 110–11, 120; achondroplasia 50, 60, 63

Eberle, Matthias 128n5, 128n10
Eisenmann, Charles 21
Eliot, T.S. 49, 58n9

Elkins, James 81n64
embodiment 136, 138, 146, 158
embryo 73, 78n18
enfreakment 113
Epstein, Marcy 189nn17–18
eroticism 9, 20, 25, 132, 133, 134, 141, 142, 153, 178, 181, 183, 184, 186, 188
ethnographic present 68
Evans, Walker 87, 89
Expressionists, German 121
exquisite corpse 133, 136, 138

Fahy, Thomas 87
Family of Man exhibition 105
Farm Security Administration (FSA) 87, 89, 95, 97n30, 97n33; *see also* New Deal
Farrell, Amy E. 190n28
fashion 21, 37, 41, 140, 141, 142, 157, 181
fat 4, 9, 178, 180, 181, 183, 186, 188, 189n5; fat activism 180; Fat Liberation Movement 180, 181, 189n5; fatshion 181
Faulkner, William 87, 89
Fausto-Sterling, Anne 172
feminism 3, 61, 77n9, 156, 178, 180, 183
femme fatale 138, 149
Ferguson, Philip M. 10n2
fetish 23, 25, 43, 133, 138, 147, 150, 152; fetishism 147, 152
Fiduccia, Barbara Waxman 189n2
Fiedler, Leslie 27n9
Fillin-Yeh, Susan 174n21, 175n36
Finkelstein, Haim 149
Finnigan, Cara A. 97n30
First Nations 47, 57n1; *see also* Native American
Flannery, Kent V. 80n41
Fleischhauer, Carl 97n30
Fluck, Winfried 95n4
form, in art 3, 5, 20, 29, 30, 31, 66, 68, 71, 99, 107, 109, 110, 153
Forrest, Tara 45n39, 45n41
Foster, Hal 6, 11n16, 133, 154n22
Foucault, Michel 75, 100, 104, 117n2
Fragonard, *The Swing* 156
Frank, Robert 105, 110, 118n27
Frankenstein 117n9, 133
freak(s) 2, 6, 7, 13, 20, 27n9, 133, 140, 142, 147, 158, 159; freak show(s) 6, 7, 20, 22, 27n16, 118n36, 158; *see also* enfreakment

Freud 132
Friedman-Pelag 131n48
Fuchs, Petra 128n18
Furst, Peter 79n31

Gabbard, Glen O. 77n8
Gade, Solveig 45n37
Gainsborough, Thomas, *The Blue Boy* 14
Garber, Margery 170,
Garelick, Rhonda 158, 173n1, 175n21, 175n33
Garland-Thomson, Rosemarie 1, 2, 6, 23, 30, 40, 46n50, 96n4, 97n34, 99, 104, 118n36, 118n39, 158, 171, 172, 173, 174n19, 177n113, 177n115, 177nn118–19
Garza, Mercedes de la 80n36
Gaza War 119, 122, 126
gaze 1, 9, 19, 20, 22, 25, 27n8, 40, 132, 150, 155, 156, 158, 162, 172, 173
gender 3, 8, 25, 26, 57, 58n2, 61, 82, 83, 85, 164, 167, 170, 172, 173n1, 180, 188
geometry, in relation to shamanic visions 54–5
Ghadessi, Touba 4
Gill, Miranda 173n1, 174n22
Gillespie-Sells, Kath 188n1, 190n35
Ginsberg, Elaine 170, 171
Giovanni Bologna 4
Glick, Elisa F. 176n76
Goldberg, Roselee 6, 178, 179
Goldberg, Vicki 95n1, 95n3
Goldberger, David 96n7
Goldman, Raymond L. 104
Goldstein, Allan 96n14
Goodwin, James 97n41
Gordon, Linda 97n32
Gowin, Emmet 26
Goya, Francisco 5
Graßmann, Kerstin 45n38
Great Depression 8, 82, 87, 89, 93, 95
Grosz, George 121, 129n20
Guillen, Abraham 58n3
Guimond, James 87, 97nn30–1, 97n41, 118n29
Guldemond, Jaap 174nn7–8, 176n89

Haberman, Irving 96n19
Hagner, Michael 129n26
Halifax, Joan 49, 58nn10–12
Harrison, S.L. 95n1
Haviland, William 79n35
Hawking, Stephen 6, 31–7, 44nn32–3

Heckel, Erich 121, 128n14
Heidegger, Martin 72
Heindl, Nina 29–46, 43n13, 44n27
Hellerstedt, Kahren jones 10n9
Herman, Todd 190n21
Herschbach, Lisa 190n43
Hevey, David 6, 27n8, 113–14, 172, 174n18; *see also* enfreakment
Higonnet, Anne 13–15, 17
Hiles, Timothy W. 99–118, 118n32
Hochreiter, Susanne 45n37, 46n61
Hoerle, Heinrich 121
Hogarth, William, *The Rake's Progress* 154, 164; *Marriage à la mode* 169
Holderbaum, James 4
Holmes, Oliver Wendell 186, 187
Holocaust 126, 127
hooks, bell 156
Horizontal axis 142
Houston, Stephen D. 78n16
Hoyng, Hans 44n32
hunchback (also kyphosis, "hunched back") 60, 63, 67, 68, 76; hunchback of Notre Dame 133
Hyler, Steven E. 77n8
hysteria 132, 150, 153

iconography 8, 31, 57, 77n5, 132, 153
idealization 5, 34, 36, 37, 130n38, 141, 155
identity 1, 2, 3, 9, 21, 23, 60, 61, 77n9, 102, 104, 110, 122, 126, 127, 134, 141, 152, 155, 157, 164, 165, 170, 171, 173, 174n13, 178, 179, 180, 183, 184, 185, 190n21
impairment 2, 5, 7, 13, 21, 23, 55, 61, 67, 69, 70, 73, 76, 80n43, 83, 87, 100, 117n4, 122, 152, 157, 158, 167, 171, 172
imprint, socio-cultural 29, 30, 31, 37, 41, 42, 43n13
inanimate form 133, 136, 138, 147, 153
Independent Living Movement 116
industrial revolution 2, 168
injuries: bodily 61, 119, 120, 121, 122; facial 120, 122; traumatic brain 122
institutionalization 4, 82, 83, 89

Jacobs, Tom 95n4
Jain, Sarah S. 190n43
Jefferson, Thomas 72
Jeffreys, Mark 171
Johnson, Lyndon B. 116
Jones, Jonathan 29, 33, 43n7, 43n16

Kafer, Alison 6, 61
Kahlo, Frida 5
Kannen, Victoria 189
Kaplan Melissa 59n37
Karloff, Boris 117n9
Kaye, Jeremy 165, 175n47
Kearney, Mary Celeste 190n23
Kellner, Clive 175nn40–1
Kennedy, John F. 116
Kent, Rachel 174n29, 175nn40–1
Kerouac, Jack 105
Kienitz, Sabine 129n22, 129nn24–5, 129n27
Kim, Eunjung 190n20
Kim, Jung-Hee 128n6
Kinzel, Lesley 181
Kirchner, Ernst Ludwig 121, 128n13
Kirkbride, Franklin 96n15
Klein, anne 128n1
Klein, Cecilia 78n10
Koerner, Morgan 39, 42, 43n16, 45nn38–9, 45n46, 46nn52–3
Krauss, Rosalind 6, 136, 141, 144, 146, 152
Krieger, Verena 31
Kruzman, Steven L. 190n43
Kubler, George 72, 79n33, 81nn49–50, 81n53, 81n62
Kuppers, Petra 6, 179, 184, 189n11

Labbé, Armand 59n31
Lamm, Nomy 9, 178–88
Lange, Dorothea 87, 89
Lapper, Alison 34; see also Quinn, Marc, *Alison Lapper Pregnant*
Lastres, Juan B. 58n3
Leen, Nina 109
leishmaniasis 50, 55, 58n2
Letchworth Village 7, 82–6, 89, 90, 95, 96, 97, 108
Lezama, Nigel 175n32, 175n34
Lieber, Maxim 89
Life magazine 82, 100, 105, 107, 110
Linkon, Sherry Lee 97n41
Linton, Simi 6, 10n4, 60, 189n14
Little, Charles S. 83, 85, 86, 96n24
Little People of America 10
Lockhart, James 81n51
Löffler, Fritz 129n30
Longmore, Paul K. 6, 21, 27n23, 39, 45n45, 96nn7–8, 97n35, 98n52
Lorch, Catrin 130n35
Lugosi, Bela 117n9
Luttikhuizen, Henry 10n9

Mackert, Gabriele 174nn7–8, 176n89
Maier, Veronica 41
man/beast in Surrealist art 136
Manet, Édouard, *Olympia* 5
Mann, Sally 26n5
mannequin, in relation to surrealist art 132, 133, 147, 149, 150, 152, 153, 156; in the work of Yinka Shonibare 156; *see also* Bellmer, Hans; doll
Mannix 27nn9–10, 27n13
March of Dimes 115–16
Marks, Ruth 154n5
Marno, Anne 119–31, 129n27
Marshall, Alan 104
Marte, Isabella 130nn32–3
Mason, John Edwin 96n20
Masschelein, Jan 117n10
Masson, André 8, 132, 134, 153
Matisse, Henri 5
Maximo and Bartola ("Lost Aztec children") 20, 21, 27
McCafferty, Sharisse D. 78n10
McCafferty, Geoffrey G. 78n10
McCallum, E.L. 147
McDonough, Paul 8, 115
McDowell, Sara 131n52
McRuer, Robert 10n6, 189n2
meditation pose in Moche ceramics 50, 55, 57
mental illness 4, 5
Mercer, Geof 39, 189n11
Mesoamerican people, Aztec (Nahua) 62, 67, 68, 77n5; Maya 62, 63, 68, 71, 81n52; Olmec 6, 7, 62, 69, 70, 73, 78n18, 80n41
Metcalf, George 80n41
Michalko, Rod 30
Michaux, Oscar 156
Milbrath, Susan 62
Miller, Mary E. 78n15, 81n52
Miller, Monica 174n12, 175n35, 175n38, 175nn51–2, 176nn90–1, 177n114
Miller, Virginia 63, 77n2, 80n35
Millett-Gallant, Ann 5, 6, 10n5, 12–28, 43n7, 43n14, 44n28, 96n4, 177n121
Minotaure 136
minstrelsy 157, 166–7; *see also* blackface
Mitchell, David 6, 179, 189n13
Mitchell, Michael 27n9
Mitchell, W.J.T. 6, 173
Moche 47, 49–50, 54–5, 57, 58n3, 59, 77n8
Moctezuma, Aztec ruler 62, 67

198 Index

Moctezuma, Eduardo Matos 77n3, 79n23
Modernism 2, 5
Modotti, Tina 23, 24
Moholy-Nagy, Hattula 79n35
Möhring, Maren 128n4
Moore, Leroy F. 190n21
Morgante (Braccio di Bartolo) 4
Morris, Errol 98n47
Morse, Ralph 8, 100, 102, 104, 105, 107, 109, 113
motherhood 15, 26
Muelle, Jorge C. 58n3
Mühlbeyer, Harald 46nn59–60
Mullen, Bill 97n41
Murdy, Carson 69, 70, 75, 77n2, 80n42, 81n45
Murray, Samantha 190n29
Muscular Dystrophy Association 116,
muse 6, 12, 13, 23, 24, 25, 26

Narby, Jeremy and Francis Huxley 58n5
narcissism 153
Native American 47, 49, 57, 57n1, 58n4, 67, 68, 72, 79n21; Navajo 58nn2–3
naturalism 5, 49, 54, 61, 71, 170
Nazi 82, 119, 127, 129n30, 130n38
neural-tube defects 69, 70, 75, 80n43
neurodiversity 22
New Deal 82, 87, 93; see also Farm Security Administration; Works Progress Administration
Nietzsche, Friedrich, Ubermensch 34
Nixon, Richard M. 116
Normal/normativity 2, 4, 5, 8, 12, 21, 30–1, 34, 36–7, 39, 40–2, 48–9, 82, 95, 99–100; 102–5, 107–11, 113–16, 133, 142, 146, 150, 152, 155, 156, 158, 165, 172, 179; culturally imprinted 30, 31, 37, 42
Nowatzki, Robert 174n28, 175n44, 175nn48–9, 175nn60–1, 175n64, 176nn67–8, 176n73, 176n77
Nussbaum, Emily 10n2
Nussbaum, Martha Craven 6, 30

Oliver, Michcael 77n8, 117n4
Ort, Nina 39, 46n51
Orvell, Miles 89
other, the 99, 100, 102, 104, 110, 114, 150, 169; otherness 2, 30, 144, 155, 158, 172

Page, Susan Harbage 6, 12–13, 16–19, 22–6
Palmer, B. Frank 186

Parks, Sarah V. 59n41
passing 9, 155, 156, 170–3; and race 170; and disability 171, 186
Pasztory, Esther 75, 80n37
pathologize 1, 2, 166
Peacock, John 175n42
Pechstein, Max 121, 128n15
Peña, Anna Marie 173n3
perfection 26, 140, 164, 171
performance 1, 2, 3, 6, 9, 20, 25, 38, 41, 45, 142, 146, 155, 157, 158, 164, 165, 166, 167, 170
performance art/artist 8, 9, 44n37, 132, 134, 138, 178–9, 180, 181, 183–8, 189n13, 190nn21–4, 191
perversity 29, 132, 153
Peterson, Jeanette Favrot 79n21
Photography: *cartes de visite* 20; commercial 14, 15, 83; documentary 82–95, 99–116; family 26; fine art 12–26, 122, 132–54, 155–72; photojournalism 36, 82–95, 99–116; pornography 15; portraiture 12, 36; snapshots 13, 14, 17; veracity of 2, 14, 104, 116, 157
physiognomy 22
Pickering, Michael 174n31, 175n44, 175n50, 175nn56–7, 175nn62–3, 175nn65–6, 176nn69–72, 176n77
Pillsbury, Joanne 81n47
Pokorny, Erwin 10n9
polio (poliomyelitis) 87, 93, 104, 115, 116
portraiture 5, 12–26, 36, 37, 38, 69, 121; Moche 50, 54, 55, 57; see also photography; Moche
Potrero Nuevo Monument 2, 61, 62
poupée 132, 149, 150, 152; see also Bellmer, Hans; doll
poverty 77n6, 82, 87, 89, 90, 93, 95
praying mantis 132, 134, 136, 138, 153
prejudice 30, 61, 165
Pressly, William L 134
Pressman, Matthew 118n41
Prose, Francine 26
prosthesis 5, 9, 120, 121, 128n9, 132, 134, 146, 152, 156, 171, 181, 183, 184, 186, 187, 188
psychoanalysis 8, 132, 133, 134, 147, 150
Puckett, John Rogers 97n43
pycnodysostosis 5

queerness 2, 165, 180, 84, 188
Quinn, Marc, *Alison Lapper Pregnant* 34, 35, 170

Rabb, Jane M. 97n41
Rabinowitz, Paula 97n30
race 3, 8, 9, 20, 61, 82, 87, 88, 113, 126, 127, 155, 156, 157, 159, 165–8, 169–70, 173
Raeburn, John 97n30, 97n41
Ratcliff, Carter 175n36
Ravenscroft, Janet 11n17
Ray, Man 136, 144
Rehabilitation Act of 1973, Section 504 of 116
Reicher, Kolja 130n45
Reichertz, Jo 41
Reinhard, Bridget 129n20
Renoir, Pierre-Auguste 5
repression 138, 153; repressed memories 138, 147, 153
retardation *see* developmental disabilities
Reynolds, Tammy 27n21
Riedesser, Peter 129n23
Riot Grrrl movement 180
Roberts, Ed 116
Robinson, Jackie 109–10
Roos, Robbert 33
Roosevelt, Franklin D. 93, 115
Rothblum, Esther 180
Rothstein, Arthur 87, 89
Rubin, Susan G. 95n1
Rugeley, Terry 79n31

Saake, Irmhild 41
Sahagún, Bernardio 79n21, 79n27
Samuels, Ellen 171, 174n13, 174n16, 176n97, 176nn99–105
Sandahl, Carrie 6, 189n2, 190n19, 190n30
Sandstrom, Alan R. 79n31
Saussure, Ferdinand de 100, 117
scarification 54
Schele, Linda 81n52
Schlingensief, Christoph 7, 29, 31, 37–42; *Freakstars 3000*, 6, 7, 29, 31, 37–42
Schmidt-Rottluff, Karl 121
Schneider, Irving 77n8
Schubert, Dietrich 128n11, 129n27, 129n31
Seeßlen, Georg 41
segregation 67, 82, 83, 86
sexuality 20, 21, 25, 61, 132, 134, 140, 141, 147, 150, 156, 163, 164, 167, 178–9, 180, 181, 183–4, 185–6, 188; sexual agency 178, 184, 186, 188, sexual culture 178, 183, 186, 188
Shahn, Been 87, 97n29
Shakespeare, Tom 6, 100, 188n1, 190n35

shaman 47–9, 50, 54–7, 58n4; shamanism 7, 47, 49, 50, 54–7, 77n8
Sherry, Mark 189n2
Shiff, Richard 79n34
Shildrick, Margrit 183
Shloss, Carol 96n4, 97n41, 98n45, 98n53
Shonibare, Yinka 9, 155–75; *Diary of a Victorian Dandy* 155–64, 167–73
Shreeve, James 58n4
Shriver, Eunice Kennedy 116; *see also* Special Olympics
Siebers, Tobin 1, 5–6, 30, 11n21, 118n38, 169, 174n24, 183, 190n33, 190n35
Silver, Larry 10n9
Simons, Martin 117n10
Sinclair, Upton 89
Sins Invalid 180, 190n21
sizeism 178, 180, 181, 188
Smith, Marquard 133, 186
Smith, Michael 79n22
Smith, W. Eugene 95, 110
Snyder, Robert 95n4, 97n41
Snyder, Sharon 6, 9, 179, 189n13
Solovay, Sondra 180
Sontag, Deborah 174n14
Sparti, Davide 117n19
Special Olympics 22, 116; *see also* Shriver, Eunice Kennedy
Spondylus 54
Stange, Maren 95n4
stare 1, 9, 115, 171, 173; at disability specifically 2, 9, 20, 40, 41, 111, 113, 114, 115, 158, 172, 173
Steichen, Edward 105
Steinbeck 87, 89, 97n40
stereotype(s) 1, 4, 7, 8, 12, 20, 29, 39, 41, 45n45, 87, 99, 100, 103, 104, 105, 107, 109, 111, 113, 115, 116, 125, 140, 158, 163, 166, 167, 173, 179, 180, 186, 188
Stirling, Matthew W. 69
Stone, Rebecca 47–59, 58nn3–7, 59n17, 59nn19–21, 59nn25–30, 59nn33–6, 59n39, 59n41, 77n8
Stott, William 97n30, 98n45, 98n53
Strobl, Andreas 129n29
Stryker, Roy 87
Sturges, Jock 26n5
Surrealism 6, 8, 132–4, 136, 138, 139, 140, 141, 142, 144, 147, 150, 152, 153, 154

Tarfán, J.M.B. 58n3
Tate, Carolyn 63, 73, 75, 78n11, 81nn57–9
Taube, Karl A. 62, 78n13, 78n15, 79n24, 80n38
Taylor, Sue 140
Titchkosky, Tanya 30
Tizoc 67, 68
Toulouse-Lautrec, Henri de 5
Touré 170
Trachtenberg, Alan 6, 89
trance 47, 49, 50, 52, 54–5, 57
transgression 7, 25, 29, 30, 31, 41, 42, 155
trauma 5, 49, 55, 90, 121, 122, 124, 126, 127, 128n8, 133, 138, 139, 153
Tremain, Shelley 117n7, 117n16
Trent, James W. 96nn10–13, 96nn15–17, 96n19, 96n21, 96n23, 97n27
Trompe, Marlene 158
Tungus 58n4

ugly laws 83
uncanny 71, 132, 133, 134, 138, 141, 142, 144, 149, 153
unconscious 140, 142, 147, 150, 153
unheimlich 133 see uncanny

Vaillant, George 81n49
Valerius, Karen 177n117
Van Gogh, Vincent 5
Vargas Llosa, Mario 58n2
Verderber, Axel 129n23
veteran, disabled 8, 119, 120–2, 123, 124, 125, 126, 127, 128nn14–18, 129nn20–8
Victorian era 76, 155, 157, 158, 165, 167, 172; perception of disability in the Victorian era 158, 168
viewer, experience of in relation to images of disability 7, 9, 13, 17, 22, 25, 29, 30, 31, 37, 39, 40, 41, 42, 43n3, 89, 90, 93, 102, 110, 113, 114, 122, 124, 127, 138, 152, 155, 158, 172, 183
visual impairment see blindness

Wagner, Monika 34, 44n27, 44n30
Walczak, Gerrit 44n35
Walker, George 167
Walker, Lisa 170, 176n98
war neurotic 120
Warnke, Martin 37
wearable art 140
Webb, Barbara 175nn53–5, 175nn58–9, 176n74
Weimar Republic 119, 121; art 121; society 122
were-jaguar 69, 80n41
White, Beatrice 104
Wilkerson, Abby L. 6, 184, 188, 189n2, 190nn35–7, 190n40
Wilkinson, Jane 173n4
Wilson, Natalie 89
Winning, Hasso Von 77n3
Winogrand, Garry 8, 113–15
Witztum, Eliezer 131n48
Wölfli, Adolf 4
Wolf Man 117n9
Works Progress Administration (WPA) 83, 87; see also New Deal
World War I 119, 121, 122, 124, 126, 128n4, 129n27
World War II 8, 99, 100
wounded healer 49, 55, 57, 58, 77n8; see also Eliot, T.S.
Wright, Beatrice 117n17

Yi, Chun-Shan (Sandie) 8, 132, 139, 140, 141, 142, 144, 146, 152, 153
Yuan, David 190n44

Żmijewski, Artur 8, 132, 150, 152–3
Zupanick, C.E. 27n21